RE/WRITING THE CENTER

RE/WRITING THE CENTER

Approaches to Supporting Graduate Students in the Writing Center

SUSAN LAWRENCE
TERRY MYERS ZAWACKI

UTAH STATE UNIVERSITY PRESS
Logan

© 2018 by University Press of Colorado

Published by Utah State University Press
An imprint of University Press of Colorado
245 Century Circle, Suite 202
Louisville, Colorado 80027

All rights reserved

The University Press of Colorado is a proud member of the Association of University Presses.

The University Press of Colorado is a cooperative publishing enterprise supported, in part, by Adams State University, Colorado State University, Fort Lewis College, Metropolitan State University of Denver, Regis University, University of Colorado, University of Northern Colorado, Utah State University, and Western State Colorado University.

ISBN: 978-1-60732-750-9 (pbk.)
ISBN: 978-1-60732-751-6 (ebook)
DOI: https://doi.org/10.7330/9781607327516

Library of Congress Cataloging-in-Publication Data

Names: Lawrence, Susan, 1960– author. | Zawacki, Terry Myers, author.
Title: Re/Writing the center : approaches to supporting graduate students in the writing center / Susan Lawrence, Terry Myers Zawacki.
Other titles: Rewriting the center
Description: Logan : Utah State University Press, [2018] | Includes bibliographical references and index.
Identifiers: LCCN 2017027946| ISBN 9781607327509 (pbk.) | ISBN 9781607327516 (ebook)
Subjects: LCSH: Writing centers. | Graduate students. | English language—Rhetoric—Study and teaching (Higher) | Academic writing—Study and teaching (Higher) | Tutors and tutoring.
Classification: LCC PE1404 .L35 2018 | DDC 808/.0420711—dc23
LC record available at https://lccn.loc.gov/2017027946

Cover illustration © Dafdes/Shutterstock.

CONTENTS

Acknowledgments vii

Prologue: Looking Back, Looking Forward
    Paula Gillespie 3

Introduction : Writing Center Pedagogies and Practices Reconsidered for Graduate Student Writers
    Susan Lawrence and Terry Myers Zawacki 7

PART I. REVISING OUR CORE ASSUMPTIONS

1. Rethinking the WAC/Writing Center/Graduate Student Connection
    Michael A. Pemberton 29

2. The Rise of the Graduate-Focused Writing Center: Exigencies and Responses
    Sarah Summers 49

3. On the Distinct Needs of Multilingual STEM Graduate Students in Writing Centers
    Steve Simpson 66

4. Getting the Writing Right: Writing/Language Centers and Issues of Pedagogy, Responsibility, Ethics, and International English in Graduate Student Research Writing
    Joan Turner 86

PART II. RESHAPING OUR PEDAGOGIES AND PRACTICES

5. Intake and Orientation: The Role of Initial Writing Center Consultations with Graduate Students
    Patrick S. Lawrence, Molly Tetreault, and Thomas Deans 107

6. Hybrid Consultations for Graduate Students: How Pre-Reading Can Help Address Graduate Students' Needs
    Elena Kallestinova 124

7   "Noticing" Language in the Writing Center: Preparing Writing Center Tutors to Support Graduate Multilingual Writers
    Michelle Cox   146

8   "Novelty Moves": Training Tutors to Engage with Technical Content
    Juliann Reineke, Mary Glavan, Doug Phillips, and Joanna Wolfe   163

PART III. EXPANDING THE CENTER

9   A Change for the Better: Writing Center/WID Partnerships to Support Graduate Writing
    Laura Brady, Nathalie Singh-Corcoran, and James Holsinger   185

10 "Find Something You Know You Can Believe In": The Effect of Dissertation Retreats on Graduate Students' Identities as Writers
    Ashly Bender Smith, Tika Lamsal, Adam Robinson, and Bronwyn T. Williams   204

11 More than Dissertation Support: Aligning Our Programs with Doctoral Students' Well-Being and Professional Development Needs
    Marilyn Gray   223

12 Revisiting the Remedial Framework: How Writing Centers Can Better Serve Graduate Students and Themselves
    Elizabeth Lenaghan   240

Epilogue: *Center*-ing Dissertation Supervision: What Was, What Is, and What Can Be
    Sherry Wynn Perdue   255

   About the Contributors   263
   Index   267

ACKNOWLEDGMENTS

We would like to thank all of the authors for their valuable contributions to this volume. We have enjoyed working with and learning from them from initial submissions to finished chapters. We extend a special thanks to Michael Spooner for his enthusiasm for the book idea when we first discussed it with him at 4Cs in 2015 and for his thoughtful guidance in the early production phase up until his retirement, including his suggestion that we replace the lengthy subtitle we'd been using, which, he gently advised, "might be almost too much of a good thing," with the current one. We must also thank Laura Furney, who shepherded the project through to completion.

We also want to acknowledge the influence of the growing body of scholarship on graduate writers in the US and internationally, which helped to inspire this collection, as well as the role played by the Consortium on Graduate Communication, which led us to identify and reach out to a number of colleagues who were previously unknown to us and who have been doing innovative work on providing writing center support to graduate writers. We are pleased that this collection, while featuring many well-known writing center scholars, also allows us to introduce the important work being done by those who might be lesser known to the writing center and WAC community.

And, of course, we must also acknowledge the insights we've gained from the graduate student writers and tutors we've worked with over the years in the writing center and in our classrooms and offices: they've challenged us to revisit some of the commonplaces of our practice, an examination that continues to open up new lines of inquiry for us.

Susan extends her thanks to Terry, who encouraged her to take on this project, and who is a collaborative partner and lifelong mentor par excellence. In turn, Terry recognizes the pleasures of collaborating with such a deeply informed scholar and meticulous editor, who, in every conversation, offered new and intriguing perspectives on the issues that are the focus of this collection.

Finally we each want to thank our partners, Jean and Bob, for their ongoing support and patience as we worked together and individually for the countless hours it took to produce this book.

RE/WRITING THE CENTER

Prologue
LOOKING BACK, LOOKING FORWARD

Paula Gillespie

For those of us who read every article and attend every conference session on graduate students and writing, we welcome this volume, as we increasingly understand the need for research and for deeper, more nuanced, and better-informed approaches to our work with and for advanced writers of extended projects such as theses and dissertations.

When I published two articles on my work with a Graduate Writing Consultant project in 2007 and 2008, the previously published offerings on working with graduate writers were few, yet writing professionals showed a lively and consistent interest in conference sessions, nationally and internationally, on the topic.

Prior to that time and dating back to the early days of the then-National Writing Centers Association, later the International Writing Centers Association (IWCA), our published articles focused for the most part on the role that graduate students, primarily English majors, played as tutors, as assistant directors, and, occasionally, as directors. Graduate students did use our writing centers, both for their work on theses and dissertations and for writing assigned in their programmatically required coursework. We did what we always do best: listened, assisted them to develop writing and tutoring goals, and worked with them on their projects—often on issues surrounding clarity as it was so subjectively defined by their teachers or advisors.

At our own Marquette center and at many centers around the country, our predominantly undergraduate tutors worked with graduate writers, and we all learned the importance of helping our tutors learn more about writing genres. So while graduate users of our centers often wanted us to give them feedback on the clarity of their writing, including issues of sentence structure and punctuation, tutors were able to draw them out to help them adhere to the genre expectations of their assignments as well. Still, many of us who did not have graduate writing centers wished for funding to start one like the excellent example at Penn State University. At the same time, we were being exposed to new ideas about tutoring—ideas relevant to working with graduate writers—as we visited or consulted with centers around the world. Our globally-based counterparts at conferences, such as those sponsored by the European Association of Teachers of Academic Writing (EATAW), and our fellow members of IWCA affiliates, such as the European Writing Centers Association (EWCA), typically had training in applied linguistics and genre studies rather than in rhetoric and composition. We learned, too, from visits to the professionally staffed writing center at Central European University in Budapest, a graduate-only, English-only university with a Center for Academic Writing.

I was the writing center director at Marquette University in 2005 when I began working on graduate support initiatives. At that time, in addition to our fifteen undergraduate peer tutors, our small center was staffed by four graduate students from English literature who, as part of their teaching assistantships, tutored for ten hours a week. Our graduate student clients liked to work with these tutors, although, if they were not available, they were also happy to work with our knowledgeable and well-trained undergraduate generalist peer tutors, most of whom were English or education majors. I was always happy when a science or social science major would take our for-credit undergraduate tutor preparation course and would be able to contribute in ways that enhanced the work of our entire center. I worked hard to try to get students from diverse majors to become tutors, but most of them had trouble fitting an extra course into their crammed schedules, unlike our English and education majors, who were able to count the prep course as part of their writing requirements.

When one of the writing center's faculty allies, a physics and engineering professor, became an associate dean of the graduate school, he and I saw the opportunity to better address the needs of our graduate student writers across the university. To that end, we met with graduate program directors to brainstorm. When some of these directors expressed the wish that their graduate students could gain expertise as consultants, my dreams morphed from hoping for a graduate writing center to hoping to train graduate TAs to be discipline-embedded tutors within their own departments.

A grant from the Council of Graduate Schools and an enthusiastic group of faculty members allowed us to proceed with a pilot program of two graduate writing consultants (GWCs) from philosophy and theology. These two pioneering consultants spent the summer reading articles and book chapters from the one-semester undergraduate tutor syllabus augmented with readings from genre studies as well as the few articles available on graduate writers. They interviewed faculty members in their programs, asking what kinds of writing they assigned in courses and why they assigned that writing. Then they made up handouts for entering graduate students and spoke to them at their orientations about the various kinds of writing their courses and their thesis or dissertation work would demand of them. The GWCs invited the new graduate students to visit them and to use the writing center as well. The grant paid the GWCs and instructor for the summer of preparation, and the GWCs' departments paid for the peer consulting offered during the academic term.

The initiative took on more GWCs the following summer and the next, as psychology, engineering, and biomedical engineering asked to have more than one of their TAs take the training. The graduate programs that participated were delighted with the results, and additional programs wanted to be part of our project. But, as the grant came to an end, the funding ended as well. The dean of the graduate school saw the value of the GWC project but did not see a way to support it without funds from the new provost, who was looking for funds to cut rather than initiatives to fund. When I left Marquette, the program left too.

My move to Florida International University (FIU) in Miami in 2009 was prompted in part by the appeal of its diverse, multilingual student population, where the white non-Hispanic student is the "other" in both the undergraduate and graduate population. In my job interview for director of the FIU writing center, it was clear that the university wanted me to increase the size and scope of their writing center, the Center for Excellence in Writing, and they were especially interested in offering more and better support for graduate student writers. The dean of the University Graduate School, the dean of Arts and Sciences (the entity I reported to), and the provost all seemed eager to have a Graduate Writing Consultant program at FIU as well as a dissertation retreat. What I did not know was that the graduate dean, then my key contact, was also on the job market and would be gone when I arrived, replaced by an interim dean for a few years.

The new permanent dean came with priorities of his own, and a vision of how his funds would be spent. And, while he continued to fund some post-masters-level tutors for our writing center to work with graduate students, he was not open to the idea of GWCs. Nor was he enthusiastic about the week-long dissertation retreat the then-assistant director and I had envisioned and planned with the interim dean, one that would bring in faculty consultants from the sciences and social sciences and provide meals for the participants. The Graduate School support was limited to having their staff screen the participants, and so we kept the retreat smaller than we had initially planned. In spite of these disappointments, the retreat allowed us to network with program and dissertation directors, contacts to keep alive as we move forward with our stellar record of participant completions.

What is the takeaway from all the plans, meetings, grant proposals, and pleadings I've detailed, all aimed to help graduate writers make their impressive work a little easier, less stressful, and more celebration-worthy? What has emerged for me is a conviction that partnerships with administrators, graduate directors, thesis and dissertation directors, and other stakeholders are vital, even though some disappointing personnel changes may occur. Writing center directors need to do more than wait for the eager graduate writer to walk through the door and tell us what they need. We must be ready to advocate for the cost-effectiveness of programming that best benefits them so that we can continue to show—and to feel—that we contribute to the degree completion and success of our graduate students, and therefore to the standing of our institutions. This volume will help us approach administrators and our faculty colleagues more effectively as well-informed writing center practitioners. It will help us be ready to share with them persuasive arguments and articles explaining what can and has been done at other places, what is possible, and what returns they might be able to expect in exchange for a relatively small but vital investment in graduate student success and completion.

Beginning with useful calls for re-examinations of our "givens," this collection also offers us innovative pedagogical moves, introduces us to initiatives that our writing center colleagues have found successful, and concludes with a call for working with the sometimes-daunting faculty advisors whose ideas of graduate writing and the needs of graduate writers may not mesh with ours. This volume will contribute toward our expertise as we try to envision what creates the best learning and writing support environment for our graduate writers.

Introduction
Writing Center Pedagogies and Practices Reconsidered for Graduate Student Writers

Susan Lawrence and Terry Myers Zawacki

Origin stories matter, as Neal Lerner (2009) tells us; they authorize endeavors and institutions and define their missions. We begin this introduction, then, with the origins of our interest in investigating writing center support for graduate students, an interest that led first to a special issue of *Writing Lab Newsletter* we co-edited in 2016, and ultimately to this volume.

Our account opens in the writing center, from our own perspective on the ground. In 2013, as a new director of George Mason University's writing center, Susan noticed that over 25 percent of the tutorial sessions were booked by graduate students, almost two thousand appointments annually, with 70 percent of those being held by writers who identified their first language as other than English, a number that was not dramatically different from when Terry had directed the center over eight years before and that has held steady to the present. Our usage data also showed that many graduate students were booking multiple sessions, suggesting that we were providing something of value. Yet we also heard our undergraduate and English masters student tutors asking how to work, within the confines of a 45-minute session, with a writer who brings a thirty-page chapter from a thesis or dissertation; whether it was acceptable to work on local concerns exclusively with a dissertation writer; or how to address substantive concerns when the dissertation genre is unfamiliar and when the text's subject matter is so specialized as to defy comprehension. Our WAC-informed writing center served students in majors across the university, but the tutors' practice, so clearly developed for undergraduate writers and writing, was frequently challenged by the advanced graduate writers they met in sessions.

Our situation was not news to writing center professionals, of course. In the mid-1990s John Thomas Farrell (1994) and Judith Powers (1995) wrote in the *Writing Lab Newsletter* about an increase in consultations with graduate students at their writing centers starting in the 1980s. And we ourselves had, before 2013, heard and responded to requests to serve graduate thesis and dissertation writers, supporting doctoral student writing groups in the mid-2000s and, more recently, offering weekly graduate student write-ins. But we hadn't taken stock; we hadn't asked how fully our existing practices and resources met—or didn't meet—the needs of the advanced graduate student writers who called on them. How could this group of writers be served with existing staff, pedagogies, and training structures? How would these resources need to be reconfigured, reinvented, or augmented to better meet the students' needs?

At almost the same time that Susan was reflecting on graduate students' use of the writing center, Terry, as then-director of Mason's Writing Across the Curriculum (WAC) program, was invited to a meeting of academic administrators to discuss concerns about high attrition rates and extended time to degree in our doctoral programs and to offer possible interventions, including those aimed at writing.[1] Before proposing any writing-related interventions, Terry suggested that a better understanding of the problem was needed, particularly related to doctoral students leaving as ABDs. Subsequently she and two colleagues received funding to study the challenges facing dissertation writers—both English L1 (first language) and English L2 (second language)—and their advisors and to provide data-driven recommendations (see Rogers, Zawacki, and Baker 2016). Among their survey, focus group, and interview findings was the discouraging, but not altogether surprising, general perception that the writing center could not adequately assist these writers with complex disciplinary tasks. While in focus groups many of the doctoral students who had sought assistance from the writing center said it was useful, they also felt the pressure to get their writing "fixed" and often minimized or failed to recognize the value of the higher-order generic and rhetorical writing instruction they described receiving.

The feedback we'd elicited from both our tutors and our graduate student clients made it clear that supporting graduate student writers would call for evaluating our existing practices. The student-centered, nondirective, generalist pedagogies that Linda Shamoon and Deborah Burns (1995) present as writing center "orthodoxy" (134) and that emerged as writing centers oriented to undergraduate writers seemed, as others have observed (Kiedaisch and Dinitz 1993; Mackiewicz 2004; Dinitz and Harrington 2014), not fully adequate for writers in the disciplines, much less for writers doing advanced disciplinary research and writing. Despite the apparent lack of congruency between orthodox writing center pedagogies and those potentially effective with advanced graduate writers, we believe that writing center foundations do bring graduate students within the ambit of writing center work. For example, Muriel Harris's (1995) landmark article on what tutors can do for writers invokes a set of activities, needs, and goals we can easily see as relevant to graduate students: the acquisition of strategic knowledge; the move toward independence fostered by talk about writing; support with the affective dimension of writing; the illumination of tacit disciplinary conventions.

With these foundations in mind, we proposed and co-edited a special issue of *Writing Lab Newsletter* (2016) focused on writing center support for thesis and dissertation writers. The process of editing this special issue, for which we received many times the number of proposals that could be included as articles, led us to envision this volume, which explores how engaging with these thesis and dissertation writers can cause us to rethink and revise the principles and practices that have been definitional in writing center theory and pedagogy, and to examine how this endeavor complicates our already complex conversations about writing center identities, pedagogies, formats, and spaces.

DEFINING IDENTITIES—GRADUATE STUDENT WRITERS AND WRITING

Writing center practices are necessarily responsive to the specific needs and circumstances of the students who lay claim to our attention. Before proceeding, then, we pause to reflect on the specific needs and circumstances of advanced graduate writers and writing, which, as we and the authors in this volume contend, call for a reconsideration of many of our core writing center practices.

As has been well documented in the literature, the development of writing expertise in a discipline is a gradual process (e.g., see Berkenkotter, Huckin, and Ackerman 1988; Carter 1990; Beaufort 2004; Thaiss and Zawacki 2006). Graduate-level writing, and theses and dissertations in particular, bring a degree of rhetorical and generic complexity that goes far beyond the simple application of general (and presumably already-learned) rules to new situations. Graduate writers, for example, must learn to pose an original question, narrow and pursue the question using appropriate resources and methods, and make original and appropriately supported claims, a set of tasks that cannot be accomplished at the level expected without a degree of knowledge transformation that far exceeds that required of most undergraduates. In addition to learning to make knowledge in their disciplines, graduate students must become familiar with the genres and moves that allow them to craft knowledge in ways appropriate to the communities of practice in which they are writing. Along the way, they are expected to have acquired the confidence to project an authoritative scholarly identity to audiences who are often disguised as "any reader" or as an "evoked" or "implicated" reader by the students' advisors or committees (Kamler and Thomson 2008; Parry 1998; Paré, Starke-Meyerring, and McAlpine 2009; Rogers, Zawacki, and Baker 2016).

All of the developmental processes described here are, of course, more complicated and difficult for English L2 writers who are struggling to acquire the correct language—vocabulary, grammar, syntax, sentence structure—for the task along with the rhetorical, sociolinguistic, and genre knowledge appropriate to advanced work in the program and field (e.g., see Prior 1991; Riazi 1997; Dong 1998, Partridge and Starfield 2007; Tardy 2009).

Yet even as these advanced graduate writers, whether English L1 or L2, are still developing, they are assumed to have already learned to write at the level expected and may accordingly receive little instruction or guidance when it comes to negotiating these challenges (Duff 2010; Gardner 2010; Paré 2011; Kamler and Thomson 2006), or even acknowledgment that the challenges exist. Further, if graduate faculty have internalized this discourse knowledge themselves, as is often the case, they may not easily access or even acknowledge it; the rhetorical situatedness of the writing they do may have become transparent (Carter 1990; Russell 2002; Paré 2011), perceived as a "normalized practice" or a "common sense" skill (Starke-Meyerring 2011; Starke-Meyerring et al. 2014). Also often transparent or "occluded" and "out of sight" are the "systems of genres" or "genre sets" (Bazerman 1994; Devitt 2009; Autry and Carter 2015) that comprise a thesis or dissertation, and that are precisely the genres and subgenres that most challenge graduate writers. The consequences are multiple: first, faculty may expect that "good writing skills" alone are adequate to the task of writing in the discipline; second, faculty are unlikely to explicitly teach knowledge that, for them, lacks visibility; and third, when writing—its genres, subgenres, moves, and conventions—is seen as normalized, decontextualized practice, graduate student writers who have not achieved proficiency are perceived as deficient and in need of remediation, by the advisor and often by the students themselves who have internalized this view (Turner 2000; Starke-Meyerring 2011; Rogers, Zawacki, and Baker 2016).

We see gaps here that writing centers can help address, but if we do not shape practices in response to graduate writers' distinct circumstances, we risk alienating them in a context that may already have them feeling alienated as writers. Enculturation must be a two-way street, as scholars focusing on English L2 graduate students have proposed: not only are graduate students enculturated into disciplinary communities; they too should transform the local academic communities in which they participate (see Leki, Cumming, and Silva 2008, 39–41, for a discussion of the literature on this issue, and Salter-Dvorak 2014 for a more recent case study), including their faculty's teaching and mentoring practices (Fujiyoka 2014). We want to think through positions and findings like this in a writing center context: by being open to changing our practices and identities in response to the distinctive qualities and needs of L1 and L2 graduate writers, writing centers can fulfill the mission of supporting them rather than leaving them to feel further estranged.

COMPLICATING IDENTITIES AND PRACTICES—PEERNESS, PEDAGOGIES, INTERACTIONS, SPACES

We propose also that the benefit is mutual: that is, to develop targeted, intentional ways of serving graduate students, writing center practitioners can discover new avenues for conceiving of writing center theory and practice. Below we consider how the turn to working with advanced disciplinary writers can inflect ongoing writing center conversations about peerness and pedagogy, higher order concerns and lower order concerns, one-to-one tutoring, and writing center spaces. Specifically, we propose that turning to graduate students complicates simple notions of peerness, augments the repertoire of pedagogies tutors use in sessions, deconstructs the opposition between higher order concerns and lower order concerns, decenters individual tutoring as the core writing center practice, and simultaneously changes and expands spaces of writing center practice.

Questioning Peerness

Already nuanced debates about generalist and specialist tutors acquire additional intricacy and depth when our clients are doing the advanced disciplinary research and writing that graduate students bring to the writing center. The shorthand "generalist/specialist" used to describe these debates can conflate issues of peerness and pedagogy, a topic Michael Pemberton addresses in his chapter in this volume, and we distinguish and treat these issues separately here. The issue of tutor identities and peerness is itself multi-layered: what does it mean, for example, to share a writer's disciplinary expertise when the research is highly specialized?

Even a tutor and writer in the same discipline may inhabit different subdisciplines, and of course most writing centers cannot hire tutors from every discipline on campus. For these reasons, Michael Carter's (2007) treatment of "metadisciplinarity" has been fruitful in theorizing and designing writing support for graduate writers, as Megan Autry and Michael Carter (2015) show. Another layer of disciplinary peerness arising with graduate writers has to do with research methods: disciplinary knowledge at the graduate level comprises research methods, and tutors who understand writers' disciplinary or even metadisciplinary methods are particularly valuable to those writers (e.g., see Phillips 2016). Yet another layer of peerness arises when we ask whether the tutor and writer are at the same degree level—is the tutor an undergraduate, masters student, PhD student in coursework, ABD (all but dissertation), or even faculty? These layers remind us how complicated the concept of peerness in the writing center can become when writers are doing advanced disciplinary work. Some of these complications are addressed in this volume in chapters by Pemberton and by Juliann Reinecke, Mary Glavan, Douglas Philips, and Joanna Wolfe.

Enlarging Pedagogical Repertoires

Related to the question "who is the tutor?" but distinct from that question, is that of the pedagogies tutors draw upon when working with advanced graduate student writers, interactions that call for a greater repertoire of practices and approaches. The lengthy disciplinary texts graduate writers can bring, for example, put pressure on the practice, used in many writing centers, of having writers read their draft aloud at the beginning of a session, as Elena Kallestinova's chapter shows. Disciplinarity is a key issue here, too, and in the literature we see a variety of approaches that allow tutors who may not share a writer's disciplinary expertise to work productively with that writer, including those we would call generalist (e.g., see Barron and Cicciarelli 2016), genre-informed (Savini 2011; Devet 2014; Vorhies 2015), and L2 pedagogies, which include greater attention to local concerns, a topic we discuss in detail below, as well as greater directivity (Reid 1994; Thonus 2004; Williams and Severino 2004; Rafoth 2015, 131). These debates about directive and nondirective methods are also complicated and enriched by advanced graduate writers, for whom directive approaches may hold particular value, especially when the tutor is a specialist who can model appropriate practice. In their argument for the potential value of directive tutoring methods, in fact, Shamoon and Burns (1995) begin with paradigm cases of graduate student writers who learned substantially from their advisors' very directive approaches to feedback (137–39). Christine Tardy (2005), too, found in her case study that heavy-handed advisors helped writers make leaps in rhetorical knowledge (331). In this volume, chapters that address pedagogies for working with advanced graduate writers on local concerns include those by Joan Turner and Michelle Cox.

If tutors need a greater repertoire of strategies for working with advanced graduate writers, then tutor training is essential—yet graduate tutors may receive less training than undergraduate peer tutors do (Phillips 2013; Summers, this volume). Even as the complexities of working with advanced graduate writers call for substantial training, the circumstances of employing graduate tutors can militate against providing such training: university financial structures along with graduate tutor commitments to their own disciplines (if they are not from writing studies) can limit the funding and time available for preparing them to tutor.

Reprioritizing Local Concerns

On its surface, the rationale for prioritizing higher order concerns (HOCs) seems well grounded in common sense: these global dimensions of a text are important to the text's quality, and they are also "early-order" concerns that should be in place before writers edit paragraphs and sentences. But working with advanced graduate writers can prompt writing center practitioners to revisit this imperative and interrogate the binary it depends on, including the priority assigned to HOCs.

While writers at all levels may ask tutors to address concerns like "grammar" and "correctness," of course, graduate writers may have unique and pressing reasons for focusing tutors' attention on local concerns. Some graduate writers deliberately elicit different kinds of feedback from their faculty instructors or advisors, their colleagues, and writing center tutors; they may ask tutors to focus on "grammar" or language, and rely on faculty and colleagues to provide feedback on elements of the project that they see as calling for disciplinary expertise (Mannon 2016).

But the idea that so-called surface issues are distinct from larger issues of meaning is deeply problematic. Indeed, anyone who actually works in depth with advanced disciplinary writers on their texts can experience the intellectual pleasure of seeing this opposition practically deconstruct itself. For example, Joan Turner's (this volume) account of working with a dissertation writer ostensibly at the sentence level shows how she and the writer, as they work phrase by phrase, tap into and disentangle issues of theory, structure, and voice in the text. Indeed, research in linguistics shows that word choice, for instance, a concern that falls decidedly within sentences, is not a local concern at all (Casanave and Hubbard 1992, 42). Choosing words, writers call on their strategic knowledge as well as intersentential and local knowledge of a text (Jonz 1990), and they deploy higher-order conceptual processing (Bachman 1982). Not surprisingly, then, Turner argues that "the [supposedly local] language work" writers and consultants perform on advanced disciplinary texts should be recognized for the "intellectual hard labour" it requires.

In addition, making missteps in so-called local features of a text may have higher-order *consequences* that are particularly salient for graduate writers. One such consequence concerns voice and disciplinary identity: subtle stance-taking moves and language, for instance, contribute to a writer's disciplinary voice and *ethos* as they arise from that writer's text (Lancaster 2014). Making these moves appropriately identifies writers as members of their disciplines, and missing the mark on such moves can identify writers as outsiders, as Michelle Cox (this volume) emphasizes in stressing the importance of teaching tutors to notice these often subtle features of professional and student texts. Again, professional identities are at stake when "correctness in writing [becomes] be a marker" of such identities—or lack of identity (Mannon 2016). These signals of appropriateness and correctness have material consequences as well: Phillips (2013) points to those visited on English L2 graduate writers, who, among all graduate students, "especially face discarded conference proposals, publication rejection, and roadblocks to dissertation completion" in fields where competition is high and fluency in language functions as a gatekeeper.

A related problem is that faculty may interpret nonstandard language use as evidence of a writer's cognitive deficiency (Zamel 1995, discussing L2 writers). Yet there is, as Leki, Cumming, and Silva (2008) write, an "enormous disparity" between language use and considerable "disciplinary knowledge and sophistication" for many L2 graduate writers on the path to acquiring English-language academic discourse (38). Twenty years later, however, researchers continue to encounter faculty informants who interpret L2 students' lack of written fluency as lack of comprehension (Zawacki and Habib 2014, 194–95) or even lack of effort (Ives et al. 2014, 219).

Decentering One-to-One Tutoring as the Core of Writing Center Practice
Definitional to writing centers is their identity as sites of individualized learning; that is, writers work one on one with a student peer or, in some

writing centers, a professional tutor, to receive feedback specific to the writing they bring to their sessions. Jackie Grutsch McKinney (2013) has argued that this thread of the writing center narrative, if it dominates the story of what writing centers are, can prevent us from fully exploring other modes of supporting writers as well as diminish the attention we might otherwise give the alternative formats we currently offer. For example, she observes, most writing centers offer workshops, but little writing center scholarship has been devoted to workshop pedagogies or practice (79).

We identify three aspects of graduate writers and writing that can prompt writing centers to explore formats beyond one-to-one consultations: first, writing centers can support graduate students' disciplinary enculturation by devising and facilitating forums in which writers can talk about writing with peers from their own disciplines (Boquet et al. 2015). Second, graduate student writers have evolving needs as they progress through a degree program, and these changing needs call for different modes of support that exceed individual consultations (Autry and Carter 2015). Finally, for graduate writers, writing will remain a high-stakes activity throughout their careers, and writing centers can help writers develop long-term habits of writing productivity. Again, such a goal may call for formats and forums that are not one-to-one conversations with a tutor.

These formats have included workshops, disciplinary and cross-disciplinary writing groups, and retreats, the latter two of which have been theorized and reported on in the literature (e.g., for writing groups, see Phillips 2012; Aitchison and Guerin 2014; Starke-Meyerring et al. 2014; Hixson et al. 2016; for retreats, see Lee and Golde 2013; Simpson 2013; and Busl, Donnelly, and Capdevielle 2015). In this volume, Steve Simpson and Elizabeth Lenaghan point to the specific benefits provided by the peer interactions that occur in such writing groups, benefits, as Simpson notes, especially valuable for L2 graduate writers. And chapters by Marilyn Gray and Ashley Bender Smith, Tika Lamsal, Adam Robinson, and Bronwyn Williams take up the benefits of workshops and writing retreats, focusing on how these forums can illuminate occluded dimensions of thesis and dissertation writing and support disciplinary identities.

Scrutinizing the Spaces of Writing Center Work

Working with advanced graduate writers has us casting a critical eye on commonplaces about writing center spaces as the center of writing center work. One such commonplace concerns access: writing centers are for all students. Our discussion in this introduction presupposes, of course, that university or writing center policies actually permit graduate students to use those spaces, an issue raised in a recent issue of *Praxis* (Madden and Eodice 2016) focusing on access and equity in graduate writing support. In some universities graduate students may not be served because funding comes from undergraduate units, as Kristina Reardon, Tom Deans, and Cheryl Maykel describe in the preamble to their program description, because university administrators believe graduate students should already possess the literacies they need, or because other exigencies (staffing, space) preclude expanding services to these writers (Reardon, Deans, and Maykel 2016). One issue related to access is taken up in the chapter by Patrick Lawrence, Molly Tetrault, and Tom Deans, who prompt us to conceive of access in terms of quality as well as quantity. These authors propose that holding an orientation "intake" meeting with graduate students before they schedule consultations, a practice that can reduce access, ensures that the writers who do secure the limited number of sessions available bring needs the center can effectively address.

Another tenet having to do with space asserts that writing centers are cozy spaces with comfortable furniture, coffee pots, and other elements that make them homelike. Graduate writers may respond to writing center spaces differently than undergraduate writers do, however, and Grutsch McKinney (2013) reminds us that spaces that look inviting to some students may not appear as welcoming to others. Writing centers with well-worn couches and armchairs, for instance, may look cozy and homelike to (middle class, domestic) undergraduates, as Grutch McKinney notes, but for graduate student writers, they can operate as visible indications of a writing center's orientation to a different student population. Graduate students entering an ostensibly undergraduate-oriented writing center may feel not only out of place, but specifically inadequate or remediated, an issue raised by Laura Brady, Nathalie Singh-Corcoran, and James Holsinger in this volume. It's also possible that cozier spaces appear less than professional to students who, as Lawrence, Tetrault, and Deans (this volume) remind us, may place a high value on professionalism. Graduate writers may seek spaces that signify both warmth *and* professionalism.

As a metaphorical space, writing centers experience a tension between inhabiting a location suggested by the name "center," on the one hand, and a perceived place as supplemental either to core writing instruction or to education in the disciplines, on the other. Collectively, many of the authors in this volume move away from a center/periphery configuration of space to envision the writing center as a key *node* in a network of graduate writing support that can include faculty advisors and program directors, upper administration, graduate student organizations, and other units on campus with a stake in graduate student success. The range and depth of the collaborations suggested in these chapters (Pemberton, Simpson, Perdue, and Brady, Singh-Corcoran, and Holsinger) may exceed those that writing centers serving predominantly undergraduate students have felt the need to develop.

* * * * *

In this introduction, we've explored how the idea of a writing center is being reshaped in response to demands—institutional, faculty, student—to assist graduate student writers with high stakes thesis and dissertation projects. In the chapters that follow, the authors take up that exploration, detailing the ways in which our core writing center pedagogies and practices are complicated by our efforts to create intentional, targeted support that responds to the circumstances and needs of advanced graduate writers. We've organized the book into three sections: Revising Our Core Assumptions, with chapters intended to situate support for graduate writers within much-rehearsed writing center arguments around effective pedagogies and practices for what has traditionally been a predominantly undergraduate clientele; Reshaping Our Pedagogies and Practices, with chapters showing how some writing centers are adapting their scheduling and tutorial practices to accommodate the complex generic, rhetorical, and linguistic support needs presented by advanced graduate student writers; and Expanding the Center, with chapters pointing to the value of gathering institutional, departmental, and programmatic data on graduate student support and partnering with those programs and offices similarly concerned with providing that support.

It seems appropriate to begin with a prologue by Paula Gillespie, past president of IWCA and among the first writing center scholars to call for systematic attention to the distinctive needs of graduate student writers. In "Looking Back, Looking Forward," Gillespie reflects on the exigencies around graduate writing that motivated the 2005 Graduate Writing Consultants initiative she developed in partnership with the graduate school at Marquette University and her subsequent experience with trying to develop a similar program at Florida International University. Gillespie's account serves not only as an early why-and-how success story but also as a cautionary tale of how tenuous such initiatives can be.

We begin Part I: Revising Our Core Assumptions, with Michael Pemberton's chapter "Rethinking the WAC/Writing Center/Graduate

Student Connection," in which he revisits his argument in the 1995 *Writing Center Journal* landmark article "Rethinking the WAC/Writing Center Connection" that well-trained generalist tutors possess the necessary expertise to work with the kinds of generic academic writing typically assigned to undergraduates across the curriculum. As he admits, however, his article failed to consider whether generalist tutors, undergraduate or graduate, are likewise equipped to handle the more discipline-specific demands of graduate writing, particularly longer projects like theses or dissertations. In reconsidering his position, he issues a call for writing centers to become fully engaged "co-sponsors" of graduate student writing, a "literal center" for writing across the university that is inclusive not only of student writers but also of faculty and administrators who share our goals and concerns for graduate students' success.

In chapter 2, the focus shifts from Pemberton's vision of what graduate-serving writing centers can be and do to what they currently are, according to Sarah Summers's findings from her 2012 survey of twenty-five writing centers that identified themselves as "primarily dedicated to serving graduate students." In "The Rise of the Graduate-Focused Writing Center: Exigencies and Responses," Summers traces the rise of institutional interest in developing specialized graduate writing support to the perceived crisis in graduate student education and to an increase in international graduate student enrollments. Developing such support requires, as she shows, an awareness of local and national conversations about program attrition and time to degree, familiarity with the emerging body of research on graduate writers and writing, an understanding of the tutorial interventions that might best meet the needs of these writers, and a willingness to gather and share information on all of these areas.

As Steve Simpson points out in his chapter "On the Distinct Needs of Multilingual STEM Graduate Students in Writing Centers," one key topic in the conversation concerns the question of whether writing centers should differentiate the writing support they offer to English L1 and L2 graduate students or provide more holistic forms of support directed at the needs of all students using our services. There are persuasive arguments to be made for each position, he explains, with one of the most compelling being that offering combined support can "shift attention from points of difference (e.g., native language) to points of overlapping need." And yet, as he argues in this chapter, focusing on overlapping writing support needs risks overlooking the distinct needs of the international and resident multilingual graduate students whose writing struggles may look similar to those of L1 writers but which can derive from very different causes.

As the final chapter in this section, Joan Turner's "Getting the Writing Right: Writing/Language Centres and Issues of Pedagogy, Responsibility, Ethics, and International English in Graduate Student Research Writing" also takes up the need for negotiation around L2 language difference and the tutorial expertise required to mediate institutional expectations for "pristine prose" in graduate student research writing. The demand for "getting the writing right" she explains, is based on an overly simplistic understanding of writing as separate from meaning making. When understood this way, it seems appropriate to assume that the responsibility for fixing "deficient" writing (and student writers) lies with writing practitioners who are schooled in attending to the "surface" features of the text and the "mechanics" of standard academic English. Turner calls out writing center professionals for their role in maintaining this assumption through their pedagogical discourse of a hierarchy of writing concerns. Her larger argument concerns the "culturally habituated expectation of a smooth read," an expectation that is not sustainable given "the multiplicity of international voices in English" and English as the lingua franca in the contemporary global economy.

In Part II: Reshaping Our Pedagogies and Practices, we turn to chapters detailing innovative and sometimes unorthodox responses to the challenge of tutoring both English L1 and L2 graduate writers on the longer, more sustained projects they present. We begin with Patrick S. Lawrence, Molly Tetreault, and Tom Deans's "Intake and Orientation: The Role of Initial Writing Center Consultations with Graduate Students," which describes the intake consultations they developed at their writing centers at the University of New Hampshire and the University of Connecticut to manage the increasing numbers of graduate students who were signing up for tutoring, often with the expectation that the tutor would "fix" their text rather than engage in a conversation about writing. Acknowledging, however, that the required consultation might be seen by the graduate students—and other writing center professionals—as a way to restrict access, they elicited feedback from graduate students who participated in the intake consultations and report on their results in this chapter.

In her data-rich chapter "Hybrid Consultations for Graduate Students: How Pre-Reading Can Help Address Graduate Students' Needs," Elena Kallestinova proposes that a hybrid consultation model consisting of "pre-reading" followed by a face-to-face session is "optimal" for working with the longer discipline-specific projects that graduate writers bring to a session. In support of this claim, she offers evidence from a wealth of usage, client evaluation, and interview data, showing that consultants and clients overwhelmingly prefer the hybrid sessions, and that issues taken up in hybrid sessions are different from those addressed in sessions that don't include pre-reading. She interprets her findings through the lens of research on reading comprehension and modalities. Kallestinova's chapter demonstrates the many ways that writing center usage and client report data can be mined to support arguments we are called on to make about the value of our graduate support services.

With Michelle Cox's chapter "'Noticing' Language in the Writing Center: Preparing Writing Center Tutors to Support Graduate Multilingual Writers," we return to a critique Turner raises in her chapter, and that we discuss earlier in this introduction, about the relevance for English L2 writers of a writing center pedagogy that privileges "higher order" or structural concerns over seemingly "lower order" or editing concerns at the sentence and language level. Drawing on the concept of "noticing" in L2 acquisition, Cox argues that working at the sentence-level with multilingual graduate student writers can honor a writing center philosophy of improving the writer, along with the writing, while at the same time promoting writer agency. She offers a range of tutor training resources in support of those goals.

The chapter "'Novelty Moves': Training Tutors to Engage with Technical Content" also concerns close attention to language, in this case the highly specialized language and content of the projects advanced graduate writers bring to the center and the demands these place on tutors. The authors Juliann Reineke, Mary Glavan, Doug Phillips, and Joanna Wolfe describe a genre-based "novelty moves" approach, adapted from John Swales's CARS model, which they train tutors to use as a question-generating heuristic in sessions with graduate writers. Drawing on interview data from tutors, the authors show that this approach allows tutors to engage with difficult technical content rather than turn to surface-level suggestions and corrections. Their findings suggest also that for tutors to be successful, they need intensive, scaffolded practice on when and how to use the novelty moves effectively, a training process the authors describe.

While writing centers have traditionally reached out beyond their walls to find allies and partner with other pedagogical initiatives to serve their predominantly undergraduate clientele, the chapters in Part III: Expanding the Center, taken together, make the argument that, for writing centers focused on graduate support, such allies and partnerships are crucial for initiating and sustaining their work, particularly given that funding can be so tenuous, as Gillespie's Prologue shows. Focusing on a partnership that will be familiar to most writing center practitioners,

Laura Brady, Nathalie Singh Corcoran, and James Holsinger's chapter "A Change for the Better: Writing Center/WID Partnerships to Support Graduate Writing" applies organization development theory to suggest a framework for change that can guide writing center directors in initiating and managing the programmatic growth that supporting advanced graduate student writers necessarily involves. They describe strategies for creating sustainable support for graduate writers, including collecting data from graduate students and faculty, analyzing organizational structures and local alliances, developing resources for tutors who work with advanced disciplinary writers, and creating opportunities for graduate faculty across the disciplines to reflect on their own scholarly identities, writing knowledge, and expectations for student writers.

In "'Find Something You Know You Can Believe In': The Effect of Dissertation Retreats on Graduate Students' Identities as Writers," Ashly Bender Smith, Tika Lamsal, Adam Robinson, and Bronwyn Williams show that focusing on graduate writers' scholarly identities may motivate writing centers to expand beyond individual consultations. The authors present findings from interviews with dissertation writers who attended a dissertation retreat; students reported that participating in the retreat made them more confident about their identities as writers and scholars, more reflective and conscious of their writing processes, and more aware of themselves as part of a community of scholarly writers. As the authors explain, their findings offer support for an approach to retreats that puts an equal emphasis on output, for example, number of pages written, and "less immediately tangible goals such as a more nuanced understanding of writing processes and an enhanced sense of agency as scholarly writers," with the latter crucial for doctoral students whose identities as scholars are still emerging.

In her chapter "More Than Dissertation Support: Aligning Programs with Professional Development and Other Doctoral Student Needs," Marilyn Gray makes a case for aligning the goals of graduate writing support with graduate student identities that go beyond the purely scholarly. In order to cultivate a broad base of support and funding, she recommends that writing centers demonstrate how the writing support they offer also contributes to academic progress, professional development, and well-being outcomes. To that end, she shows how writing center directors can explore a range of data on doctoral students' general support needs, including reports on students' perceptions and concerns about their own academic progress, mental health, and career prospects, as well as professional development competencies that are increasingly being adopted by institutions. Gray's chapter explains how

UCLA's graduate writing center, located in Student Affairs, has drawn on these data to inform their support initiatives, focusing in particular on discipline-specific dissertation retreats they offer.

Elizabeth Lenaghan's chapter "Revisiting the Remedial Framework: How Writing Centers Can Better Serve Graduate Students and Themselves" is similarly concerned with how writing centers frame the work they do with graduate writers. She argues against situating the need for support for graduate writing within concerns around program attrition and time to degree, as many centers—and chapters in this book—have done. She maintains that evoking these concerns as exigencies for our work with graduate writers risks confirming the already widely held perception of writing centers as remedial, product-oriented "fix-it" shops, a perception which, in turn, marginalizes the role centers can play in graduate student education. In her chapter, Lenaghan explains how she counters this perception in the development and marketing of graduate center services, including a well-funded Graduate Writing Fellows initiative. In support of her claims for the effectiveness of all of these efforts in changing perceptions of the center, she offers evidence from graduate client surveys, Fellows' session reports, and increasing numbers of students booking multiple appointments.

Many of the chapters in this collection, most notably the opening chapter by Michael Pemberton, address the need for writing centers to connect with faculty advisors who may perceive thesis and dissertation writing as merely a matter of "writing up" the research and who are often unprepared to give meaningful feedback on writing issues that go beyond surface-level fixes. We close, then, with an epilogue by Sherry Wynn Perdue that takes up the call for support for faculty supervisors as co-sponsors of graduate students' writing literacy development. In "Centering Dissertation Supervision; What Is, What Can be," Perdue describes the theoretical framework that guided her design and implementation of a dissertation supervision fellowship program she piloted through her writing center and her plans for an empirical investigation of how the program may have enhanced the faculty fellows' beliefs, supervision experiences, genre knowledge, and feedback practices—in sum, the degree to which interventions like hers might build upon the work presented in this and other scholarship on graduate writing support.

Collectively, the chapters in this volume suggest that advanced graduate student writers present an exigence for writing centers that differs from that presented by undergraduate writers, and that responding to this exigence has given writing centers the occasion to reconsider many of the principles and practices that have emerged from our work with undergraduate writers. This kind of reconsideration, we propose, not only benefits graduate writers but also writing centers as we identify and pursue new possibilities for inquiry and practice.

NOTE

1. Conversations like this were also happening at the national (and international) level, precipitated by reports from the Council of Graduate Schools on its PhD Completion project (e.g., see 2008) as well as by universities' recruitment of increasing numbers of international graduate students as a part of institutional strategic goals, as Summers (this volume) discusses.

REFERENCES

Aitchison, Claire, and Cally Guerin, eds. 2014. *Writing Groups for Doctoral Education and Beyond: Innovations in Practice and Theory*. London: Routledge.

Autry, Megan Kittle, and Michael Carter. 2015. "Unblocking Occluded Genres in Graduate Writing." *Composition Forum* 31. http://compositionforum.com/issue/31/north-carolina-state.php.

Bachman, Lyle. 1982. "The Trait Structure of Cloze Test Scores." *TESOL Quarterly* 16 (1): 61–70. https://doi.org/10.2307/3586563.

Barron, Paul, and Louis Cicciarelli. 2016. "Stories and Maps: Narrative Tutoring Strategies for Working with Dissertation Writers." *WLN: A Journal of Writing Center Scholarship* 40 (5–6): 26–29.

Bazerman, Charles. 1994. "Systems of Genres and the Enactment of Social Intentions." In *Genre and the New Rhetoric*, ed. Aviva Freedman and Peter Medway, 79–101. London: Taylor & Francis.

Beaufort, Anne. 2004. "Developmental Gains of a History Major: A Case for Building a Theory of Disciplinary Writing Expertise." *Research in the Teaching of English* 39:136–85.

Berkenkotter, Carol, Thomas N. Huckin, and John M. Ackerman. 1988. "Conventions, Conversations, and the Writer: Case Study of a Student in a Rhetoric PhD Program." *Research in the Teaching of English* 22 (1): 9–41. https://wac.colostate.edu/atd/graduate_wac/busletal2015.cfm.

Boquet, Elizabeth, Meredith Kazer, Nancy Manister, Owen Lucas, Michael Shaw, Valerie Madaffari, and Cinthia Gannett. 2015. "Just Care: Learning from and with Graduate Students from a Doctor of Nursing Practice Program." *Across the Disciplines* 12 (3). https://wac.colostate.edu/atd/graduate_wac/boquetetal2015.cfm.

Busl, Gretchen, Kara Lee Donnelly, and Matthew Capdevielle. 2015. "Camping in the Disciplines: Assessing the Effect of Writing Camps on Graduate Student Writers." *Across the Disciplines: Graduate Writing Across the Disciplines* 12 (3).

Carter, Michael. 2007. "Ways of Knowing, Doing, and Writing in the Disciplines." *College Composition and Communication* 58 (3): 385–418.

Carter, Michael. 1990. "The Idea of Expertise: An Exploration of Cognitive and Social Dimensions of Writing." *College Composition and Communication* 41 (3): 265–86. https://doi.org/10.2307/357655.

Casanave, Christine, and Philip Hubbard. 1992. "Writing Assignments and Writing Problems of Doctoral Students: Faculty Perceptions, Pedagogical Issues, and Needed Research." *English for Specific Purposes* 11 (1): 33–49. https://doi.org/10.1016/0889-4906(92)90005-U.

Council of Graduate Schools. 2008. *PhD Completion and Attrition: Analysis of Baseline Program Data from the PhD Completion Project*. Washington, DC: Council on Graduate Schools.

Devet, Bonnie. 2014. "Using Metagenre and Ecocomposition to Train Writing Center Tutors for Writing in the Disciplines." *Praxis: A Writing Center Journal* 11 (2). http://www.praxisuwc.com/devett-112.

Devitt, Amy. 2009. "Teaching Critical Genre Awareness." In *Genre in a Changing World*, ed. Charles Bazerman, Adair Bonini, and Debora Figueiredo, 337–51. West Lafayette, IN: Parlor Press.

Dinitz, Sue, and Susanmarie Harrington. 2014. "The Role of Disciplinary Expertise in Shaping Writing Tutorials." *Writing Center Journal* 33 (2): 73–98.

Dong, Yu Ren. 1998. "Non-Native Graduate Students' Thesis/Dissertation Writing in Science: Self-reports by Students and Their Advisors from Two U.S. Institutions." *English for Special Purposes* 17 (4): 369–90.

Duff, Patricia. 2010. "Language Socialization into Academic Discourse Communities." *Annual Review of Applied Linguistics* 30:169–92.

Farrell, John Thomas. 1994. "Some of the Challenges to Writing Centers Posed by Graduate Students." *Writing Lab Newsletter* 18 (6): 3–5.

Fujioka, Mayumi. 2014. "L2 Student–U.S. Professor Interactions through Disciplinary Writing Assignments: An Activity Theory Perspective." *Journal of Second Language Writing* 25: 40–58.

Gardner, Susan K. 2010. "Faculty Perspectives on Doctoral Student Socialization in Five Disciplines." *International Journal of Doctoral Studies* 5:39–53. https://doi.org/10.28945/1310.

Grutsch McKinney, Jackie. 2013. *Peripheral Visions for Writing Centers*. Logan: Utah State University Press. https://doi.org/10.2307/j.ctt4cgk97.

Harris, Muriel. 1995. "Talking in the Middle: Why Writers Need Writing Tutors." *College English* 57 (1): 27–42. https://doi.org/10.2307/378348.

Hixson, Cory, Walter Lee, Dierdre Hunter, Marie Paretti, Holly Matsovich, and Rachel McCord. 2016. "Understanding the Structural and Attitudinal Elements That Sustain a Graduate Student Writing Group in an Engineering Department." *WLN: A Journal of Writing Center Scholarship* 40 (5–6): 18–25.

Ives, Lindsey, Elizabeth Leahy, Anni Leming, Tom Peirce, and Michael Schwartz. 2014. "'I Don't Know If That Was the Right Thing to Do': Cross-Disciplinary/Cross-Institutional Faculty Respond to L2 Writing." In *WAC and Second Language Writers: Research towards Linguistically and Culturally Inclusive Programs and Practices*, ed. Terry Myers Zawacki and Michelle Cox, 211–32. Fort Collins, CO: The WAC Clearinghouse.

Jonz, John. 1990. "Another Turn in the Conversation: What Does Cloze Measure?" *TESOL Quarterly* 24 (1): 61–83. https://doi.org/10.2307/3586852.

Kamler, Barbara, and Pat Thomson. 2006. *Helping Doctoral Students Write: Pedagogies for Supervision*. London: Routledge.

Kiedaisch, Jean, and Sue Dinitz. 1993. "Look Back and Say, 'So What?' The Limitations of the Generalist Tutor." *Writing Center Journal* 14 (1): 63–75.

Kamler, Barbara, and Pat Thomson. 2008. "The Failure of Dissertation Advice Books: Towards Alternative Pedagogies for Doctoral Writing." *Educational Researcher* 37 (8): 507–14. https://doi.org/10.3102/0013189X08327390.

Lancaster, Zak. 2014. "Making Stance Explicit for Second Language Writers in the Disciplines: What Faculty Need to Know about the Language of Stance-Taking." In *WAC and Second Language Writers: Research towards Linguistically and Culturally Inclusive Programs and Practices*, ed. Terry Myers Zawacki and Michelle Cox, 269–98. Fort Collins, CO: The WAC Clearinghouse.

Lawrence, Susan, and Terry Myers Zawacki, eds. 2016. Special issue *Writing Lab Newsletter* 40 (5–6).

Lee, Sohui, and Chris Golde. 2013. "Completing the Dissertation and Beyond: Writing Centers and Dissertation Boot Camps." *Writing Lab Newsletter* 37 (7–8): 1–6.

Leki, Ilona, Alister Cumming, and Tony Silva. 2008. *A Synthesis of Research on Second Language Writing in English*. New York: Routledge.

Lerner, Neal. 2009. *The Idea of a Writing Laboratory*. Carbondale: Southern Illinois University Press.

Mackiewicz, Jo. 2004. "The Effects of Tutor Expertise in Engineering Writing: A Linguistic Analysis of Tutors' Comments." *IEEE Transactions on Professional Communication* 47 (4): 316–28. https://doi.org/10.1109/TPC.2004.840485.

Madden, Shannon, and Michele Eodice, eds. 2016. "Access and Equity in Graduate Writing Support." Special issue, *Praxis: A Writing Center Journal* 14 (1). http://www.praxisuwc.com/new-page-29/.

Mannon, Bethany Ober. 2016. "What Do Graduate Students Want from the Writing Center? Tutoring Practices to Support Dissertation and Thesis Writers." *Praxis: A Writing Center Journal* 13 (2). http://www.praxisuwc.com/mannon-132.

Paré, Anthony. 2011. "Speaking of Writing: Supervisory Feedback and the Dissertation." In *Doctoral Education: Research-Based Strategies for Doctoral Students, Supervisors, and Administrators*, ed. Lynn McAlpine and Cheryl Amundsen, 59–74. New York: Springer.

Paré, Anthony, Doreen Starke-Meyerring, and Lynn McAlpine. 2009. "The Dissertation as Multi-Genre: Many Readers, Many Readings." In *Genre in a Changing World: Perspectives on Writing*, ed. Charles Bazerman, Adair Bonini, and Débora Figueiredo. Fort Collins, CO: The WAC Clearinghouse and Parlor Press. Electronic version. https://wac.colostate.edu/books/genre/.

Parry, Sharon. 1998. "Disciplinary Discourse in Doctoral Theses." *Higher Education* 36 (3): 273–99. https://doi.org/10.1023/A:1003216613001.

Partridge, Brian, and Sue Starfield. 2007. *Thesis and Dissertation Writing in a Second Language: A Handbook for Supervisors*. New York: Routledge.

Phillips, Talinn. 2016. "Writing Center Support for Graduate Students: An Integrated Model." In *Supporting Graduate Student Writers: Research, Curriculum, & Program Design*, ed. Steve Simpson, Nigel A. Caplin, Michelle Cox, and Talinn Phillips, 159–70. Ann Arbor: University of Michigan Press.

Phillips, Talinn. 2013. "Tutor Training and Services for Multilingual Graduate Writers: A Reconsideration." *Praxis: A Writing Center Journal* 10 (2). http://www.praxisuwc.com/phillips-102.

Phillips, Tallin. 2012. "Graduate Writing Groups: Shaping Writing and Writers from Student to Scholar." *Praxis: A Writing Center Journal* 10 (1). http://www.praxisuwc.com/phillips-101.

Powers, Judith K. 1995. "Assisting the Graduate Thesis Writer Through Faculty and Writing Center Collaboration." *Writing Lab Newsletter* 20 (2): 13–16.

Prior, Paul. 1991. "Contextualizing Writing and Response in a Graduate Seminar." *Written Communication* 8 (3): 267–310. https://doi.org/10.1177/0741088391008003001.

Rafoth, Ben. 2015. *Multilingual Writers and Writing Centers*. Logan: Utah State University Press.

Reardon, Kristina, Tom Deans, and Cheryl Maykel. 2016. "Finding a Room of Their Own: Programming Time and Space for Graduate Student Writing." *WLN: A Journal of Writing Center Scholarship* 40 (5–6): 10–17.

Riazi, Abdolmehdi. 1997. "Acquiring Disciplinary Literacy: A Social-Cognitive Analysis of Text Production and Learning among Iranian Graduate Students of Education." *Journal of Second Language Writing* 6 (2): 105–37. https://doi.org/10.1016/S1060-3743(97)90030-8.

Reid, Joy. 1994. "Responding to ESL Students' Texts: The Myths of Appropriation." *TESOL Quarterly* 28 (2): 273–92. https://doi.org/10.2307/3587434.

Rogers, Paul, Terry Myers Zawacki, and Sarah E. Baker. 2016. "Uncovering Challenges and Pedagogical Complications in Dissertation Writing and Supervisory Practices: A Multimethod Study of Doctoral Students and Advisors." In *Supporting Graduate Student*

Writers: Research, Curriculum, & Program Design, ed. Steve Simpson, Nigel A. Caplan, Michelle Cox, and Talinn Phillips, 52–77. Ann Arbor: University of Michigan Press.

Russell, David. 2002. *Writing in the Academic Disciplines: A Curricular History*. 2nd ed. Carbondale: Southern Illinois University Press.

Salter-Dvorak, Hania. 2014. "'I've Never Done a Dissertation Before Please Help Me': Accommodating L2 Students Through Course Design." *Teaching in Higher Education* 19 (8): 847–59. https://doi.org/10.1080/13562517.2014.934344.

Savini, Catherine. 2011. "An Alternative Approach to Bridging Disciplinary Divides." *Writing Lab Newsletter* 35 (7–8): 1–5.

Shamoon, Linda K., and Deborah H. Burns. 1995. "A Critique of Pure Tutoring." *Writing Center Journal* 15 (2): 134–52.

Simpson, Steve. 2013. "Building for Sustainability: Dissertation Boot Camp as a Nexus of Graduate Writing Support." *Praxis: A Writing Center Journal* 10 (2). http://www.praxisuwc.com/simpson-102.

Starke-Meyerring, Doreen. 2011. "The Paradox of Writing in Doctoral Education: Student Experiences." In *Supporting the Doctoral Process: Research-Based Strategies*, ed. Lynn McAlpine and Cheryl Amundson, 75–95. New York: Springer. https://doi.org/10.1007/978-94-007-0507-4_5.

Starke-Meyerring, Doreen, Anthony Paré, King Yan Sun, and Nazih El-Bezre. 2014. "Probing Normalized Institutional Discourses about Writing: The Case of the Doctoral Thesis." *Journal of Academic Language and Learning* 8 (2): A13–A27.

Tardy, Christine M. 2005. "'It's Like a Story': Rhetorical Knowledge Development in Advanced Academic Literacy." *Journal of English for Academic Purposes* 4 (4): 325–38. https://doi.org/10.1016/j.jeap.2005.07.005.

Tardy, Christine M. 2009. *Building Genre Knowledge*. West Lafayette, IN: Parlor Press.

Thaiss, Chris, and Terry Myers Zawacki. 2006. *Engaged Writers and Dynamic Disciplines: Research on the Academic Writing Life*. Portsmouth, NH: Heinemann.

Thonus, Terese. 2004. "What Are the Differences? Tutor Interactions with First- and Second-Language Writers." *Journal of Second Language Writing* 13 (3): 227–42. https://doi.org/10.1016/j.jslw.2004.04.012.

Turner, Joan. 2000. "Academic Literacy and the Discourse of Transparency." In *Students Writing in the University: Cultural and Epistemological Issues*, ed. Carys Jones, Joan Turner, and Brian Street, 149–60. Philadelphia: John Benjamins Publishing Company. https://doi.org/10.1075/swll.8.14tur.

Vorhies, Heather Blaine. 2015. "Building Professional Scholars: The Writing Center at the Graduate Level." *Writing Lab Newsletter* 39 (5–6): 6–9.

Williams, Jessica, and Carol Severino. 2004. "The Writing Center and Second Language Writers." *Journal of Second Language Writing* 13 (3): 173–201. https://doi.org/10.1016/j.jslw.2004.04.009.

Zamel, Vivian. 1995. "Strangers in Academia: The Experiences of Faculty and ESL Students Across the Curriculum." *College Composition and Communication* 46 (4): 506–21. https://doi.org/10.2307/358325.

Zawacki, Terry Myers, and Anna Habib. 2014. "Negotiating 'Errors' in L2 Writing: Faculty Dispositions and Language Difference." In *WAC and Second Language Writers: Research towards Linguistically and Culturally Inclusive Programs and Practices*, ed. Terry Myers Zawacki and Michelle Cox, 183–210. Fort Collins, CO: The WAC Clearinghouse.

PART I

Revising Our Core Assumptions

1
RETHINKING THE WAC/ WRITING CENTER/GRADUATE STUDENT CONNECTION

Michael A. Pemberton

Questions about whether tutoring sessions are enhanced when tutors and students share disciplinary expertise have long troubled writing center praxis and have usually been described as the core of the "generalist/specialist" debate. Some scholars, particularly those in centers staffed by undergraduate peer tutors who are not routinely matched with students by major or discipline, have made a strong case for the value of non-disciplinary, generalist readers. On the one hand, they say, disciplinary "outsiders" can sometimes provide insights into texts that "insiders" might overlook; on the other hand, a tutor's lack of disciplinary expertise can also help to balance the power dynamics in a conference, investing authority in student writers as "content experts" and thereby enhancing the possibilities for true collaboration in tutoring sessions (Bruffee 1984; Hubbuch 1988; Healy 1993; Adler-Kassner and Wardle 2015). Other scholars, though, have argued that familiarity with field-specific genres and disciplinary discourse can be extremely useful in tutorial conferences, especially when writing centers are housed in institutions with strong WAC/WID programs that promote the use of writing as a tool for disciplinary enculturation (Kiedaisch and Dinitz 1993; Shamoon and Burns 1995; Dinitz and Harrington 2014).

In my 1995 *Writing Center Journal* article, "Rethinking the WAC/ Writing Center Connection," I argued that writing centers need not trouble themselves overmuch about hiring undergraduate tutors with expertise in a broad spectrum of majors to work with students from WAC/WID courses. Aside from the practical problems of staffing and scheduling qualified tutors this approach would require, some interesting research (Geisler 1994[1]) suggested that most assignments in most departments, even within nascent WAC programs, did not ask undergraduate students to write or think like experts, so writing centers could continue their pre-disciplinary "generic" conferencing pedagogies relatively guilt-free. What my article failed to consider, however, were the needs and interests of graduate students—students who make frequent use of writing centers; who are working on long-term, lengthy projects like theses and dissertations; who need assistance and advice that neither pre-disciplinary undergraduates nor generic tutorial strategies can adequately provide; who generally write well but are not yet fluent in specialized discourses; and whose lives, communities, contexts, and learning styles may require flexible tutoring opportunities that go well beyond the standard single-visit, thirty- to sixty-minute conference that randomly pairs them with an undergraduate tutor.

Before I move on, it is worth noting the difficulty of making clear-cut distinctions between undergraduate and graduate tutors, particularly with regard to disciplinary expertise. Undergraduate tutors may range from those completing general education requirements to those enrolled in upper-division courses in their majors while graduate students may display a similar range with some doing coursework and others working independently on lengthy long-term projects such as theses or dissertations. In our research, we often elide these important distinctions, discussing them as if they were homogeneous groups except when describing research on department-embedded centers, discipline-embedded tutors and writing fellows, or "major-matching" scheduling.

In this chapter, I will examine the relationship between writing centers and graduate student writing somewhat more deeply than was possible in 1995, incorporating recent research into graduate student writing processes, expectations, networks of disciplinary enculturation, liminality, and rhetorical demands, and then discussing some of the ways writing centers have used this research to better meet graduate student needs. I will begin with a brief overview of writing center scholarship about disciplinarity and address the specific question of whether our strategies for working with undergraduates are equally efficacious with graduate students and, if they are not, what should be done instead. Lastly, I discuss a number of initiatives at writing centers around the country that are striving to meet advanced graduate students' distinct writing needs.

DECONSTRUCTING GENERIC/GENERALIST TUTORING

In retrospect, overlooking graduate student needs in a 1995 article about WAC/Writing Center connections is unsurprising, as nearly all postsecondary WAC initiatives at the time were focused on changes to the undergraduate curriculum, the need for ongoing faculty development, and strategies for negotiating faculty resistance. In two of the most significant WAC collections in this early period, *Strengthening Programs for Writing across the Curriculum* (McLeod, 1988) and *Writing across the Curriculum: A Guide to Developing Programs* (McLeod and Soven, 1992) graduate students and graduate programs are not referred to at all, and nine years later, in *WAC for the New Millennium* (McLeod et al., 2001), contributors' chapters continue to focus on undergraduate initiatives exclusively

A few years after my 1995 WAC/Writing Center article saw print, I published a short chapter in the *Writing Center Resource Guide* on "Working with Graduate Students in the Writing Center" (1998), in which I extended my earlier argument about undergraduate peer tutors, generalist tutoring, and WAC. I asserted that graduate students could still benefit from a "naïve" reading of their texts because the difference in academic positions (undergraduate tutor/graduate student writer) and complementary skill sets (writing expert/content expert) could balance power relationships and make the conferencing experience more collaborative and equitable. I also argued that questions asked by a disciplinary outsider could often help writers discover new connections and encourage them to reflect on their audience and rhetorical stance more carefully. Admittedly, these arguments were as much an expression of pragmatism as pedagogy because it was far easier to rationalize the value of the field's current practices than to grapple with the thorny issue of disciplinarity in graduate student writing and the level of tutor expertise necessary to engage with complex, context- and content-specific rhetorical needs. Talinn Phillips (2016) has recently critiqued my position in that chapter, saying that while my advice "isn't false . . . it does belie important differences in the role of writing for graduates versus undergraduates as well as differences in the complexity of their respective writing tasks. It also masks the limitations that even excellent and well-trained undergraduate tutors face in working with graduate writers" (160).

To be fair (to myself), there was relatively little research into the specifics of graduate student writing and writing processes available in the early to mid-1990s, and even less about the possible contributions of undergraduate tutors to that process (Farrell 1994). A few early studies of graduate students' writing and learning practices (Berkenkotter, Huckin, and Ackerman 1988, 1991; Torrance, Thomas, and Robinson 1992) identified some significant differences between undergraduate and graduate students' understanding of disciplinary discourse conventions, but the general consensus among writing center scholars in the mid-1990s was that undergraduate student tutors could work productively with graduate students despite their lack of disciplinary expertise.

In large measure, this position was an extension of the argument about whether or not tutors needed to be familiar with the "subject area" of the paper they were working on. Susan Hubbuch (1988) and Bonnie Devet et al. (1995), for example, both maintained that tutors frequently did their "best work" when they responded to discipline-specific writing as non-experts. And though Hubbuch and Devet et al. were careful to acknowledge that there were some content-related aspects of writing that tutors could not help with, they felt that tutors could still address rhetorical matters such as organization, development, use of evidence, and tone.[2] This is not to say that there weren't dissenting voices in this debate, however. In "Look Back and Say, 'So What?': The Limitations of the Generalist Tutor," Jean Kiedaisch and Sue Dinitz argued that tutorial strategies which addressed only generic rhetorical issues operated under the assumption that all academic papers shared a set of common features (Kiedaisch and Dinitz 1993). Given the variety of genres and discipline-specific conventions that inflected and sometimes violated these generic structures, they claimed that it was possible that non-expert tutors could provide ineffective or inaccurate advice.

Kiedaisch and Dinitz's critique of generic tutorial strategies seems to be even more pertinent with regard to graduate students who are generally expected to write like disciplinary professionals. And while it might be true that graduate student writers, even those working on lengthy research projects that demand fluency with disciplinary genres and conventions, could profit from a "naïve" reading of their texts and generic tutoring strategies employed by an undergraduate writing tutor, it also seems likely that the benefits they derive would be of limited value, inadequate for the rhetorical and discourse needs that accompany their specialized texts.

GRADUATE STUDENT WRITING AND DISCIPLINARY ENCULTURATION

So what are the rhetorical and discourse needs that might distinguish graduate student writers from undergraduates and that could also be used to reframe writing center pedagogy to address them? Perhaps one way to begin answering that question is to consider the role writing plays as a part of graduate study—not just in terms of the texts that must be produced, but in terms of their larger educational and professional purpose. One of the distinct differences between graduate student writing and undergraduate writing is the degree to which texts are used both as tools for disciplinary enculturation and as the bases for assessing writers' qualifications to become members of a professional discourse community.

Early studies of graduate student writers highlighted the complex nature of such professional enculturation, which spanned not only the development and production of written texts, but the rich network of relationships, conversations, histories, and negotiations with peers and experts that shape graduate students' professional identities. Among these relationships are understandings of foundational knowledge structures (Berkenkotter, Huckin, Ackerman 1991);[3] appropriate discourse conventions and methodologies (Parry 1998); issues and conflicts that appear in disciplinary "microsocieties" (Prior 1991);[4] and new, sometimes conflicting, audiences for their work, such as departments and advisors (Lundell and Beach 2003; Starke-Meyerring 2011). It is not hard to imagine that writing centers in their traditional configurations—typically staffed by undergraduate peer tutors and typically offering thirty- to sixty-minute conferences on an ad hoc rather than ongoing basis—would be ill-suited for the kinds of writing assistance that graduate students require at the thesis- or dissertation-writing stage of their academic careers. This is not to say that traditional writing centers are superfluous to graduate education. Feedback from many different readers and audiences can be valuable to writers as they compose and revise drafts. But these readers may not be well positioned to provide the most beneficial feedback to pre-professional writers whose primary goal is to become active, participating members of a disciplinary discourse community.

GRADUATE STUDIES AS A LIMINAL, YET INADEQUATELY SUPPORTED, EXPERIENCE

Unlike undergraduate students, whose programs of study are for the most part introductory to the field, graduate students occupy a transitional, liminal space between disciplinary novice and disciplinary professional. Though a portion of their studies will incorporate seminars and short papers, the crux of their work as graduate students will hinge on a single written product—the thesis or dissertation, which, along with the composing contexts in which it is written, is likely to be unfamiliar and daunting to most graduate students. In addition to program- and institution-based demands around length, form, and format, the scholarly goals embodied by theses and dissertations are also quite different from those required in typical undergraduate research papers. The writer is expected (a) to demonstrate a comprehensive understanding of the chosen topic, largely through an extensive literature review that synthesizes research from a wide range of relevant sources, and (b) to make an original contribution to the field that is reflective of, but clearly distinct from, the published work that has come before. Understanding these goals and achieving them is at the core of most graduate programs of study, and the process of conducting independent research and writing about that research for a disciplinary audience is, largely, what helps graduate students begin to develop their own sense of professional identity.

And yet, because that identity is still developing, they often find themselves in the uncomfortable position of having to act like experts without the requisite writing knowledge or resources that would enable them to do so with confidence. Some graduate students, in fact, "may not [have been] exposed to the scholarly writing process until the dissertation" (39), according to Rosemary Caffarella and Bruce Barnett, which, in many cases, may lead to their feeling a profound sense of anxiety about their ability to provide helpful writing feedback as disciplinary experts to their peers (Caffarella and Barnett 2000, 43), a finding that has clear implications for writing centers and the presumed benefits of generic peer tutoring strategies employed by generalist tutors. If graduate students are anxious and uncertain about their ability to critique written work by students in their own programs, even when they are collectively engaged in advanced study in a shared disciplinary field, it is not hard to see why they would be skeptical about the quality and utility of advice offered by generalist tutors, especially when those tutors are undergraduates. Recent research confirms, in fact, that graduate students generally want to work with more "expert" tutors than undergraduate writing centers can normally provide (Phillips 2016, 162).

And here is the crux of the problem for both graduate students and writing centers: the need for writing assistance is crucial, particularly given the liminal, transitional space that advanced graduate students occupy; however, most writing centers—in particular those staffed by undergraduate tutors and designed to address the writing and rhetorical needs of students in an undergraduate curriculum—are not structured or staffed in ways that will allow them to provide discipline-specific writing assistance relevant to advanced graduate students in a wide variety of professional discourse communities. Even more problematic is the fact that a great many graduate programs have, historically, failed to provide a systematic support structure for graduate student writing assistance, though the need for such support has been recognized for many years. Indeed, as early as 2001, Mike Rose and Karen McClafferty made "A Call for the Teaching of Writing in Graduate Education," arguing that although some research had been done investigating the connections between graduate student writing and disciplinary enculturation, "there is little professional discussion of what we can do to help our students write more effectively. And though some graduate faculty spend a good deal of time working with their students on their writing, there are few proposals to address writing specifically in the graduate curriculum" (Rose and McClafferty 2001, 27).

Studies of graduate education have noted that there is frequently more of a focus on the best way to teach graduate students about research methods than there is on writing (Sallee, Hallett, and Tierney 2011, 67), and that most institutional discourse about writing at the graduate level seems to consider writing only as a product or as an easily transferable skill that should have been learned before admission to a graduate program (Starke-Meyerring et al. 2014; Rogers, Zawacki, and Baker 2016). When graduate writing support programs do exist in institutions, they are typically focused on the writing needs of second-language students, either through individual tutoring or a supplemental course on basic English writing skills (Simpson 2012; Fairbanks and Dias 2016).

In many graduate programs, the thesis or dissertation advisor is expected to assume responsibility for mentoring individual graduate students, coaching them through their writing and research projects and modeling frameworks of inquiry and discourse in the profession. But while this apprenticeship model may be the perceived norm in postgraduate study and may be a vision of mentorship and collaboration that exists for a great many graduate students, this ideal case rarely attends for everyone. Gillian Fergie et al. (2011) observed that "for many PhD students, the challenge of writing their theses (and thus developing an academic identity) is undertaken without a great deal of guidance. While supervisors provide insight into crucial subject debates and advice on research design, they do not always create a space in which to discuss and engage with issues of reading and writing, an awareness of which is critical during the transition from student to academic" (236). Further, graduate advisors may have difficulty articulating writing expectations or disciplinary discourse features explicitly, and they may see their roles as primarily product-oriented rather than process-based (Starke-Meyerring 2011; Rogers, Zawacki and Baker 2016). As Helen Snively (2008) notes in her study of graduate student writers' experiences, faculty members' focus on end products often times obscures the importance of supporting the writing process. As one student in the study remarked, her faculty mentors "were not willing to brainstorm" with her (91).

I point out these limitations in the mentoring/apprenticeship model not to argue that thesis and dissertation advisors are unimportant or even to minimize their roles in graduate education. They are extremely important in ways that go far beyond the production of a single written document. What seems evident, however, is that this model is likely insufficient for the full range of intellectual, professional, emotional, and writing-related needs that many graduate students have (as Gray discusses in this volume), and writing centers that are willing to adapt to the contexts and demands of graduate student writing are also well positioned to help meet some of those needs when their academic mentors do not or cannot.

THE ROLE(S) OF THE WRITING CENTER

So what should the role of the writing center be, given the challenges posed by—and faced by—advanced graduate students: undergraduate tutors unfamiliar with the conventions and expectations of specialized discourse communities, limitations inherent to generic tutoring strategies, and institutions and advising structures that provide insufficient writing support? That is a question that writing centers have been grappling with for many years, as I've noted, but as is the case with most questions about writing center praxis, specific answers will always depend on local circumstances and contexts. Location, funding, institutional histories, resources, and perceived needs vary widely and resist any one-recommendation-fits-all answer. A flexible, context-sensitive set of approaches to graduate student writing support is likely to be the most productive and the most responsive to divergent, often shifting needs.

One thing the research shows conclusively, as I've said, is that graduate student enculturation into a discipline can be an uncomfortable, sometimes solitary endeavor, especially when there are few support structures in place to help them with their "ticket" to disciplinary success: the master's thesis or the dissertation. But, as Chris Casanave (1995) argues, based on case studies of graduate students in sociology, real enculturation takes place through conversations, dialogues, and discussions with others in a kind of "intellectual village" (89), and this perspective resonates quite strongly with Kenneth Burke's (1941) metaphor of the "parlor," Ken Bruffee's (1984) notion of "the conversation of mankind," and David Bartholomae's (1986) view of "inventing the university," which characterize how we learn to participate as aspiring members of new discourse communities. Talk is as important as writing, and talk *about* writing is more important still. So writing centers, whose epistemology is grounded in the centrality of dialogue to cognitive growth and writing development, have the potential to be key players in graduate students' educational experiences.

That said, however, the dialogic role that writing centers staffed by undergraduate tutors can play in an advanced graduate writer's development and enculturation into a professional community of practice is likely to be limited, given that these require, at least to some degree, the intervention of disciplinary experts who can model conventions and forms and provide feedback about discipline-specific norms related to micro- and macro-structures in writing. However, with appropriate training and explicit instruction in disciplinary genres and rhetorical genre approaches (e.g., see Reineke et al. and Brady, Singh-Corcoran, and Holsinger, this volume) generalist tutors can learn how to engage in beneficial conversations with graduate student writers. Rather than detailing what that training might involve, here I want to consider some of the additional programmatic options that writing centers are offering to meet graduate students' specific needs.

CONSIDERING THE OPTIONS

Over the years, writing centers have proposed and implemented numerous initiatives for graduate student writers: dissertation retreats ("boot camps"), on-site writing groups (e.g., see Hixson et al. 2016), seminar courses (see Reardon, Deans, and Maykel 2016), and partnerships with WAC/WID programs (e.g., see Brady, Singh-Corcoran, and Holsinger, this volume). In the sections that follow, I describe several of these initiatives and their particular benefits for graduate students, but, by doing so, I do not intend to imply that these are mutually exclusive options; as a number of chapters in this volume show (Lawrence, Tetreault, and Deans; Smith et al.; Gray), many writing centers are employing more than one of these approaches.

Web Resources for Graduate Student Writers

One of the earliest graduate writing center support roles (and the one centers have most frequently adopted) is that of web content provider, that is, creating informational pages on the main writing center website that are typically aimed at graduate students working on major projects. Particularly noteworthy are resources offered by writing centers at UNC Chapel Hill, Indiana University at Pennsylvania, the University of South Florida, and the especially robust sites at Texas A&M and Claremont Graduate University, which offer advice on writing the dissertation proposal, preparing for a defense, and working with a dissertation committee.

Dissertation Retreats ("Boot Camps")

A face-to-face program that many writing centers have created for graduate students is the dissertation retreat (most often called "boot camps"), a carefully organized and sometimes strictly enforced setting for graduate students to work on their theses and dissertations. The idea for these dissertation writing retreats originated at the University of Pennsylvania's Graduate Student Center (Mastroieni and Cheung 2011), though the concept was drawn primarily from the "Scholar's Retreat" run by the University of Colorado at Denver since 1997 (Lee and Golde 2013). Sohui Lee and Chris Golde identify two prominent models that structure these retreats, one of them the "Just Write" model in which students are provided with the time, place, and opportunity for focused writing over an extended period of time, and the "Writing Process" model in which students also participate in discussions, keep writing logs, and receive some form of individualized tutorial help (Lee and Golde 2013). The "Just Write" boot camps report "great success" and affirm that "graduate students make great progress in their dissertation writing" (Lee and Golde 2013, 4), while a recent study of the "Writing Process" boot camp at New Mexico Tech indicated that "most students report finishing most of their writing plans . . . [and] satisfaction with both the quantity . . . and quality . . . of the work completed during the week" (Simpson 2013, 4).

Enthusiasm for the retreat/boot camp initiative has been expressed in several WCenter listserv discussion threads, with a number of posters describing their programs and sharing overviews and agendas (e.g., see http://lyris.ttu.edu/read/messages?id=24640473). Despite a few misgivings expressed on the listserv about the "boot camp" military metaphor (http://lyris.ttu.edu/read/archive?id=24640482), a great many writing centers have embraced retreats as a beneficial approach to providing graduate student writing assistance, most often to those writing their dissertations.

Writing Groups

A related approach that a number of writing centers are pursuing is helping graduate students to form their own small writing groups so they can share their work in progress and get feedback (and encouragement!) from peers. Though these groups often comprise students in similar disciplinary communities, a homogeneous makeup is not an absolute requirement since it can be useful to have "outside" members in these groups, both to provide new perspectives and to discuss research and writing that can be a break from what often seems like unrelenting disciplinary immersion. The value of writing groups for graduate students across disciplines has been well documented in the literature. For example, Damien Maher et al. (2008) describe how their writing group functioned as "a community of discursive social practice" (263), and in a similar fashion, Michelle Maher, Amber Fallucca, and Helen Halasz observed that when graduate students became active members of a focused writing group, they formed a "vibrant intellectual community" in which scholarly productivity and commitment to degree completion "soared" (Maher, Fallucca, and Halasz 2013, 193).

Writing centers seem well positioned to foster graduate writing groups, especially when the need is urgent and opportunities for active participation in writing-related discussions are limited. Citing a "newly recognized institutional need" for graduate student writing assistance, Talinn Phillips (2012) reiterates the point—made earlier in this chapter—that "traditional tutoring can't always provide the long-term, extensive support that graduate writers need as they spend years working on theses and dissertations," and so writing groups can be a "productive means of providing that long-term support" (1). According to a survey conducted by Rebecca Jackson and Jackie Grutsch McKinney on the WCenter listserv in 2010, in fact, approximately 10 percent of writing centers who responded said they had organized or coordinated some form of graduate writing groups at their institutions (Jackson and McKinney 2011, 2), one notable example of such a group being the Virginia Tech Engineering Education Writing Group (EEWG), sponsored by the VT Engineering Communication Center and hosted by the VT Writing Center (Hixson et al. 2016).

One intangible but extremely important benefit of these groups, cited by Sherry Gradin, Jennifer Pauley-Gose, and Candace Stewart, is that, along with support for writing, they can help graduate students escape the sense of isolation that many of them experience, while also providing a collaborative support structure as they move through the transitional experience of graduate study and toward professional disciplinary enculturation (Gradin, Pauley-Gose, and Stewart 2006). Most of this support and camaraderie, as would be expected, is provided by the members of the groups themselves, with writing center consultants being peripheral participants at most, typically acting only as facilitators in initial meetings and showing the participants how to comment on and critique each other's texts productively. In general, most writing centers limit their roles to organizational matters—coordinating groups as noted, handling signups, scheduling, and arranging places for groups to meet.

Graduate Writing Centers

While many centers may offer support to graduate students, some institutions have created specialized "graduate writing centers." These centers, often housed in locations separate from a "main" writing center and typically staffed by professional tutors and/or graduate students, are intended to address the special needs and circumstances of students engaged in advanced study and writing extended research documents (e.g., see Summers, Cox, Kalestinova, Gray, and Lenaghan, this volume). In "Writing Centers for Graduate Students," Helen Snively, Tracy Freeman, and Cheryl Prentice describe several such graduate writing centers (GWCs) which address the needs of graduate students in ways that undergraduate centers generally cannot, including, for example, extended, long-term writing support (Snively, Freeman, and Prentice 2006). They may allow students to work with a highly skilled graduate "peer tutor" who can engage with and discuss content in specialized fields. In addition to being a better reader and discussant of content, Snively (2008) argues, the graduate tutor can also be a "surrogate audience" whose feedback will more closely resemble that of an advisor or disciplinary expert (97).

In addition to the benefits GWCs can provide for graduate students working on lengthy research projects, GWCs can also be an important mechanism for the graduate student tutor's professional enculturation. By working with and tutoring others, graduate student tutors enhance their disciplinary communication skills. By sharing their knowledge about disciplinary norms and expectations with students (and other tutors), they contribute to the overall quality of tutoring in the writing center. The more opportunities they have to think and talk about their discipline and their research, the more quickly they will begin to enculturate into their own disciplinary communities, as Paula Gillespie (2007) shows in her description of the GWC project she developed at

Marquette University (see Gillespie's "Prologue," this volume, for a brief description of the GWC project). In the tutor-training course she developed for the graduate consultants, they "analyze, discuss, and describe for their peers the disciplinary conventions of course papers, conference papers, papers for submission to journals, and other genres such as posters and presentations. During their training they work with writers from outside their disciplines, but after they complete the course, they work only with their peers in their PhD programs" (6). According to Gillespie, this project led to the writing center emerging "as the source of valuable disciplinary knowledge, and tutor training has taken on a whole new life as it helps the Graduate School, the graduate faculty, the graduate students, and the university to meet its goals, present and future" (6).

More recently, Steve Simpson et al. (2015) describe a similar approach taken at New Mexico Tech in their article "Creating a Culture of Communication: A Graduate-Level STEM Communication Fellows Program at a Science and Engineering University." This program of embedded graduate tutors, like Marquette's, emerged from collaborative work conducted by the Center for Graduate Studies, the Technical Communication program, and the Writing and Oral Presentation Center, and it eventually grew to encompass several campus departments with graduate programs. The benefits of this program were clear, as "overwhelmingly, students and advisors indicated improvement in students' communication abilities," but even more interestingly, this program helped to resolve some of the apprentice/mentorship problems that I referred to earlier in this chapter. In their discussion of results, the authors note that "facilitating discussion on writing between advanced and beginning students builds an architecture of apprenticeship into the program, wherein more advanced students are given opportunities to share their knowledge with newcomers. Not only is such student-centered design potentially more sustainable, but it is potentially more persuasive to graduate students, who might be more resistant to support mechanisms that seem to be imposed on them from faculty" (under "Discussion").

Despite the benefits and accomplishments of such programs, however, not all institutions are well suited for graduate writing centers, and not all institutions are able to commit the funding that is necessary to create and maintain them. Professional staff and TA lines are expensive, far more expensive than undergraduate tutors who are paid by the hour, and funding challenges can easily demand more effort and attention from writing center directors than they are willing to commit.

At University of Texas at Austin, for example, in 2001 the proposers of a new graduate writing center were told to solicit TA lines from the departments that would be served (Snively, Freeman, and Prentice 2006, 156). And at Saint Mary's University of Minnesota, the graduate writing center was staffed by one full-time director who did all the conferencing and was expected to "generate offset revenue, mainly by teaching workshops" (157). While graduate writing centers may be a great way to meet many of the specialized needs that graduate students present, getting them started may be a challenging task, even those at institutions with very active graduate programs (e.g., see Brady, Singh-Corcoran, and Holsinger, this volume). Nevertheless, the keyword here is "challenging," not "impossible." Bureaucratic and economic hurdles can be overcome, and the number of graduate writing centers across the country continues to grow, as chapters in this volume illustrate.

LOOKING AHEAD AND EXPLORING NEW POSSIBILITIES

In essence, then, writing centers that work with graduate students face many of the same challenges that I talked about regarding disciplinarity twenty-plus years ago in "Rethinking." In the contexts of their own institutions, writing centers still need to identify students' particular needs, recognize the center's strengths and limitations, confront the problems of expertise and disciplinarity, acquire resources, build networks of support, educate faculty and administrators about the need for specialized student writing assistance, and provide tutor training that enables—rather than accidently undermines—students' writing goals. As I discussed earlier in this chapter, some writing centers have opted to support graduate student writing with direct interventions and tutoring solely from fellow graduate students, while other centers have, for economic as well as pedagogical reasons, assumed primarily organizational and facilitative roles, creating contexts for writing and conversations rather than being directly engaged with students and their written texts. Both of these approaches contribute meaningfully to graduate students' progress toward their degrees and the contexts in which they write, but my concern is that they may often be implemented as reactive "fixes" to momentary needs rather than as component pieces of a more extensive, unified framework for graduate student writing support. Ideally, I want to argue, the writing center, no matter how it is configured or staffed, should be the literal "center" for writing on campus. It should be a resource not just for the student body—undergraduates and graduate students alike—but for faculty across the disciplines and administrators as well. In other words, it should be a place where everyone comes and everyone participates in writing as a shared, collaborative, multidisciplinary activity. Too idealistic? Maybe. Unrealistic? Probably (at least according to Stephen North [1994]). A goal to work toward? Unquestionably.

The place to begin, it seems to me, is for writing centers to start thinking of themselves, or maybe re-envision themselves, as "co-sponsors" of graduate students' disciplinary enculturation through the medium of writing. Their mission should not just be to prop up or give supplemental support to writing tasks that are assigned and produced for "other disciplines." Their mission should be to become an integral part of the enculturation process itself, to be fully engaged writing mentors, not just supportive, encouraging bystanders. Many of us do this sort of thing already, when we talk with disciplinary faculty about WAC and writing in the disciplines (WID). We share our expertise about writing, but we also make sure to emphasize that they, the faculty, are writing experts as well, even though they may not, at first, think of themselves in those terms. We stress the importance of interdisciplinary collaboration in WAC/WID programs, and we emphasize our shared interest in improving students' writing and critical thinking. "We're all in this together," we say, "and we can all learn from one another." And the writing center is right there in the center of it all, metaphorically and literally, working with students in classes from all parts of campus, collaborating with faculty, and giving workshops to address specialized writing needs.

There is no reason this same type of involvement can't take place with graduate programs, graduate faculty, and graduate students as well. A first step might be for a writing center director and interested WAC/WID faculty to meet with administrators and departments to determine interest and identify pockets of need (e.g., see Brady, Singh-Corcoran, and Holsinger, this volume). Deans of graduate colleges and/or directors of graduate programs, in particular, would also be great places to start. These preliminary conversations could be used to identify some specific writing issues with which graduate writers need help—not just grammar or English L2 problems—and begin formulating some collaborative approaches to address them. (I use the term "collaborative" pointedly here, because the writing center director should absolutely refuse to take full responsibility for doing this work alone.) Directors can ask for the names of advisors and/or additional faculty who might be willing to help plan and participate, and they can also inquire about internal and external funds that might be available in their units to support new initiatives. The key feature of this approach would be to create an institution-wide framework for graduate student writing support to include directors of graduate programs; key administrators, including those overseeing graduate studies at the institutional level; the writing program (composition, WAC) and writing center; other relevant support units; and representatives of the graduate students themselves. The role of the writing center director in these discussions would be partly informational—presenting a range of programs, collaborations, and approaches used at other institutions—and partly strategic, considering (with colleagues) which options might work best and how different campus units can support each other's efforts and goals programmatically.

Meeting the challenges posed by advanced graduate student writers will not be an easy task, even in a fully (and ideally) collaborative setting like the one I'm recommending here. Not everyone will agree, different constituencies will have different perspectives and sometimes competing needs, and it may be a struggle to identify connections and places where participants share common ground and mutual interests. In essence, then, these conversations pose exactly the same kinds of challenges that writing centers have long faced regarding the issue of disciplinarity and graduate student writing. Different knowledge sets, different areas of expertise, and different understandings of procedural and pedagogical norms can make communication difficult, as we all know. But as writing center directors and scholars, we are used to this, and we have learned through experience that differences can be overcome or negotiated, and that understanding—and learning—is possible with focused effort and a willingness to transcend disciplinary boundaries in order to achieve a shared, desirable goal. Though I was reluctant to acknowledge this point of view in my 1995 "Rethinking" article, I find it an inescapable truth today.

So twenty years after its initial publication, I have learned, perhaps unsurprisingly, that my "Rethinking" article is . . . about twenty years out of date. Writing centers still struggle with the issues around graduate student support, disciplinarity, and expertise, and I suspect we always will, but it appears that we now have a much richer assortment of approaches and long-term strategies we can employ to address them. The success of multiple graduate student writing initiatives—writing groups, GWCs, dissertation writing retreats, and others—as well as the continued growth of WAC/WID programs across the country (Thaiss and Porter 2010) attest to the ongoing interdisciplinary interest in writing support at all levels, and writing centers are clearly positioned to play key roles in creating and developing that support.

NOTES

1. In their 2006 study, Chris Thaiss and Terry Myers Zawacki reported similar findings from faculty interviews (Thaiss and Zawacki 2006).
2. A number of relatively recent articles and tutoring manuals continue to make this case, for example, Paula Gillespie and Neal Lerner in *The Longman Guide to Peer Tutoring* (Gillespie and Lerner 2008), Alexis Greiner's chapter in *A Tutor's Guide: Helping Writers One to One* (Greiner 2005), and, most recently, Lauren Fitzgerald and Melissa Ianetta in *The Oxford Guide for Writing Tutors* (Fitzgerald and Ianetta 2015). Fitzgerald and Ianetta approach the generalist/specialist issue through the lens of *genre*, which allows them to recognize the benefits and drawbacks of both approaches and suggest a middle ground where the best qualities of each can be blended into discussions of disciplinary genres to which both conference participants can contribute (148–53).
3. Akin to threshold concepts; see, for instance, *Naming What We Know* (Adler-Kassner and Wardle 2015).
4. "Microsocieties" in this context are disciplinary subgroups that exist within a larger disciplinary domain, each with its own sets of accepted conventions and practices. In psychology, for example, microsocieties might include clinical psychology, child psychology, abnormal psychology, cognitive psychology, behavioral psychology, etc.

REFERENCES

Adler-Kassner, Linda, and Elizabeth Wardle. 2015. *Naming What We Know: Threshold Concepts of Writing Studies*. Logan: Utah State University Press.

Bartholomae, David. 1986. "Inventing the University." *Journal of Basic Writing* 5 (1): 4–23.

Berkenkotter, Carol, Thomas Huckin, and John Ackerman. 1991. "Social Context and Socially Constructed Texts: The Initiation of a Graduate Student Writer into a Writing Research Community." In *Textual Dynamics of the Professions: Historical and Contemporary Studies of Writing in Professional Communities*, ed. Charles Bazerman and James Paradis, 191–215. Madison: University of Wisconsin Press.

Berkenkotter, Carol, Thomas N. Huckin, and John M. Ackerman. 1988. "Conventions, Conversations, and the Writer: Case Study of a Student in a Rhetoric PhD Program." *Research in the Teaching of English* 22 (1): 9–41.

Bruffee, Kenneth. 1984. "Collaborative Learning and the 'Conversation of Mankind.'" *College English* 46 (7): 635–52. https://doi.org/10.2307/376924.

Burke, Kenneth. 1941. *The Philosophy of Literary Form*. Berkeley: University of California Press.

Caffarella, Rosemary S., and Bruce G. Barnett. 2000. "Teaching Doctoral Students to Become Scholarly Writers: The Importance of Giving and Receiving Critiques." *Studies in Higher Education* 25 (1): 39–52. https://doi.org/10.1080/030750700116000.

Casanave, Christine Pearson. 1995. "Local Interactions: Constructing Contexts for Composing in a Graduate Sociology Program." In *Academic Writing in a Second Language: Essays on Research and Pedagogy*, ed. Diane Dewhurst Belcher and George Braine, 83–110. Westport, CT: Greenwood.

Devet, Bonnie, Peter Cramer, Alice France, Forest Mahon, Mary-Jane Ogawa, Tammy Raabe, and Brandon Rogers. 1995. "Writing Lab Consultants Talk about Helping Students Writing across the Disciplines." *Writing Lab Newsletter* 19 (9): 8–10.

Dinitz, Sue, and Susanmarie Harrington. 2014. "The Role of Disciplinary Expertise in Shaping Writing Tutorials." *Writing Center Journal* 33 (2): 73–98.

Fairbanks, Katya, and Shamini Dias. 2016. "Going Beyond L2 Graduate Writing: Redesigning an ESL Program to Meet the Needs of Both L2 and L1 Graduate

Students." In *Supporting Graduate Student Writers: Research, Curriculum, and Program Design*, ed. Steve Simpson, Nigel A. Caplan, Michelle Cox, and Talinn Phillips, 139–58. Ann Arbor: University of Michigan Press.

Farrell, John Thomas. 1994. "Some of the Challenges to Writing Centers Posed by Graduate Students." *Writing Lab Newsletter* 18 (6): 3–5.

Fergie, Gillian, Suzanne Beeke, Colleen McKenna, and Phyllis Crème. 2011. "'It's a Lonely Walk': Supporting Postgraduate Research Through Writing." *International Journal on Teaching and Learning in Higher Education* 23 (3): 236–45.

Fitzgerald, Lauren, and Melissa Ianetta. 2015. *The Oxford Guide for Writing Tutors*. Oxford: Oxford University Press.

Geisler, Cheryl. 1994. "Literacy and Expertise." *Language and Learning across the Disciplines* 1 (1): 35–57.

Gillespie, Paula. 2007. "Graduate Writing Consultants for PhD Programs." *Writing Lab Newsletter* 32 (2): 1–6.

Gillespie, Paula, and Neal Lerner. 2008. *The Longman Guide to Peer Tutoring*. 2nd ed. New York: Longman.

Gradin, Sherrie, Jennifer Pauley-Gose, and Candace Stewart. 2006. "Disciplinary Differences, Rhetorical Resonances: Graduate Writing Groups beyond the Humanities." *Praxis: A Writing Center Journal* 3 (2): 2–6. http://www.praxisuwc.com/new-page-83.

Greiner, Alexis. 2005. "Tutoring in Unfamiliar Subjects." In *A Tutor's Guide: Helping Writers One to One*, ed. Ben Rafoth, 115–20. Portsmouth, NH: Boynton/Cook.

Healy, David. 1993. "A Defense of Dualism: The Writing Center and the Classroom." *Writing Center Journal* 14 (1): 16–29.

Hixson, Cory, Walter Lee, Dierdre Hunter, Marie Paretti, Holly Matsovich, and Rachel McCord. 2016. "Understanding the Structural and Attitudinal Elements That Sustain a Graduate Student Writing Group in an Engineering Department." *WLN: A Journal of Writing Center Scholarship* 40 (5–6): 18–25.

Hubbuch, Susan. 1988. "A Tutor Needs to Know the Subject Matter to Help a Student with a Paper: __Agree __Disagree __Not Sure." *Writing Center Journal* 8 (2): 23–30.

Kiedaisch, Jean, and Sue Dinitz. 1993. "Look Back and Say, 'So What?': The Limitations of the Generalist Tutor." *Writing Center Journal* 14 (1): 63–75.

Jackson, Rebecca, and Jackie Grutsch McKinney. 2011. "Beyond Tutoring: Mapping the Invisible Landscape of Writing Center Work." *Praxis: A Writing Center Journal* 9 (1): 1–11. http://www.praxisuwc.com/journal-page-91.

Lee, Souhi, and Chris Golde. 2013. "Completing the Dissertation and Beyond: Writing Centers and Dissertation Boot Camps." *Writing Lab Newsletter* 37 (7): 1–5.

Lundell, Dana Britt, and Richard Beach. 2003. "Dissertation Writers' Negotiations with Competing Activity Systems." In *Writing Selves/Writing Societies: Research from Activity Perspectives*, ed. Charles Bazerman and David R. Russell, 483–514. Fort Collins, CO: The WAC Clearinghouse and Mind, Culture, and Activity.

Maher, Damian, Leonie Seaton, Cathi McMullen, Terry Fitzgerald, Emi Otsuji, and Alison Lee. 2008. "'Becoming and Being Writers': The Experiences of Doctoral Students in Writing Groups." *Studies in Continuing Education* 30 (3): 263–75. https://doi.org/10.1080/01580370802439870.

Maher, Michelle, Amber Fallucca, and Helen Mulhern Halasz. 2013. "Write On! Through to the PhD: Using Writing Groups to Facilitate Doctoral Degree Progress." *Studies in Continuing Education* 35 (2): 193–208. https://doi.org/10.1080/0158037X.2012.736381.

Mastroieni, Anita, and DeAnna Cheung. 2011. "The Few, the Proud, and the Finished: Dissertation Boot Camp as a Model for Doctoral Student Support." *NASPA Excellence in Practice* (Fall): 4–6.

McLeod, Susan, ed. 1988. *Strengthening Programs for Writing across the Curriculum*. San Francisco: Jossey-Bass.

McLeod, Susan, and Margo Soven, eds. 1992. *Writing across the Curriculum: A Guide to Developing Programs.* Newbury Park, CA: Sage Publications.

McLeod, Susan, Eric Miraglia, Margot Soven, and Christopher Thaiss, eds. 2001. *WAC for the New Millennium: Strategies for Continuing Writing-across-the-Curriculum Programs.* Urbana, IL: National Council of Teachers of English.

North, Stephen. 1994. "Revisiting 'The Idea of a Writing Center.'" *Writing Center Journal* 15 (1): 7–18.

Parry, Sharon. 1998. "Disciplinary Discourse in Doctoral Theses." *Higher Education* 36 (3): 273–99. https://doi.org/10.1023/A:1003216613001.

Pemberton, Michael A. 1995. "Rethinking the WAC/Writing Center Connection." *Writing Center Journal* 15 (2): 116–33.

Pemberton, Michael A. 1998. "Working with Graduate Students in the Writing Center." In *The Writing Center Resource Manual,* ed. I. V. Bobbie Bayliss Silk, 3.1–3.5. Emmitsburg, MD: NWCA Press.

Phillips, Talinn. 2012. "Graduate Writing Groups: Shaping Writing and Writers from Student to Scholar." *Praxis: A Writing Center Journal* 10 (1): 1–7. http://praxis.uwc.utexas.edu/index.php/praxis/article/view/81.

Phillips, Talinn. 2016. "Writing Center Support for Graduate Students: An Integrated Model." In *Supporting Graduate Student Writers: Research, Curriculum, and Program Design,* ed. Steve Simpson, Nigel A. Caplan, Michelle Cox, and Talinn Phillips, 159–70. Ann Arbor: University of Michigan Press.

Prior, Paul. 1991. "Contextualizing Writing and Response in a Graduate Seminar." *Written Communication* 8 (3): 267–310. https://doi.org/10.1177/0741088391008003001.

Reardon, Kristina, Tom Deans, and Cheryl Maykel. 2016. "Finding a Room of Their Own: Programming Time and Space for Graduate Student Writing." *Writing Lab Newsletter* 40 (5–6): 10–17.

Rogers, Paul M., Terry Myers Zawacki, and Sarah E. Baker. 2016. "Uncovering Challenges and Pedagogical Complications in Dissertation Writing and Supervisory Practices: A Multimethod Study of Doctoral Students and Advisors." In *Supporting Graduate Student Writers: Research, Curriculum, and Program Design,* ed. Steve Simpson, Nigel A. Caplan, Michelle Cox, and Talinn Phillips, 52–77. Ann Arbor: University of Michigan Press.

Rose, Mike, and Karen A. McClafferty. 2001. "A Call for the Teaching of Writing in Graduate Education." *Educational Researcher* 30 (2): 27–33. https://doi.org/10.3102/0013189X030002027.

Sallee, Margaret, Ronald Hallett, and William Tierney. 2011. "Teaching Writing in Graduate School." *College Teaching* 59 (2): 66–72. https://doi.org/10.1080/87567555.2010.511315.

Shamoon, Linda, and Deborah Burns. 1995. "A Critique of Pure Tutoring." *Writing Center Journal* 15 (2): 134–52.

Simpson, Steve, Rebecca Clemens, Drea Rae Killingsworth, and Julie Dyke Ford. 2015. "Creating a Culture of Communication: A Graduate-Level STEM Communication Fellows Program at a Science and Engineering University." *Across the Disciplines* 12 (3). http://wac.colostate.edu/atd/graduate_wac/simpsonetal2015.cfm.

Simpson, Steve. 2012. "The Problem of Graduate-Level Writing Support: Building a Cross-Campus Graduate Writing Initiative." *WPA: Writing Program Administration* 36 (1): 95–118.

Simpson, Steve. 2013. "Building for Sustainability: Dissertation Boot Camp as a Nexus of Graduate Writing Support." *Praxis: A Writing Center Journal* 10 (2): 1–8. http://www.praxisuwc.com/journal-page-102.

Snively, Helen. 2008. "A Writing Center in a Graduate School of Education: Teachers as Tutors, and Still in the Middle." In *(E)Merging Identities: Graduate Students in the Writing Center,* ed. Melissa Nichols, 89–102. Southlake, TX: Fountainhead Press.

Snively, Helen, Traci Freeman, and Cheryl Prentice. 2006. "Writing Centers for Graduate Students." In *The Writing Center Director's Resource Book*, ed. Christina Murphy and Byron L. Stay, 153–64. Mahwah, NJ: Lawrence Erlbaum Associates.

Starke-Meyerring, Doreen, Anthony Pare, King Yan Sun, and Nazih El-Bezre. 2014. "Probing Normalized Institutional Discourses about Writing: The Case of the Doctoral Thesis." *Journal of Academic Language and Learning* 8 (2): A13–A27.

Starke-Meyerring, Doreen. 2011. "The Paradox of Writing in Doctoral Education: Student Experiences." In *Supporting the Doctoral Process: Research-Based Strategies*, ed. Lynn McAlpine and Cheryl Amundsen, 75–95. New York: Springer. https://doi.org/10.1007/978-94-007-0507-4_5.

Thaiss, Christopher, and Tara Porter. 2010. "The State of WAC/WID in 2010: Methods and Results of the US Survey of the International WAC/WID Mapping Project." *College Composition and Communication* 61 (3): 534–70.

Thaiss, Christopher, and Terry Myers Zawacki. 2006. *Engaged Writers and Dynamic Disciplines: Research on the Academic Writing Life*. Portsmouth, NH: Boynton/Cook Heinemann Press.

Torrance, Mark, Glyn V. Thomas, and Elizabeth J. Robinson. 1992. "The Writing Experiences of Social Science Research Students." *Studies in Higher Education* 17 (2): 155–67. https://doi.org/10.1080/03075079212331382637.

2
THE RISE OF THE GRADUATE-FOCUSED WRITING CENTER
Exigencies and Responses

Sarah Summers

Since the early 2000s, institutions of higher education have become increasingly aware of and concerned about graduate student attrition and time to degree. In 2007, the Council of Graduate Schools reported that only 57 percent of doctoral candidates finished their degree within ten years, a number that drops to 49 percent in the humanities (4). In part because completion numbers influence the National Research Council's ranking of doctoral programs, universities want to help graduate students complete their programs successfully, and they recognize that, for many students, writing the dissertation is a problem. For that reason, administrators at many universities have turned to writing support programs as part of the solution.

The need for more and better-informed graduate writing support has led scholars and practitioners in higher education, rhetoric and composition, and writing centers to turn their attention to the particular writing demands and rhetorical situations encountered by graduate writers, particularly at the doctoral level, and the programs that might best serve them, including, for example, initiatives such as writing groups and dissertation retreats (Palmer and Major 2008; Phillips 2012; Lee and Golde 2013). The kinds of individualized writing support that might be optimal for advanced graduate students has also been explored by writing center professionals over the past twenty-plus years (e.g., see Gillespie 2007; Powers 1995; and Snively 2008). With the recent focus on graduate program completion, however, writing center scholarship has become increasingly attentive to the needs of these writers, as demonstrated, for example, by this volume, along with 2016 special issues of *WLN* and *Praxis*, both focused on writing centers' intentional support for thesis and dissertation writers. In addition, we are seeing a growing number of writing centers dedicated to serving only graduate students.

These graduate writing centers (GWCs) are the focus of this chapter, in which I report on the landscape of graduate student writing support a decade after the Council of Graduate Schools launched its national conversation on doctoral education in 2002. I first identify some of the public conversations that contributed to the growing awareness of and interest in graduate students as writers who need (and deserve) support from writing programs. I focus on the early part of the 2000s, which sees two related trends: first, a perceived crisis in graduate student education, one effected by a convergence of low completion rates, a desire to improve national rankings, and an increase in international students; and second, the resulting demand for writing support from institutions and from graduate students themselves, a demand that, in turn, contributed to a rise in GWCs across the country. Following my discussion of these trends, I present findings from a survey I conducted in 2012 about day-to-day GWC[1] practices. This examination of external pressures and internal operations highlights the tensions that shape GWCs and their practices. From their locations on campus to their staffing and appointment structures, GWCs must balance three perspectives: an awareness of external conversations about graduate completion, an attention to local institutional needs and contexts, and a commitment to employ or develop practices that best fit the needs of graduate writers and the lengthy projects they are undertaking. As I suggest in the discussion of my survey data, these three perspectives do not always neatly align.

The challenge to balance external, local, and pedagogical perspectives in the GWC has been further complicated by the limited venues for writing center professionals to share practical and specific data about the day-to-day operations of existing GWCs. Writing support for graduate students has certainly existed prior to the 2000s: in the mid-1990s, for example, John Thomas Farrell (1994) and Judith Powers (1995) published articles in the *Writing Lab Newsletter* that discussed their work with graduate students in their writing centers, and Penn State's GWC opened in 1999 (Penn State Department of English Program in Writing and Rhetoric 2016). But the first comprehensive description of GWCs was not provided until 2006, in an article by Helen Snively, Traci Freeman, and Cheryl Prentice entitled "Writing Centers for Graduate Students." Given the dearth of scholarship on GWCs, in 2012 I set out to update and extend Snively, Freeman, and Prentice's work by conducting an online survey to gather data from GWCs about how they respond to students' and institutions' concerns about graduate writing. The goal of the survey was to collect useful information that could help guide GWC directors' decision making about key areas in writing center administration—location, services, staffing, administration, and funding. The findings also suggest how these key areas are shaped by broader national and institutional exigencies.

GRADUATE WRITING CRISIS, GRADUATE WRITING CENTERS

From 2002 to 2003, the Council of Graduate Schools (CGS) (2007) initiated a "national discussion," as they called it, about PhD completion and attrition, which included an April 2003 conference, assessments of doctoral programs, analyses of institutional data, and surveys of doctoral students. The conference and these data resulted in the publication of four reports from 2004 to 2010. Reports on the state of US doctoral education were also issued by the Carnegie Foundation (Golde and Walker 2006) and the Andrew W. Mellon Foundation (Ehrenberg et al. 2009). These, coupled with the 2007 Council of Graduate School's report showing only a 57 percent completion rate for doctoral students, as I noted earlier, led to widespread—and often public—concern about the efficacy of graduate education.

In 2006, for example, the *Washington Post* published "As Many Dropouts as Degrees: Poor PhD Completion Rate Prods Group to Evaluate What's Lacking" (V. Strauss 2006). In 2007, the Canadian publication *University Affairs* published "PhDs in Science Finish Faster in Canada than in U.S.," a headline that calls to mind the international competition over K–12 education outcomes (S. Strauss 2007). The same year, the *New York Times* published "Exploring Ways to Shorten the Ascent to a PhD," which begins with a caricature of the frazzled dissertator: "The hair is well-streaked with gray, the chin has begun to sag, but still our tortured friend slaves away at a masterwork intended to change the course of civilization that everyone else just hopes will finally get a career under way. We even have a name for this sometimes pitied species—the A.B.D.—All But Dissertation" (Berger 2007, par. 1–2). Articles from *The New York Times* (Cohen 2010) to *The Chronicle of Higher Education* (Berube 2013) identified graduate education and individual disciplines as facing a crisis, a situation that calls to mind earlier crisis rhetoric in higher education, for example, "Why Johnny Can't Write" (Sheils 1975), and subsequent responses. Writing centers themselves, as I discuss shortly, have historically gained traction in response to perceived crises in education (Boquet 1999), a response that demonstrates that the crisis label—while complicated and subjective—can also create opportunities for change.

As the problems surrounding PhD completion became a part of the public discourse about higher education, pressures mounted within institutions to address attrition and time to degree. One such response to these concerns was a focus on doctoral student writing. In fact, the CGS's 2010 report explicitly mentioned the importance of writing support and highlighted institutions that had developed programs for graduate writers since the start of—and implicitly as a result of—their study: "There is widespread recognition that students at the dissertation stage feel isolated and vulnerable and universities are putting into place a number of efforts to help students overcome these feelings and remain on track" (57). The report noted "promising practices" including face-to-face tutoring and workshops on both writing and project management (59). Not only, then, did these reports identify a need for graduate student writing support, they also reinforced graduate writing programs as "promising practices" for emulation. In other words, GWCs and other initiatives aimed at graduate writers, in particular doctoral student writers, became one potential solution to the crisis facing graduate education.

According to data from a survey I administered—described in detail in the following section—the largest swell of GWCs occurred from 2006 to 2010, when ten GWCs opened, a time frame that corresponds to the initial reports from the CGS. While these centers may have opened for a complex array of reasons, artifacts from some GWCs suggest they were responding directly to the results of the CGS studies and the subsequent pressure put on institutions to improve PhD retention and completion in order to increase or maintain national rankings. As Dana Ferris and Chris Thaiss explain in "Writing at UC Davis: Addressing the Needs of Second Language Writers," the development of writing support for graduate students at University of California, Davis, and elsewhere "reflects the gradual realization by U.S. graduate schools that lack of such assistance has kept retention and degree completion rates at disappointing levels" (Ferris and Thaiss 2011, under "Workshops and Tutoring"). Paula Gillespie (2007) references the CGS report directly in her description of the conversations that led to the development of Marquette's GWC. She also notes the importance of PhD productivity for Marquette's national reputation: "Because of Marquette's size, our status in the research community, for grant and recruitment purposes, could diminish with just a small drop in PhD productivity. The university wishes not merely to maintain its ranking, but to advance in the rankings. Increasing and strengthening the PhD programs are central aspects in our strategic plan" (4). Even more recent programs for graduate writers, like the expansion of West Virginia University's Eberly Writing Studio to include graduate tutoring, find themselves responding to institutional recognition that doctoral student writers, like all writers, need support (Brady, Singh-Corcoran, and Holsinger, this volume).

The increase in new GWCs from 2006 to 2010 also coincides with an increase in international student admissions into US graduate programs. In the years following September 11, 2001, international student applications to US graduate programs dropped by as much as 30 percent, in part because of stricter visa regulations imposed by the United States (Fischer 2010, 1). According to the CGS's study of international graduate student acceptances and enrollments from 2003 to 2011, numbers of international graduate student applications began to rise again after the 2003–2004 academic year and showed the largest percentage increase in 2005–2006 (Bell 2011, 1). While most international students pass English language proficiency exams like the TOEFL or IELTS exams prior to beginning their graduate work in the United States, many are still unfamiliar with American academic writing conventions (Phillips 2013; Zhang 2011). GWCs were—and continue to be—one way to support these students as they take on extensive writing projects.

The institutional context surrounding the peak period of GWC development—widespread concerns about graduate student writing as a cause of program attrition, as well as a fast-growing population of international students—recalls a similar period in the history of undergraduate writing centers (UWCs), which grew in number and visibility during the 1970s following Open Admissions policies. As Elizabeth Boquet explains in "'Our Little Secret': A History of Writing Centers, Pre- to Post-Open Admissions," many writing centers during this time "were created largely to fix problems that university officials had difficulty even naming, things like increasing enrollment, larger minority populations, and declining (according to the public) literacy skills" (470). While the GWCs in my survey did not list their mission as increasing PhD productivity, retention, and completion, a mission that Elizabeth Lenaghan (this volume) cautions against adopting, they must be mindful of these institutional concerns and expectations as they develop the writing center pedagogies that best serve their graduate student clients.

Although we have seen a rise in the numbers of GWCs since 2006, when I designed my 2012 study, there was limited scholarship about the specialized writing and rhetorical demands encountered by advanced graduate writers, and GWC directors had similarly limited means of sharing research and experiential knowledge, assessments, and other resources that would help them develop well-informed support for graduate writers. With the goal of gathering and disseminating some of this knowledge and information, I developed a survey that elicited GWC directors' accounts of their centers' administrative and pedagogical practices. In addition to presenting survey findings about GWC structures and practices, this chapter intends to provide a better understanding of the key issues faced by GWCs, their directors, their tutors, and their clients.

SURVEY DETAILS

Through internet searches, posts on the writing center listserv, and word of mouth, I identified twenty-eight potential GWC directors to participate in an IRB-approved survey about the administrative and pedagogical practices of GWCs. The survey, distributed electronically in February 2012, also asked respondents to name any other GWCs they knew of, allowing me to identify an additional six potential GWC directors. In total, I sent thirty-five surveys and received twenty-five responses, twenty-one of which identify respondents' centers as "a writing center primarily dedicated to serving graduate students." The purpose and goal of the survey was to identify GWCs, their administrative structures, their clientele, and their pedagogical practices so that potential or current GWC directors could use that information to adopt common practices, advocate for institutional support based on data, and anticipate the issues they would need to address in their own programs.

The survey comprised a combination of thirty brief quantitative and qualitative questions, asking respondents about their GWCs' staffing, funding, tutors, and tutoring practices. It was not meant to be evaluative since I felt it was too early in our knowledge of GWC practices to assess efficacy. Instead, the questions focused on gathering fairly straightforward data, including numbers of students served and kinds of services. I also used survey data as a starting point to determine data-rich sites to conduct subsequent case studies of several GWCs during 2012 and 2013 (e.g., see Summers 2016, for my study of the UCLA GWC, directed by Marilyn Gray, who also has a chapter in this volume).

In the remainder of this chapter, I draw on survey data to show how the GWCs have been organized within their local institutional contexts and in light of current writing center research and praxis.

KEY ISSUES IN GWC RESEARCH AND PRACTICE

While GWCs may have been set up in response to concerns shared by institutions nationally around graduate program attrition and time to degree, they must also adapt to their own institutional contexts (number and focus of graduate programs, funding streams, graduate program demands, and so on) and to the particular needs of the graduate writers at their institutions. This need to respond and adapt to both institutional and graduate student writers' concerns works in tandem at times and in sharp contrast at others, pointing to the challenges of balancing the demands that shape GWCs, their administration, and their practices. To illuminate the tensions among external, local, and pedagogical needs, I organize my data using the five categories that Snively, Freeman, and Prentice (2006) identify as important considerations for GWCs as they adapt to their institutions and to graduate writers: services, location, staff, administration, and funding. In the discussion of my findings below, I take up their call for a deeper understanding of each of these areas, which represent key decision points for GWC administrators as well as key areas for reflection and innovation, given what we know from the scholarship about graduate writers and their needs.

In the subsections that follow I provide a snapshot of the GWCs that participated in this study, highlighting shared practices and potential areas for innovation. It has been particularly important to me to highlight shared practices in light of one of my most critical survey findings: the lack of professional visibility of GWCs in 2012, which I determined to be the case based on the last question of my survey which asked respondents to name other GWCs. Twelve respondents did not name any other GWCs, and five respondents named centers that are no longer open (e.g., Harvard) or UWCs that also serve graduate students. From their responses, I infer that GWC directors may feel somewhat isolated and, by extension, that they may have limited means of collaborating and sharing best practices, hence my goal to identify local practices, challenges, and solutions that might be useful to GWC administrators more generally.

Services

GWCs report high demand for services and rely primarily on individual consultations to fulfill their missions, no surprise given the national statistics about the role of writing in graduate completion rates, as well as writing centers' traditional emphasis on face-to-face appointments. Of the eighteen survey respondents who provided data on appointment numbers, fourteen indicated that they routinely fill over 75 percent of appointments offered, with six respondents filling 100 percent. Year-end reports from two GWCs support the finding that GWCs consistently experience high demand: Penn State's well-established GWC consistently filled 85 percent of appointments offered during the fall 2010 semester (Belk 2010) while the Graduate Writing Studio at California State University, Fresno, a center that only opened in the fall of 2010, consistently had a waitlist during the spring of 2011 and, by the spring of 2012, regularly filled 100 percent of weekly appointment (2011–2012 year-end report provided by survey respondent). Collectively, these data suggest that GWCs are fulfilling an otherwise unmet need at their institutions. In other words, the national conversation about the need for writing support for graduate students seems to be borne out in local institutional contexts.

In addition to face-to-face appointments, the GWCs represented in the survey attempt to meet demand by offering

- handouts (85%)
- online resources (85%)
- writing workshops focused on academic writing (other than dissertations) (75%)
- presentations to graduate-level courses (55%)
- writing workshops focused on dissertation writing (55%)
- coordinated graduate student writing groups (29%)

Many of these are traditional services that would also be available at UWCs, for example, online resources, handouts, and academic writing workshops. Less frequently offered, however, are sponsored writing groups, which Snively, Freeman, and Prentice (2006) suggest are both a good use of consultant time and helpful to graduate students who can "benefit greatly from the mutual feedback and camaraderie such groups provide" (160).

Given space and budget constraints as well as the fact that advanced graduate students may complete their research or writing away from campus, I expected to find that most GWCs also provide one-to-one synchronous online tutoring or email tutoring. Approximately half of the centers offer these services, and only 40 percent of respondents use web-based communication software (i.e., Skype or Google Chat) in their centers. Even fewer use distance tutoring software (15%) or video conferencing (10%). Thus, the range of services provided and the media used to provide them are areas where GWCs might adopt new or innovative practices, especially in light of the high demand placed on individual centers. (See Kallestinova, this volume, for a description of the hybrid consultation model her GWC employs.)

Location
The array of services GWCs offer—and the high demand for those services—is consistent with those provided by writing centers at all levels. However, other dimensions of GWCs are more complex. The question of GWC location is a good starting point for demonstrating the tensions between external pressures to support graduate students, local contexts, and writing center praxis. The issue that surfaced most commonly in my survey was whether GWCs share their location with a UWC. Five of the respondents reported that, although their GWC operates separately from their UWC, they are housed in the same building, sometimes in the same space. GWCs sometimes share administrative staff or have joint staff meetings and tutor training, and are often "start-up" operations cobbling together funding and support; thus sharing space with a UWC makes sense logistically in those institutional contexts, as, for example, the chapter by Laura Brady, Nathalie Singh-Corcoran, and James Holsinger in this volume suggests.

Some scholars, however, including Brady, Singh-Corcoran, and Holsinger, acknowledge that co-locating a GWC with a UWC may influence the attitudes of graduate students seeking writing support and thus be at odds with graduate students' needs and, accordingly, the best practices for serving them. As Tom Hemmeter and Carolyn Mee found in their ethnographic study of writing centers, space and location communicate a message about the center (Hemmeter and Mee 1993). Sharing space with a UWC may influence graduate students' perceptions of the center and their willingness to use it. While undergraduate students may feel anxious and insecure about their writing, these insecurities may be heightened for graduate students because, as Laura Micciche and Allison Carr point out, they may perceive their writing problems as "private, shameful, or an indicator of unfitness for graduate school" (Micciche and Carr 2011, 479). Having to seek out help amid first-year composition students, often the most frequent writing center clientele, may only exacerbate graduate writers' sense of failure.

There are, however, potential institutional benefits to sharing space with a UWC, including the ability to share resources and take advantage of a visible, central space. For example, according to a follow-up interview with Liberty University's GWC director, the GWC there recently relocated to share a space with the Undergraduate Writing Center, Online Writing Center, and Foreign Language Lab, collectively forming the Center for Writing and Languages, part of the larger Center for Academic Support and Advising, which now funds their GWC. The move has been beneficial in terms of providing more space and support for the GWC, and the director believes that most graduate students do not even realize that both centers share the space. The convenience of the location and the proximity to parking and the library, she argues, outweigh the potential association with undergraduate writing for graduate students. However, she also believes that becoming part of the Center for Academic Support and Advising contributes to the perception of the GWC as remedial, particularly among faculty. A consideration of location needs to be more complex than physical space and take into account institutional spaces and affiliations, along with the meanings that may be read into those spaces and affiliations as well.

Staff

Staffing the GWC—and training that staff—represents another area where GWCs can and should develop new practices but are potentially limited by their institutional contexts. As others in this volume argue, graduate writers will benefit more from tutoring that is tailored to their needs (see in this volume, Kallestinova; Lawrence, Tetreault, and Deans; Simpson; Cox) and informed by the genres they must compose (see in this volume, Cox; Brady, Singh-Corcoran and Holsinger; Reineke et al.), which suggests that tutors might be drawn from a range of disciplines representing the graduate programs offered by the institution and that specialized training is necessary. Yet, as the findings from my survey indicate, these potential best staffing and training practices may not match with local realities, including a center's funding structure.

In response to the survey question "From what disciplines do the majority of your GWC's tutors come?" eighteen of the twenty-five GWCs that responded selected English (86%). Other popular disciplines from which to draw tutors included other humanities disciplines (48%) and social sciences disciplines (37%).[2] Follow-up interviews with directors for my case studies revealed that it is often easier to hire tutors from English because funding for GWCs, and thus their tutors, is often linked to English departments or humanities initiatives. Because well under half of the respondents' clients actually come from English and other humanities disciplines (31%), tutors are often working outside their disciplinary areas of expertise.

Many GWC respondents indicated that their staff receives little formal tutor training to address this disparity in disciplinary knowledge. Nine respondents wrote that they provide either no training for their tutors or rely on their tutors' previous experience working as tutors in UWCs. In discursive responses, some respondents listed shadowing or observing current tutors (eight responses), conducting practice tutorials (three responses), and holding in-service meetings prior to or throughout the semester (five responses) as kinds of training provided to tutors. In response to questions about training tutors in areas of specialization relevant to writing center practice—writing in the disciplines, multilingual writing, and tutoring with technology—the ten centers that reported offering such specialized training listed readings from collections written for UWCs, for example, *The Bedford Guide for Writing Tutors* and *ESL Writers: A Guide for Writing Center Tutors*. While these collections undoubtedly provide valuable theoretical insights and practical advice for all tutors, reliance on UWC texts for training indicates an underlying assumption that UWC experience or liberal arts training is specialized enough to support graduate writers. The question of the staffing—who should the tutors be—and training—what should they read/learn/do—specifically for GWCs is one that requires more research in the context of the practical considerations I've described, and, among the five categories discussed in this chapter, it is the one that would most benefit from a more focused sharing of practices across GWCs.

Administration

None of the twenty-one dedicated GWCs that responded to my survey was coordinated by a tenure-line faculty member. Eleven of the centers have staff members in administrative roles. Graduate students, non-tenure-line faculty members, or a combination of the two coordinate the remaining centers. I did not anticipate this finding, so the survey did not provide opportunities for follow-up comments on this issue. However, it is likely that the criteria for and selection of administrators is bound up in other local institutional considerations, including funding and the structure of academic and student services. As with staffing, the administration of GWCs is an area in need of more investigation to determine how these centers' leadership is structured by local exigencies as well as by broader perceptions of writing centers as sites of service rather than education and research.

Past writing center scholarship on undergraduate writing centers indicates that centers that are led by non-tenure-line faculty or administrators could leave them in a vulnerable position. As Gary Olson and Evelyn Ashton-Jones argue, "The future of the writing center and the integrity of the larger writing program are directly linked to the professional status accorded their directors" (Olson and Ashton-Jones 1995, 52). While Olson and Ashton-Jones's work is focused on UWCs, their warning has proven historically true for GWCs as well. For example, the GWC at the University of Texas at Austin was coordinated by a series of graduate students and eventually closed when a new dean took over their graduate school and their center "got lost in the shuffle" (Snively, Freeman, and Prentice 2006, 157). This case demonstrates that temporary labor, such as that provided by graduate students, can be inadequate to provide the continuity or administrative clout needed to protect GWCs when those centers fall into jeopardy. Professionalization of UCW directors, as well as the problematic reliance on contingent faculty as GWC administrators, is an ongoing conversation, one that GWC directors, however they may be situated, should be joining.

Funding

One of the primary reasons GWCs are coordinated by staff members and graduate students is to reduce costs. Finding funding can be difficult for GWCs, even as university administrators perceive that GWCs can benefit their institution's ranking and PhD productivity, as I explained earlier. The survey results suggest that the most difficult part of securing funding may be the lengthy process of identifying and lobbying possible sources, as there is no standard source of funding for GWCs. Of the twenty-one responses to the survey question "How is your GWC funded?" there were twelve different answers, ranging from a special President's Fund and government fees paid by graduate students to subsets of Academic Affairs and various academic departments. GWC funding, then, is not only linked to the local institutional contexts of each center, as Chris Anson (2002) points out for writing programs in general, but also may reflect the lack of knowledge and research about GWCs and how they operate, as I explained earlier. That is, when administrators of new GWCs look for funding options, they may not have clear examples of the range of options. Inconsistency in funding, like contingent administrators, also puts GWCs in vulnerable positions. For example, the Writing, Research, and Teaching Center (WRTC) at the Harvard Graduate School of Education closed in 2004 after five years, when TA lines were redistributed and writing services became the responsibility of the library (Snively, Freeman, and Prentice 2006, 159).[3]

Even promising external funding sources, like federal grants, provide only short-term solutions for GWCs. For example, at least three GWCs, those at Colorado State University Pueblo, the University of La Verne, and the University of New Mexico, are funded by Department of Education Title V Post-Baccalaureate Opportunities for Hispanic

Americans (PPOHA) grants. These Title V grants are awarded to Hispanic-serving institutions to improve services and instruction, and PPOHA grants fund services specifically designed for Hispanic graduate students. At Colorado State University–Pueblo (CSU Pueblo), PPOHA grants fund a Graduate Student Support Center, the primary function of which is to support graduate student writers. The grant funds one full-time staff member—the coordinator—while the Provost's office funds an additional writing consultant for twenty hours per week (Roy Jo Sartin, pers. comm.). The grant, however, provides funds for only five years. As Peggy Jolly (1984) notes in "The Bottom Line: Financial Responsibility," federal funds are a boon to writing centers, but "once these monies are depleted, the director is again faced with the necessity of keeping the program going" (113). While the Provost's investment in CSU Pueblo's GWC is promising, the need for GWCs to discover other funding sources underscores the importance of making information about how GWCs are funded more readily accessible, so GWC administrators have multiple funding models to consider as they seek to sustain existing GWCs or to create new centers.

Rather than drawing exclusively from federal or university resources, three GWC survey respondents said they offset costs by charging students for services. Teachers College-Columbia University charges students $25 per session, Brenau University charges $23 per hour, and the University of St. Thomas charges students after four hours of tutoring per semester. As Snively, Freeman, and Prentice (2006) argue, however, charging students for writing center services "raises serious ethical questions . . . because it presents a clear problem for financially strapped students" (162). Some of the alternatives they suggest, on the other hand, including using volunteer tutors and conducting workshops for fees, seem equally problematic. Yet, as the University of Connecticut found, charging students a deposit for workshops and boot camps can mitigate the problem of high demand. When they experienced no-shows and attrition after initially having 150 students apply for twenty spots in their workshop series, they implemented a one hundred dollar deposit that was refunded to students who attended all sessions (Reardon, Deans, and Maykel 2016, 11–12). Creative fiscal solutions like these help address budget cuts and increasing financial strain on individual departments and institutions as a whole. Still, the landscape portrayed by the responses to this survey is one in which funding for GWCs is varied and frequently unstable. In light of these funding challenges, considerations of long-term and stable funding are at the forefront of GWC's administrative planning and are bound up in how long the ongoing conversations about graduate completion will hold the attention of administrators and decision makers.

CONCLUSION: THE NEED FOR A SUSTAINABLE GWC COMMUNITY

While the number of GWCs is increasing in response to external concerns about both degree completion and graduate writing and internal demands from doctoral students and their faculty to provide greater writing support, we need to know much more about how these external and internal exigencies are shaping the core practices of GWCs related to services, location, staff, administration, and funding. Only when we have more data to demonstrate the unique forces that shape GWCs and the challenges that result from those forces, can we make compelling recommendations about the training needed for GWC tutors, the need for more tenured GWC directors, and the possibilities for stable GWC funding that reflect the interests of both administrators and graduate students. This chapter serves as one starting point to illuminate how GWC practices and structures are influenced by external pressures, internal constraints, and current scholarship. However, each of the categories I've described and the exigencies that shape our practices are in need of further research.

This research is already underway and GWC administrators may no longer feel as isolated as some of my survey respondents did. Scholarship about graduate writers across writing center journals and scholarly collections like Simpson et al.'s (2016) *Supporting Graduate Student Writers: Research, Curriculum, and Program Design*, is burgeoning, while a *Praxis* (Madden and Eodice 2016) special issue on access and equity demonstrates another step forward with the editors focusing on students of color, students with disabilities, multilingual students, and first-generation college students. This issue—coupled with other scholarship on specific populations, such as Talinn Phillips's work on multilingual graduate writers (2016)—indicates that our field is also moving beyond descriptions of programs and attention to graduate students as a whole to consider more specific needs within the diverse populations of graduate students.

Another recent development is the Consortium on Graduate Communication (CGC), an association created from the ground up by and for educators who teach speaking and writing to graduate students. The CGC's mission is to "create online and face-to-face opportunities to discuss and share resources, ideas, research, and program models for this vital segment of international higher education" (Consortium on

Graduate Communication 2015, para. 2). In addition to the extensive resources provided on their website, they have begun to host annual colloquiums, the first having been offered in 2015. Groups like the CGC can become partners with GWCs to build the kinds of collaborative communities that provide the internal and external visibility they need in order to sustain their work. Such community-building, an endeavor consistent with the collaborative history and praxis of writing centers, can highlight not only the challenges faced by GWCs but also the pioneering work they are doing to define and meet the needs of advanced graduate students. GWCs are now well positioned to assist our constituencies in moving beyond crisis mode and to help determine the ways that graduate educators and the public understand, support, and cultivate graduate student writing.

NOTES

1. For the purposes of my study, I defined GWCs as university writing centers that offer individual, one-to-one, peer consultations to a clientele composed primarily of graduate students across the disciplines. GWCs are not the only writing initiatives for graduate students, but these centers are easier to identify and study than more diffuse, ground-up initiatives for graduate writers, such as departmental writing groups.
2. The survey did not pose questions about the process of selecting tutors. Instead I asked mainly about the number and demographics of existing tutors. Survey responses to the numbers of tutors in the GWC indicate that they have anywhere from one to fifteen tutors. In nineteen of the centers, these tutors are all graduate students. Staff members and non-tenure line faculty members sometimes tutor as well, as three smaller centers indicated in discursive comments.
3. The Harvard Graduate School of Arts and Sciences has recently opened a Center for Writing and Communicating Ideas.

REFERENCES

Anson, Chris. 2002. "Figuring It Out: Writing Programs in the Context of University Budgets." In *The Writing Program Administrator's Resource: A Guide to Reflective Institutional Practice*, ed. Stuart C. Brown, Theresa Enos, and Catherine Chaput, 233–52. Mahwah, NJ: Lawrence Erlbaum Associates.
Belk, John. 2010. *Report of Graduate Writing Operations, Fall 2010*. State College, PA: Penn State Graduate Writing Center.
Bell, Nathan E. 2011. *Findings from the 2011 CGS International Graduate Admissions Survey. Phase II: Final Applications and Initial Offers of Admissions*. Washington, DC: Council of Graduate Schools.
Berger, Joseph. 2007. "Exploring Ways to Shorten the Ascent to a PhD." *New York Times*, October 3, 2007. https://www.nytimes.com/2007/10/03/education/03education.html.
Berube, Michael. 2013. "Humanities Unraveled." *Chronicle of Higher Education*, February 18, 2013. https://www.chronicle.com/article/Humanities-Unraveled/137291/.

Boquet, Elizabeth. 1999. "'Our Little Secret': A History of Writing Centers, Pre- to Post-Open Admissions." *College Composition and Communication* 50 (3): 463–82. https://doi.org/10.2307/358861.

Cohen, Patricia. 2010. "The Long-Haul Degree." *New York Times*, April 16, 2010. https://www.nytimes.com/2010/04/18/education/edlife/18phd-t.html.

Consortium on Graduate Communication. 2015. "About the Consortium." https://www.gradconsortium.org/.

Council of Graduate Schools. 2007. *PhD Completion and Attrition: Analysis of Baseline Program Data from the PhD Completion Project*. Washington, DC: Council of Graduate Schools.

Ehrenberg, Ronald G., Harriet Zuckerman, Jeffrey A. Groen, and Sharon A. Brucker. 2009. "Changing the Education of Scholars: An Introduction to the Andrew W. Mellon Foundation's Graduate Education Initiative." In *Doctoral Education and the Faculty of the Future*, ed. Ronald Ehrenberg and C. V. Kuh, 15–34. Ithaca, NY: Cornell University Press. Electronic version.

Farrell, John Thomas. 1994. "Some of the Challenges to Writing Centers Posed by Graduate Students." *Writing Lab Newsletter* 18 (6): 3–5.

Ferris, Dana, and Chris Thaiss. 2011. "Writing at UC Davis: Addressing the Needs of Second Language Writers." *Across the Disciplines* 8 (4). http://wac.colostate.edu/atd/ell/ferris-thaiss.cfm.

Fischer, Karin. 2010. "Graduate-Admissions Offers to Foreign Students Bounce Back." *Chronicle of Higher Education*, April 19, 2010. https://www.chronicle.com/article/Graduate-Admissions-Offers-to/123987/.

Gillespie, Paula. 2007. "Graduate Writing Consultants for PhD Programs Part I: Using What We Know: Networking and Planning." *Writing Lab Newsletter* 32 (2): 1–6.

Golde, Chris, and George Walker, eds. 2006. *Envisioning the Future of Doctoral Education: Preparing Stewards of the Discipline—Carnegie Essays on the Doctorate*. San Francisco: Jossey-Bass.

Hemmeter, Tom, and Carolyn Mee. 1993. "The Writing Center as Ethnographic Space." *Writing Lab Newsletter* 18 (3): 4–5.

Jolly, Peggy. 1984. "The Bottom Line: Financial Responsibility." In *Writing Centers: Theory and Administration*, ed. Gary A. Olson, 101–14. Urbana: National Council of Teachers of English.

Lee, Sohui, and Chris Golde. 2013. "Completing the Dissertation and Beyond: Writing Centers and Dissertation Boot Camps." *Writing Lab Newsletter* 37 (7–8): 1–5.

Madden, Shannon, and Michele Eodice, eds. 2016. ""Access and Equity in Graduate Writing Support." Special issue." *Praxis (Bern)* 14 (1).

Micciche, Laura R., and Allison Carr. 2011. "Toward Graduate-Level Writing Instruction." *College Composition and Communication* 62 (3): 477–501.

Olson, Gary, and Evelyn Ashton-Jones. 1995. "Writing Center Directors: The Search for Professional Status." In *Landmark Essays on Writing Centers*, ed. Christina Murphy and Joe Law, 47–56. Davis, CA: Hermagoras Press.

Palmer, Betsy, and Claire Howell Major. 2008. "Using Reciprocal Peer Review to Help Graduate Students Develop Scholarly Writing Skills." *Journal of Faculty Development* 22 (3): 163–69.

Penn State Department of English Program in Writing and Rhetoric. 2016. "GWC Services." http://pwr.la.psu.edu/resources/graduate-writing-center/GWC#Services.

Phillips, Tallin. 2012. "Graduate Writing Groups: Shaping Writing and Writers from Student to Scholar." *Praxis: A Writing Center Journal* 10 (1). http://www.praxisuwc.com/phillips-101.

Phillips, Tallin. 2013. "Tutor Training and Services for Multilingual Graduate Writers: A Reconsideration." *Praxis: A Writing Center Journal* 10 (2). http://www.praxisuwc.com/phillips-102.

Powers, Judith K. 1995. "Assisting the Graduate Thesis Writer Through Faculty and Writing Center Collaboration." *Writing Lab Newsletter* 20 (2): 13–16.

Reardon, Kristina, Tom Deans, and Cheryl Maykel. 2016. "Finding a Room of Their Own: Programming Time and Space for Graduate Student Writing." *WLN: A Journal of Writing Center Scholarship* 40 (1): 10–17.

Sheils, Merrill. 1975. "Why Johnny Can't Write," *Newsweek*, December 8, 1975.

Simpson, Steve, Nigel A. Caplan, Michelle Cox, and Talinn Phillips, eds. 2016. *Supporting Graduate Student Writers: Research, Curriculum, and Program Design*. Ann Arbor: University of Michigan Press. https://doi.org/10.3998/mpub.8772400.

Snively, Helen. 2008. "A Writing Center in a Graduate School of Education: Teachers as Tutors, Still in the Middle." In *(E)Merging Identities: Graduate Students in the Writing Center*, ed. Melissa Nicolas, 89–102. Southlake, TX: Fountainhead Press.

Snively, Helen, Traci Freeman, and Cheryl Prentice. 2006. "Writing Centers for Graduate Students." In *The Writing Center Director's Resource Book*, ed. Christina Murphy and Byron Stay, 153–64. Mahwah, NJ: Lawrence Erlbaum Associates.

Strauss, Stephen. 2007. "PhDs in Science Finish Faster in Canada than in U.S." *University Affairs*, November 5, 2007. https://www.universityaffairs.ca/news/news-article/phds-in-science-finish-faster-in-canada-than-us/.

Strauss, Valerie. 2006. "As Many Dropouts as Degrees: Poor PhD Completion Rate Prods Group to Evaluate What's Lacking." *Washington Post*, April 18, 2006. www.washingtonpost.com/wp-dyn/content/article/2006/04/17/AR2006041701123.html?noredirect=on.

Summers, Sarah. 2016. "Building Expertise: The Toolkit in UCLA's Graduate Writing Center." *Writing Center Journal* 37 (2): 117–45.

Zhang, Zheng. 2011. "A Nested Model of Academic Writing Approaches: Chinese International Graduate Students' Views of English Academic Writing." *Language and Literature* 31 (1): 39–60.

3
ON THE DISTINCT NEEDS OF MULTILINGUAL STEM GRADUATE STUDENTS IN WRITING CENTERS

Steve Simpson

Recent scholarship in graduate writing support has opened the discussion of whether support for first language (L1) and second language (L2) graduate students should be separated or combined, or a little of both (Simpson et al. 2016). Because the pioneering work on graduate writing support emerged from English language institutes and other TESOL-related contexts, much of the early research and pedagogical resources focused more directly on the needs of multilingual students, particularly international students. (E.g., see Canseco and Byrd 1989; Swales 1990; Casanave and Hubbard 1992; Belcher 1994; Swales and Feak 1994, 2012; Canagarajah 2002). Given the importance of written communication to the success and employability of all graduate students regardless of linguistic background, institutions across the United States and overseas have now embraced more holistic forms of support that satisfy the combined needs of L2 *and* L1 students. This trend is important not only because it enables access to writing support to so-called monolingual resident students, but also because it accounts for linguistically-diverse students not easily served in intensive English programs (e.g., underrepresented minority populations such as Latina/o and Native American students in the United States, students from Anglophone countries in Africa who have used English throughout their academic careers, etc.).

A critical move in arguing for combined support mechanisms is to shift attention from points of difference (e.g., native language) to points of overlapping need. For example, Mary Jane Curry (2016) deftly argues that all graduate students regardless of linguistic background struggle to acquire generic conventions in their field. While I have also argued for combined forms of support, I also believe that there can be a danger when combining L2 and L1 support services in that overlooking points of difference might result in multilingual students feeling lost in the mix. Writing centers must be particularly sensitive to points of difference, as in many institutions they play a crucial role in filling in gaps in coverage between other campus resources. In this chapter, I would like to shift attention from the writing support needs of graduate students in general and back to some distinct needs of international and resident multilingual graduate students. Given my role as a writing center director and department chair at a science and engineering research university, I am especially interested in multilingual students in Science, Technology, Engineering, and Mathematics (STEM) disciplines, which also comprise a large percentage of international students in the United States.

I open with recent statistics on international student trends in the United States and on multilingual student populations in graduate programs to paint a complex portrait of the needs and goals of internationals and resident multilingual graduate students in STEM disciplines. I then pull from case studies of multilingual graduate students in an interdisciplinary environmental sciences doctoral program learning graduate-level scientific writing genres[1] and from personal anecdotes from my own writing center work in opposite corners of the United States to draw attention to a few salient differences in the needs of multilingual graduate students. I close with some recommendations for how these differences might affect how we structure writing center support for graduate students and how we train writing center consultants. My goal is to present a nuanced understanding of how we can still account for the distinct needs of multilingual students in combined English L1 and L2 graduate support programs such as writing centers.

MULTILINGUAL STUDENT TRENDS AND GRADUATE STUDENT TRAJECTORIES

As US universities have ramped up international recruitment, and as emerging economies such as China, India, and Brazil have sought to build their own research and educational infrastructures by sending students abroad (Downie 2011; Levy 2013), our graduate programs and STEM fields in particular have become increasingly diverse. It is critical for writing centers and other student support services to understand the nature of this diversity and these students' educational and professional goals. Naturally, international students comprise a visible portion of the multilingual graduate students writing centers encounter, and, according to the 2016 National Science Foundation Science and Engineering Indicators, more than half of these graduate student were enrolled in

STEM fields (National Science Foundation 2016). An interesting trend to watch in the United States is the growing number of international students in STEM remaining in the United States after completing their degrees. As of 2014, two-thirds of temporary visa holders earning a doctorate in the United States remained in the United States for at least five years. Seventy-five percent of international students receiving a PhD from a US university planned to remain in the United States. Eighty-eight percent of Chinese doctoral students reported planning to stay in the United States (National Science Foundation 2016). While many students return to their home countries after graduating—in fact, many are required either to return home or return their government scholarships—many of these students are joining the United States workforce and interacting in a variety of languages as part of their jobs. Thus, as writing center professionals, we should be aware of the linguistic needs of the students who intend to remain in the United States and the range of genres with which they will need assistance as they prepare to enter US research or industry positions.

When discussing the needs of multilingual graduate students, however, we must expand our scope beyond just international students, as resident students bring considerable linguistic diversity to graduate programs as well. As an administrator at a Hispanic Serving Institution (a US Department of Education designation for schools with greater than 25% Latino/a enrollment), I am particularly interested in these students' diverse array of linguistic backgrounds. According to the National Center for Education Statistics (n.d.), Latino/a enrollment in post-baccalaureate programs has risen by 25 percent in the period between 2009 to 2014 (229,800 total). In particular, minority enrollment in master's programs and professional master's programs (i.e., master's programs designed to prepare students for the workplace rather than further graduate work) is particularly high, with some programs reporting 25 percent minority enrollment (Council of Graduate Schools 2013). Thus, some (though certainly not all) Latino/a students will be interested in industry versus academic careers. Further, their linguistic backgrounds vary considerably depending on a variety of factors, including educational background and the number of generations the students' family has been in the United States (Pew Research Center 2015). From my own experience, I have found that some might report being much more comfortable with Spanish and thus identify as ESL (particularly first-generation students), some might be perfectly bilingual, and still others (especially third generation students) might identify more with their "monolingual" American counterparts.

Taken together, these statistics give us a complex picture of graduate students who might use writing center services. These students come to us with wide-ranging linguistic experiences, and they may be more focused on non-academic careers than what many of us may expect of graduate students. Yes, they might need help completing their theses or dissertations, which is often our focus in graduate student support, but they might have other needs as well, especially if they are anticipating a career in which they will need to interact with multilingual audiences in multiple registers and in their L2. Less than half of PhD students in STEM fields, in fact, go on to work in the education sector. The majority enter jobs in industry—often in the private sector—or leave research altogether (National Science Foundation 2016).

MULTILINGUAL GRADUATE STUDENTS IN THE WRITING CENTER

Not only must writing center professionals understand the demographics and career goals and trajectories of multilingual graduate students using the center, they must also account for their distinct linguistic and writing needs at the graduate level. In the following sections, I review three critical differences that should be recognized when working with multilingual students in writing centers, with a particular focus on STEM students. This review is not exhaustive. Rather it is meant to be representative of the different kinds of needs that we might uncover when we shift our attention from combined English L2 and L1 graduate writing support back to support for multilingual students. It is further important to note that some of these writing support needs might seem to apply both to L1 and L2 students across the board; however, recognizing degrees of difference can often be very important when assessing student needs. For multilingual students, for example, when the typical difficulties of writing a methods section are compounded by limited fluency in the target language and different previous educational experiences with scientific conventions, the task can become profoundly complex. Thus, it is important to remember—and to stress to disciplinary faculty and to writing center consultants—that just because an English L1 and an L2 student are each struggling with the same task, this does not mean that the two students are struggling for the same reasons.

The Complexities of Graduate Student Linguistic Proficiency in Writing Centers
Linguistic proficiency would seem to be an obvious goal shared by all multilingual students; however, the challenges involved in attaining this

goal may vary considerably among international students and between international and resident multilingual students, all of whom may express similar difficulties but with different symptoms. Among international students who do not use English as one of their primary languages, the challenges may be quite varied. At the graduate level, for example, it has become increasingly common for advisors to accept some students who are promising researchers but whose TOEFL or IELTS scores do not yet meet university requirements. While some universities have responded by developing graduate-level bridge programs that support students' transition into graduate programs (Habib, Haan, and Mallett 2015; Mallett, Haan, and Habib 2016), in other cases, students may simply be accepted into graduate programs either with the understanding that they will enroll in EAP classes or that they will "catch up" on their own, as was the case with "Paulo," a forestry student from Brazil at a Northeastern Land Grant University (NLGU) who was an informant for my study of writing for publication in an environmental sciences program (Simpson 2013). Very often, such students find their way to writing centers.

This notion of language proficiency needs unpacking, however, as students' complex language needs are often hard to capture in proficiency tests, particularly when it comes to graduate-level or discipline-specific writing tasks. For example, Suresh Canagarajah (2018) studied twenty-four Chinese scholars in STEM fields at a Midwestern university who reported being successful writing for their disciplines despite having low proficiency in everyday interactional English. Pulling from sociolinguistics, Canagarajah describes this phenomenon as "truncated multilingualism," which, in his words, refers to "the possibility that multilinguals might find a few resources from many languages suitable for meaning-making and accomplishing their activities, separated from the grammatical systems of which they are a part, and without advanced or complete proficiency in those systems" (Canagarajah 2018). That is, students might have enough familiarity with disciplinary language to write a scientific paper but might not be successful using English to, for example, interact with English-speaking colleagues at a conference, teach a university class, or write the "Broader Impacts" section of a National Science Foundation grant, which requires a less jargon-filled account of research implications.

Forestry student Paulo, for example, reported having an easier time with discipline-specific language tasks than with everyday English demands. In his case, Portuguese was the medium of instruction for both his undergraduate and master's programs, and, while he had written his master's thesis in Portuguese, his textbooks and most of the research literature were in English. He reported feeling fairly comfortable writing specialized articles in English, which often confounded many of the NLGU writing tutors when he came in for assistance. But he also reported feeling much less comfortable talking about his research to non-specialist audiences and so had developed the habit of reading articles in popular science magazines to improve his English fluency. Paulo ended up securing a prestigious post-doctorate position after completing his degree despite being admitted with a low TOEFL score. However, he struggled as a language learner in graduate school along the way, and, while he visited the writing center several times, he said that he never felt that the writing tutors with whom he worked understood his complex linguistic needs.

Conversely, international multilingual graduate students may excel with their everyday interaction in English and with providing very colloquial descriptions of their research but experience difficulties mastering academic register or using disciplinary conventions appropriately. Many of these students come from countries in which English is one of several languages used or may be the primary language of instruction in educational settings (e.g., India, Pakistan, Nepal), and, while they have extensive experience using English, they might have limited experience with formal academic writing or formal scientific presentations. Interestingly, in writing center conferences, these students' ease with spoken English might mask their confusion about core concepts in their field. "Salman," an oceanology student from Pakistan and another informant in my NLGU study, reported a lifelong disconnect between his everyday use and academic use of English and the concepts the latter was used to represent. In his primary school years, for example, he reported that many of the English textbooks used in class were originally published in England and made reference to places or items he had never seen (e.g., descriptions of lush wooded settings). When he first started graduate school in Pakistan, he reported applying to a program in oceanology due to the availability of a scholarship. It wasn't until much later in his education that he actually saw an ocean for the first time (Simpson 2010).

Many of the resident Latino/a students and native students at my current institution express similar difficulties, albeit with different symptoms. Unlike other students in their programs who may have parents who work for one of New Mexico's many national labs, some resident students are first-generation college students who may come from rural backgrounds. One of my graduate students was a second-generation US resident and the child of migrant laborers from Mexico, for example. While proficient in everyday interactional English, she struggled with language use in her writing, especially academic writing. Perhaps most significantly, as with many of her peers from underrepresented backgrounds, she struggled with a lack of confidence writing in an academic register and for academic audiences. As a result, her writing did not communicate how much she actually knew about her subject matter. Writing tutors working with such students may need to spend more time helping them develop ideas orally to flesh out their written explanations.

For this reason, a more robust framework for assessing linguistic proficiency is needed. While, for international L2 students, for example, TOEFL or IELTS scores may be useful in the initial placement, they provide only a one-dimensional view of the students' needs, and they miss some student populations altogether (e.g., refugee students who attend American high schools). Further, resident students' linguistic proficiencies can be incredibly complex and are not adequately captured on any proficiency metric currently in use in higher education.

I propose looking at proficiency as occurring along two interrelated spectra. The first spectrum is what I will call "interactional proficiency"—a student's ability to use English in everyday situations, oral interactions, informal emails, and so on. The second spectrum is "disciplinary proficiency"—a student's ability to understand and use the language specific to their discipline. One might find that student writers with whom one works can fall anywhere along these spectra, and that a student's proficiency in one area (e.g., a proficiency in the disciplinary language) may not correspond with proficiency in the other (e.g., interactional proficiency), and that resident students and international students vary in linguistic strengths and weaknesses. Further, we must recognize that language is not simply something one accomplishes and then moves on from there. Rather, multilingual students will continue to negotiate these language demands throughout their acquisition process, and likely for their entire academic careers. Several foreign-born advisors in my study reported that even after publishing in English for ten or twenty years, they still make use of colleagues to help with editing.

Negotiating Different Cultural Views of Authority in the Writing Center

While interviewing faculty in the environmental sciences program at NLGU about their advisees' experiences writing about their research, I was struck by a recurring theme in faculty's description of international students. This theme is captured best in a quote from "John," a Professor of Oceanology, speaking of interactions with "Girmit," an Indo-Fijian graduate student whom he had brought into his personal research:

> The biggest cultural issues that are important here are, to what extent is he doing my work, to what extent is he doing his own creative work? When should he ask for help? In the past, I've found he hasn't asked for help soon enough, and he hasn't objected soon enough when I've given lousy advice. He has gone off and worked on lousy advice well past the point where he realized I was wrong—where it would be better to say, John, or Sir, or whatever, are you sure you meant to say that? Or are you completely baked? (Simpson 2010)

John further reported that he was waiting for Girmit to take greater "ownership of the problem" that they were researching.

The passage above presents a conundrum for students. On one hand, students may be working on their advisor's project, which is often expected in STEM disciplines, and yet they are expected to "own" the problem and challenge the professor—to be an "irreverent graduate student," as another professor in the program stated—or at least to feel comfortable asking challenging questions. Granted, John's statement requires qualification. One must be careful with essentialist claims about a student's cultural background and their willingness—or not—to challenge authority. Numerous factors contribute to students' responses to authority including a student's personality. I have encountered both painfully shy American students and appallingly brash international students who challenged authority too much. Moreover, working with first-generation Latina/o and native students has impressed on me how wary students can be of the professor-student power differential, though I have likewise had minority students who did not have this problem at all. Professors, on the other hand, can make any number of assumptions about students who don't ask questions or who seemingly disappear while awaiting "instructions" from a professor, as Chris Casanave (2016) writes of her interactions with Japanese graduate students at Temple University's Japan campus.

At first glance, these issues of authority might seem outside the bounds of writing center work. However, from my own experiences working with graduate students in writing centers, I have often found that students have been willing to tell me when they are confused by their advisors' instructions, and often it can be painfully clear in conferences when the student and her advisor are not on the same page. Advisor feedback is critical to a student's successful completion of a writing project, especially when a student is working on her or his advisor's project. If a student is not understanding her advisor's instructions or is not asking the right questions, she may be at a loss for what to write, or may be producing considerable text that the advisor finds unusable.

This situation can be delicate for writing tutors, as one does not want to direct students further down the wrong path or exacerbate the confusion between the advisor and advisee. While this confusion can also haunt interactions between any graduate student and her advisor, multilingual students might have extra layers of cultural or linguistic barriers that exacerbate communication difficulties. In these cases, the writing tutor's most important role can be helping multilingual graduate students frame questions for their advisors—especially if the student struggles with interactional English, as discussed in the last section—or at least helping flag parts of students' writing that they could discuss further with advisors. In general, one goal of graduate writing support should be to augment the relationship between advisors and advisees, and writing tutors, because of the intimate nature of one-on-one or small group tutoring, are uniquely situated to help students negotiate some of the cultural barriers to working with advisors.

The Conundrum of Multilingual Students and Plagiarism in the Writing Center

Plagiarism and ethical source use are perhaps even more delicate issues than the advisor-advisee relationship for graduate writing consultants working with multilingual writers. Concerns about plagiarism surface continually in discussions of multilingual graduate writers on college campuses and have become a top concern for many graduate deans, particularly after several high-profile cases of doctoral degrees being rescinded years after the fact due to plagiarism charges (Howard 2008). An essay on the iThenticate (2014) website—"Ph.D. in 'Copy-and Paste'? Addressing the Rise of Plagiarism in Graduate Programs"—fuels these concerns about plagiarism being a "growing" problem, particularly among international students and in STEM disciplines. Granted, as the leading anti-plagiarism software for graduate-level work, iThenticate has a vested interest in portraying plagiarism in catastrophic terms.

Many writing center administrators would agree that the focus on multilingual students plagiarizing is unfair; the stark contrast between an L2 student's prose and unparaphrased text can make plagiarism easier to catch in an L2 writer's manuscript than in an L1 writer's manuscript. Because plagiarism can have severe repercussions for multilingual graduate students' career trajectories, we do need to take this concern seriously, and we need to reflect on both our assumptions of graduate student plagiarism and our method of teaching students ethical citation practices, particularly in writing centers where we have opportunities to intervene before a student's problematic text gets too far down the road. In my own institution, early intervention has become even more critical, since our graduate school now requires every completed thesis or dissertation to be run through iThenticate and since many advisors work under the assumption that graduate students should already know well enough how to cite properly.

Perhaps the first step for writing centers is to discuss with writing tutors the pros and cons of common explanations for multilingual student plagiarism. The most common explanation for plagiarism among international students—particularly among Asian students—is their different cultural perceptions of intellectual property and the emphasis on memorization and repetition in the Confucian educational system (Chien 2014). While these cultural differences are certainly accurate and well documented, this explanation can lead many tutors and educators to uncritical conclusions. First, it can lead to sweeping generalizations of "Eastern" and "Western" cultures. I have even encountered one writing center consultant leading a training workshop who went as far as to assume that European students should understand plagiarism better as they come from a "Western" rather than an "Eastern" tradition and have an "individualist" versus "collectivist" perspective on intellectual property. Second, this explanation can lead educators to overlook the importance of previous educational experiences. As Wendy Sutherland-Smith (2008) shows, plagiarism policies have begun to change worldwide as many universities have standardized their curricula to allow for greater student mobility. A student's previous experience with plagiarism will vary depending on where they attended school and how diligently plagiarism policies were taught and enforced.

Perhaps the greatest assumption that educators draw from the cultural explanation is that information is the antidote to plagiarism—that, if we make policies clear and accessible and explain to students that "this is how we do things here," then students should no longer have problems. However, many scholars have found that there is little correlation between knowing about plagiarism and not plagiarizing (Sutherland-Smith 2008). Thus, while it certainly does not hurt to discuss university plagiarism policies with students in the writing center, tutors should not rely on explanation as the only tool in the toolkit.

Writing centers must lead the way in thinking of paraphrasing and citing as something that must be learned both through explicit instruction and practice (Howard, Serviss, and Rodrigue 2010) and through exposure to disciplinary practice (Pecorari 2006). Rebecca Howard's extensive research on plagiarism (e.g., Howard 2008; Howard, Serviss, and Rodrigue 2010) has demonstrated that "patchwriting"—the act of copying chunks of source text into one's work and paraphrasing small parts—is a learning strategy for many students. In Canagarajah's (2018) study of twenty-four Chinese scholars writing scientific papers, several participants reported using sophisticated patchwriting techniques in successfully published work. It can be expected that novice multilingual writers—particularly those who are still developing the linguistic repertoire needed to successfully paraphrase, or students employing a "truncated multilingualism"—will lean heavily, and unsuccessfully, on these strategies. Writing centers can play a pivotal role not only in helping graduate students understand university plagiarism policies but also in working with students at the sentence level to help them better integrate source material.

Also critical to understand, as both Salman and Paulo pointed out to me in my study of the NLGU environmental sciences program, is that many multilingual graduate students might not have received previous instruction in writing as a process. I would argue that what many multilingual students need is better scaffolding of the writing process itself, from collecting and organizing information from texts to organizing and drafting manuscripts. Writing centers might not traditionally see themselves in the role of working with students on process-related strategies, especially if graduate students are accustomed to visiting writing centers toward the end of the drafting stage. However, many of the issues with unethical uses of citation can be avoided when tutors work with graduate students on earlier stages of their drafts and provide advice on composing and note-taking strategies. Earlier interventions with multilingual students' work also helps counter the common assumption in many STEM disciplines that the "writing up" stage is something that happens quickly at the very end of the research process (Kamler and Thomson 2006), rather than understanding writing as a tool for thinking through the research while it is being conducted and throughout all stages of composing.

IMPLICATIONS FOR WRITING CENTER PEDAGOGY AND DESIGN

The growing number of graduate writers using writing centers necessitates our rethinking traditional undergraduate writing center pedagogy and design, an argument that is the focus of this collection and which has been made elsewhere by a number of writing center scholars, for example, Talinn Phillips (2013). Further, the growing diversity of the graduate student population forces us to strike a balance between designing centers to accommodate the combined needs of both L1 and L2 students and to allow opportunities to meet multilingual students' distinct needs head on. In the following section, I highlight just a few essential shifts in writing center practice.

Conducting Institution-Wide Needs Analyses

Naturally, many writing centers keep fastidious records of writing center usage. While these data can provide writing center administrators with critical insight into changing student needs, they still only describe students who actually come to the center. These data do not always capture the needs of students not using the center—the unmet needs—and this may particularly be the case for advanced graduate writers who may be reluctant to admit to the need for writing assistance. Writing centers can benefit from a periodic institution-wide needs analysis that surveys graduate students and faculty advisors about on potential unmet needs and the particular writing experiences and challenges they face. Moreover, writing centers can use this survey opportunity to collect information on students' career trajectories and other communicative contexts for which they might benefit from writing center services, needs often not considered, particularly when graduate student writing support is framed by concerns about attrition and time to degree (see chapters by Gray and Lenaghan, this volume, about expanding the focus of our arguments around graduate writing support).

A number of examples of survey-based needs analyses can be found on the Consortium on Graduate Communication website (Consortium on Graduate Communication n.d.). One should note that many of these surveys were conducted alongside focus group sessions to collect more qualitative insight. For example, when I conducted a graduate student needs analysis at New Mexico Tech, I also visited with academic departments at department meetings and conducted an information session with our school's graduate student association. (See also Brady, Singh-Corcoran, and Holsinger's chapter, this volume, and Rogers, Zawacki, and Baker 2016.) When conducting these needs analyses, writing centers can partner with other campus entities that might benefit from this data and who might be able to assist with circulating the survey and/or pool resources, for example, graduate schools, writing programs, international student services, institutional research departments, and so on.

Further, considering how incomplete admissions data can be on student demographics and student language use—particularly regarding resident multilingual student populations—such needs analyses can provide a more robust portrait of multilingual students and their linguistic and educational backgrounds. Questions that would be useful to ask might concern, for example, multilingual graduate students' backgrounds in writing and speaking in scientific and academic contexts (e.g., have they published or co-authored a paper in English? What role did they have in writing the paper? How confident do they feel in their abilities to use English academically? How would they describe their abilities with English outside of academic contexts?) and their perceptions of themselves as an English language user (e.g., would they consider English to be one of their first languages? Was English a medium of instruction in their former education context? How long have they used English academically?). They too might have other interactional communicative needs, as described earlier, for which they may never even have considered visiting the writing center.

Positioning the Writing Center as Graduate Student Resource

Writing centers face the perennial issue of being seen as the last-stop fix-it shop for writing on campus. This problem assumes a few new nuances when working with multilingual graduate students. Indeed, writing center administrators must think strategically about how they would like to be positioned on their campus as a graduate student resource—and not just a site of thesis or dissertation support—and how they advertise their services to multilingual students. Positioning the center as the place for thesis or dissertation support can unintentionally communicate to students and advisors that it is the place for last-minute edits, or the place where students go to "fix those language issues" before turning in the final product. (See Turner, this volume, for implications of the fix-it shop perception for L2 writers, tutors, and supervisors.)

On the surface, this last-minute fix-it problem is reminiscent of what writing centers have experienced for years working with undergraduate writers. However, until one has experienced zombie-like graduate students staggering into the writing center on the last week of the semester with 200-page documents, one might have trouble envisioning how epically monstrous this problem can become. In addition, many multilingual student drafts can be difficult to comment on at such a late stage, particularly if the student had trouble successfully paraphrasing source materials. At our writing center, we have found that multilingual students in particular are much better served when they come to us over several sessions while drafting their work so that our consultants can help with these concerns along the way, as I discussed earlier related to plagiarism and patchwriting.

It is critical, then, to talk to multilingual students and advisors about the writing center being a useful resource throughout the process of generating and composing the thesis or dissertation. One way of communicating this message is to position the writing center as a graduate student resource available for consultation on needs that are not being explicitly met anywhere else on campus. Some of these needs might not be *directly* related to writing (e.g., using bibliographic software such as Endnote and Mendeley, using statistics, learning code-based documentation preparation software such as LaTex, etc.), but they are important to graduate-level writing tasks. In some cases, writing centers have hired tutors that can advise on some of these other areas. Talinn Phillips (2016) reports hiring a statistics tutor for her graduate writing center. Granted, some administrators might see these types of workshops as being outside the purview of a writing center. However, for many students in STEM disciplines—and especially for international students still learning the expectations of a US educational context—these concerns are inextricable from the writing process. Many writing centers, including my own, have also partnered with other entities on campus to host small graduate student development workshops (e.g., see Gray, this volume). Discounting these additional kinds of consulting and development workshops can be a disservice to students, and it can be a missed opportunity to meet students early in the drafting process.

Writing center administrators must also consider ways of positioning themselves as a resource for advisors and graduate faculty, as well, and perhaps moving away from the model of the writing center being a place to outsource support that could be provided in programs, as discussed by Jerry Stinnett and Shannon Madden (Stinnett and Madden 2016). (Related to this point, see also chapters by Pemberton and Perdue, this volume.) Particularly at larger schools, it might not be feasible for writing centers to function as the sole source of writing support, even if they are a resource for graduate students. It is particularly important to talk to disciplinary faculty about working with multilingual graduate students, as faculty can often hold a variety of assumptions about students' language proficiency and understanding of ethical source use and their expectations of the advisor-advisee relationship, as I've discussed. Often, international faculty in the disciplines can be powerful allies in these conversations.

Moving beyond the Tutor Dyad Model
While one-on-one consulting will always have a role in graduate student writing center work, there are good reasons for moving away from the dyad model with graduate students in general—and multilingual students in particular—and moving toward hybrid tutorial sessions involving writing and discussion groups. Given the complexity of graduate student projects, it might prove difficult for any one person without the disciplinary expertise to provide sufficient feedback to the writer. Often, one-on-one sessions create the impression with students and advisors that the writing consultant has the "silver bullet" piece of advice that will solve all problems in the text, and, while I have had graduate consultants give sterling advice, this expectation places undue pressure on the session. Rather, many graduate students benefit from hybrid sessions structured as a writing group discussion moderated by a writing center consultant in which diverse students can contribute advice from their own experiences. This format often allows for a more integrated discussion of both content and language-related concerns better suited to the nature of scientific writing. For example, it is often difficult to talk about the readability of a figure without also discussing what the data in the figure represent, the latter also being a discussion to which participants from the field might be better able to contribute than the consultant. Moreover, at a more basic level, it is difficult to discuss the language and writing concerns in a scientific paper while skipping over the figures, which is the tendency of many consultants who come from a humanities background. Thus, as Phillips (2012) described in her study of graduate writing groups, the feedback is mediated through the language of negotiation.

This more distributed consultation model is also another tool for meeting some of multilingual students' more distinct concerns. It can, first of all, provide students with additional ways to satisfy other needs that might bring them to the writing center and that might not be met with a more traditional one-on-one session. For example, much of the research on Latino/a student success in graduate school has stressed the need for mentoring opportunities, particularly for first generation students (Castellanos, Gloria, and Kamimura 2006). A distributed model may allow graduate students opportunities to establish these types of relationships and may also allow individual students to assume a mentoring or expert role on topics on which they feel more confident. In my own experiences, these sessions have also led to students sharing advice on how to approach certain advisors or where to go for specific questions on graduate school procedures or expectations. Further, this distributed model more closely resembles workplace feedback sessions and provides students with strategies that they can continue to use in industrial settings.

At my institution, we have gravitated toward a graduate STEM Communication Fellows program to deliver these distributed consultation sessions (Simpson et. al. 2015). The STEM Fellows, in addition to serving as writing consultants in our writing center, seek out opportunities to host informal writing groups—sometimes organized by discipline or related discipline—with options for one-on-one sessions during or after the group meeting. Multilingual students, in particular, can benefit from a larger group discussion that integrates content and writing and then from a follow up with a STEM Fellow for specific language questions or to receive additional feedback on paraphrasing source material. In this arrangement, graduate students also find opportunities to mentor each other. For example, in one Earth Sciences proposal writing group organized by communication fellow Drea Rae Killingsworth, a more senior graduate student in the group recognized at one point that another student was working on the same New Mexico Geological Society grant that he had received, and he quickly stepped into the role of mentoring his colleague.

The group format can be particularly beneficial for multilingual students who struggle with "interactional proficiency," which I described earlier, or who lack the fluency in English to explain their research to non-specialized audiences or to paraphrase it sufficiently in a literature review. One particularly good conversation starter that helps all students but multilingual students in particular with these issues is a visualization exercise that I borrowed from a close colleague and from a book on visual problem-solving: Dan Roam's (2013) *The Back of a Napkin*. Quite simply, discussion participants are provided with a stack of cocktail napkins and Sharpies and asked to draw their research and explain their drawings to one another. This exercise serves a number of purposes. First, it helps the graduate consultant and the others in the group better understand each other's projects, which enables them to provide more specific feedback. Second, the activity encourages them to experiment with alternate ways of explaining their research, which is particularly useful for multilingual writers struggling with fluency. Third, it helps students better understand critical concepts about which they are trying to write, and, fourth, it can serve as a guide for conversations and questions in meetings with advisors about their projects. In one case, an advisor emailed me to say that an advisee brought her napkin to an advising session and that it was a useful way for her to gauge how well her advisee understood the topic. Last, many students find the napkin exercise a good starting point for planning their writing. As Curry (2014) has argued from her ethnographic work with engineers writing about research, visuals often serve as a rhetorical invention strategy for scientists and engineers—that is, many scientists and engineers start an article by creating graphs and diagrams of their findings and organizing the text around them. Many graduate students I have worked with on this task have, in fact, digitized and integrated these visuals, or at least have found the discussion useful both for practicing their interactional proficiency and starting the drafting process.

CONCLUSION

While this chapter has discussed the combined needs of graduate students and the distinct needs of multilingual graduate students, particularly those in STEM fields, my ultimate vision is for a writing center space designed to accommodate students from a range of linguistic backgrounds and disciplinary backgrounds. Designing this space, however, requires writing center researchers to continually shift focus between areas where student needs overlap and where they are distinct, as I have had to do in this chapter. I would argue further that graduate student writing support, in general, requires a broader view of student needs and student success. We focus our attention on writing because we are writing specialists, but in doing so we might be overlooking how writing fits in with other needs students may have. Multilingual graduate students' needs are complex, and we would do well to take stock of their many needs first, and then look for ways, some of which I've suggested here, that writing centers can provide more holistic, nuanced support.

NOTE

1. Data come from a case study of five multilingual doctoral students in an interdisciplinary environmental sciences program at a Northeastern Land Grant University (NLGU). This qualitative study involved a survey of all international students in the program, interviews with program faculty and advisors, a series of semi-structured interviews with and observations of study participants, and textual analysis. Participants include "Ana" (Fisheries Management, Colombia), "Salman" (Oceanography, Pakistan), Girmit (Oceanography, Fiji), Gabi (Hydrology, Brazil), and Paulo (Forestry, Brazil). For more on this study, please see Simpson (2010, 2013)

REFERENCES

Belcher, Diane. 1994. "The Apprenticeship Approach to Advanced Academic Literacy Graduate Students and Their Mentors." *English for Specific Purposes* 13 (1): 23–34. https://doi.org/10.1016/0889-4906(94)90022-1.

Canagarajah, Suresh. 2018. "English as a Spatial Resource: Explaining the Claimed Competence of Chinese STEM Professionals." *World Englishes* 37 (1): 34–50.

Canagarajah, Suresh. 2002. "Multilingual Writers and the Academic Community: Towards a Critical Relationship." *Journal of English for Academic Purposes* 1 (1): 29–44. https://doi.org/10.1016/S1475-1585(02)00007-3.

Canseco, Grace, and Patricia Byrd. 1989. "Writing Required in Graduate Courses in Business Administration." *TESOL Quarterly* 23 (2): 305–16. https://doi.org/10.2307/3587338.

Casanave, Christine Pearson, and Philip Hubbard. 1992. "The Writing Assignments and Writing Problems of Doctoral Students: Faculty Perceptions, Pedagogical Issues, and Needed Research." *English for Specific Purposes* 11 (1): 33–49. https://doi.org/10.1016/0889-4906(92)90005-U.

Casanave, Christine Pearson. 2016. "What Advisors Need to Know about the Invisible, 'Real Life' Struggles of Doctoral Dissertation Writers." In *Supporting Graduate Student Writers: Research, Curriculum, and Program Design*, ed. Steve Simpson, Nigel A. Caplan, Michelle Cox, and Talinn Phillips, 97–116. Ann Arbor: University of Michigan Press.

Castellanos, Jeanett, Alberta M. Gloria, and Mark Kamimura, eds. 2006. *The Latino/a Pathway to the Ph.D.: Abriendo Caminos*. Sterling, VA: Stylus.

Chien, Shih-Chieh. 2014. "Cultural Constructions of Plagiarism in Student Writing: Teachers' Perceptions and Responses." *Research in the Teaching of English* 49 (2): 120–40.

Council of Graduate Schools. 2013. *Completion and Attrition in STEM Master's Programs: Pilot Study Findings*. Washington, DC: Council of Graduate Schools.

Consortium on Graduate Communication. n.d. www.gradconsortium.org.

Curry, Mary Jane. 2014. "Graphics and Invention in Academic Engineers' Writing for Publication." In *Language, Literacy, and Learning in STEM Education: Research Methods and Perspectives from Applied Linguistics*, ed. Mary Jane Curry and David I. Hanauer, 87–106. Philadelphia: John Benjamins Publishing Company. https://doi.org/10.1075/lsse.1.06cur.

Curry, Mary Jane. 2016. "More than Language: Graduate Student Writing as 'Disciplinary Becoming'." In *Supporting Graduate Student Writers: Research, Curriculum, and Program Design*, ed. Steve Simpson, Nigel A. Caplan, Michelle Cox, and Talinn Phillips, 78–96. Ann Arbor: University of Michigan Press.

Downie, Andrew. 2011. "Latin American Countries Push More Students to Study Abroad." *Chronicle of Higher Education*, August 9. http://chronicle.com/article/Latin-American-Countries-Push/128584/.

Habib, Anna S., Jennifer Haan, and Karyn Mallett. 2015. "The Development of Disciplinary Expertise: An EAP and RGS-informed Approach to the Teaching and Learning of Genre at George Mason University." *Composition Forum* 31. http://compositionforum.com/issue/31/george-mason.php.

Howard, Rebecca Moore. 2008. "Plagiarizing (from) Graduate Students." In *Pluralizing Plagiarism: Identities, Contexts, Pedagogies*, ed. Rebecca Moore Howard and Amy E. Robillard, 92–100. Portsmouth, NH: Heinemann.

Howard, Rebecca Moore, Tricia Serviss, and Tanya K. Rodrigue. 2010. "Writing from Sources, Writing from Sentences." *Writing & Pedagogy* 2 (2). https://doi.org/10.1558/wap.v2i2.177.

iThenticate. 2014. "Ph.D. in 'Copy-and Paste'? Addressing the Rise of Plagiarism in Graduate Programs." http://www.ithenticate.com/hs-fs/hub/92785/file-1696075998-pdf/resources/iThenticate-Plagiarism-Graduate-Paper.pdf?submissionGuid=ade0270e-ea09-4b1e-ad31-c7e6232bb8a5.

Kamler, Barbara, and Pat Thomson. 2006. *Helping Doctoral Students Write: Pedagogies for Supervision.* New York: Routledge.

Levy, Harold O. 2013. "Why China and India Love U.S. Universities." *Scientific American*, December 1, 2013. https://www.scientificamerican.com/article/why-china-and-india-love-us-universities/.

Mallett, Karyn, Jennifer Haan, and Anna S. Habib. 2016. "Graduate Pathway Programs as Sites for Strategic, Language-Supported Internationalization: Four Pedagogical Innovations." In *Supporting Graduate Student Writers: Research, Curriculum, and Program Design,* ed. Steve Simpson, Nigel A. Caplan, Michelle Cox, and Talinn Phillips, 118–38. Ann Arbor: University of Michigan Press.

National Center for Education Statistics. n.d. *Fast Facts: Degrees Conferred by Sex and Race.* https://nces.ed.gov/fastfacts/display.asp?id=72.

National Science Foundation. 2016. "National Science Board: Science and Engineering Indicators 2016." https://www.nsf.gov/statistics/2016/nsb20161/#/L.

Pecorari, Diane. 2006. "Visible and Occluded Citation Features in Postgraduate Second-Language Writing." *English for Specific Purposes* 25 (1): 4–29. https://doi.org/10.1016/j.esp.2005.04.004.

Pew Research Center. 2015. "English Proficiency on the Rise Among Latinos." Pew Research Center: Hispanic Trends. http://www.pewhispanic.org/2015/05/12/english-proficiency-on-the-rise-among-latinos/.

Phillips, Talinn. 2012. "Graduate Writing Groups: Shaping Writing and Writers from Student to Scholar." *Praxis: A Writing Center Journal* 10 (1). http://www.praxisuwc.com/phillips-101/.

Phillips, Talinn. 2013. "Tutor Training and Services for Multilingual Graduate Writers: A Reconsideration." *Praxis: A Writing Center Journal* 10 (2). http://www.praxisuwc.com/phillips-102/.

Phillips, Talinn. 2016. "Writing Center Support for Graduate Students: An Integrated Model." In *Supporting Graduate Student Writers: Research, Curriculum, and Program Design,* ed. Steve Simpson, Nigel A. Caplan, Michelle Cox, and Talinn Phillips, 159–71. Ann Arbor: University of Michigan Press.

Roam, Dan. 2013. *The Back of the Napkin: Solving Problems and Selling Ideas with Pictures. Expanded edition.* New York: Penguin.

Rogers, Paul M., Terry Myers Zawacki, and Sarah E. Baker. 2016. "Uncovering Challenges and Pedagogical Complications in Dissertation Writing and Supervisory Practices: A Multimethod Study of Doctoral Students and Advisors." In *Supporting Graduate Student Writers: Research, Curriculum, and Program Design,* ed. Steve Simpson, Nigel A. Caplan, Michelle Cox, and Talinn Phillips, 52–77. Ann Arbor: University of Michigan Press.

Simpson, Steve. 2010. "Learning Systems: An Ecological Perspective on Advanced Academic Literacy Practices of Multilingual Writers." PhD diss., University of New Hampshire.

Simpson, Steve. 2013. "Systems of Writing Response: A Brazilian Student's Experiences Writing for Publication in an Environmental Sciences Doctoral Program." *Research in the Teaching of English* 48 (2): 228–49.

Simpson, Steve, Rebecca Clemens, Drea Rae Killingsworth, and Julie Dyke Ford. 2015. "Creating a Culture of Communication: A Graduate-Level STEM Communication Fellows Program at a Science and Engineering University." *Across the Disciplines* 12 (3). http://wac.colostate.edu/atd/graduate_wac/simpsonetal2015.cfm.

Simpson, Steve, Nigel A. Caplan, Michelle Cox, and Talinn Phillips, eds. 2016. *Supporting Graduate Student Writers: Research, Curriculum, and Program Design.* Ann Arbor: University of Michigan Press.

Stinnett, Jerry, and Shannon Madden. 2016. "Entrepreneur Versus Expert: How Offshored Consulting Prevents Writing from Being Fully Integrated into the Academic Curriculum." *Writing Center Journal Blog Community,* July 2016. http://www.writingcenterjournal.org/community/.

Sutherland-Smith, Wendy. 2008. *Plagiarism, The Internet, and Student Learning: Improving Academic Integrity.* New York: Routledge.
Swales, John M. 1990. *Genre Analysis: English in Academic and Research Settings.* Cambridge: Cambridge University Press.
Swales, John M., and Christine B. Feak. 1994. *Academic Writing for Graduate Students: Essential Tasks and Skills.* Ann Arbor: University of Michigan Press.
Swales, John M., and Christine B. Feak. 2012. *Academic Writing for Graduate Students: Essential Tasks and Skills.* 3rd ed. Ann Arbor: University of Michigan Press. https://doi.org/10.3998/mpub.2173936.

4
GETTING THE WRITING RIGHT
Writing/Language Centers and Issues of Pedagogy, Responsibility, Ethics, and International English in Graduate Student Research Writing

Joan Turner

My focus in this chapter is on the writing of English second language (L2) graduate students and the challenges that writing or language center practitioners face in their mediating role between student and institutional expectations. In particular, I foreground the tension between over-simplistic assumptions of what is involved in getting the writing right, encapsulated in the demand for proofreading, and the complex contemporary reality of writing in English. It seems that the issue of proofreading steps into the breach between the improbability of perfect prose in an additional language and the cultural demand for pristine prose in high stakes academic contexts such as doctoral programs. At the same time, the underlying issues are being blurred, enabling institutional policy makers to avoid making difficult decisions in relation to international English.

In my discussion of the issues, it should be noted that I conflate the role of the US writing center with that of the UK English language center. This is not to gloss over differences in institutional heritage and modes of delivery, nor in professional pathways for their practitioners, but rather to accentuate the similarities in their student-centered educational principles as well as in some of the challenges each faces in the contemporary international university. Writing centers as such are relatively scarce in the United Kingdom, but the need for the kind of work that they do is increasing across the spectrum of degree provision. As a result, attention to writing is included in a range of recent overarching terminologies relating to student support. These include *academic skills, academic practice,* or *learning development centers.* There is currently a great deal of flux and merger around these areas, including English language centers, so it is difficult to be definitive either with regard to terminology

DOI: 10.7330/9781607327516.c004

or exactly what is being provided. As a further point of contrast, there is no widespread tradition of peer tutoring for writing in the United Kingdom, although this has been increasing at the undergraduate level with regard to helping students familiarize themselves in general with what studying involves.

English language centers, albeit with varying terminologies, have a longer heritage based on the provision of English for Academic Purposes (EAP) to international L2 students (see Swales 1985; Dudley-Evans and St. John 1998; Benesch 2001 for historical overviews). Recently, such centers have also increasingly been working with what in the United Kingdom are known as "home" students, especially with regard to writing. Home students may have English either as their first language or as an additional language, that is, they may speak a different language with their parents. In any event, as Pierre Bourdieu and Jean-Claude Passeron have famously pointed out, academic language is nobody's mother tongue (Bourdieu and Passeron 1994). Most students struggle to a greater or lesser extent with the exigencies of academic writing, especially given the increasing plethora of genres that they are asked to write in. While curricular emphases may differ for home or international students, the principles of practice are similar, especially where student needs are at the forefront. Catering for a wide range of needs and deciding what to prioritize is a perennial issue for writing support practitioners.

The area of language center provision which most marries up with writing center issues is what is known as "in-sessional" provision. In-sessional provision is for students who are enrolled in different programs throughout the university in contrast to intensive preparatory programs run by the language center for international students before they join their future degree courses. In-sessional provision usually consists of weekly writing support classes of two-hour duration. While attempts are made to tailor such classes to specific discipline-based programs, this is not always possible, so there might be, for example, a class for students in the social sciences rather than a class for each discipline. Historically, most in-sessional provision has been focused on master's students because, in the United Kingdom, master's programs are only one year in duration, and so there is a limited length of time for students to be able to develop their language and particularly their writing skills to meet the expectations of genre and required length. Most master's programs in the humanities and social sciences require students to produce four essays of around five thousand words in length, plus a dissertation of up to fifteen thousand words.

Language centers usually also put on a class for PhD students, drawing for example on the work of Brian Paltridge, Brian Paltridge and Sue Starfield, John Swales and Christine Feak, Barbara Kamler and Pat Thomson, and Claire Aitchison and Alison Lee (Paltridge 2002; Kamler and Thomson 2006; Aitchison and Lee 2006; Paltridge and Starfield 2007; Swales and Feak 2012). In many cases, there will also be provision for one-to-one consultations, either by appointment or at regular drop-in sessions. In this chapter, I include examples from such one-to-one consultations from my own experiences as a writing practitioner in the language center at Goldsmiths University in London.

I use the term "writing practitioner" throughout this chapter to refer to this professional experience regardless of specific tradition and the institutional logistics of delivery; it is my contention that, although the professional pathways for practitioners in language centers and writing centers vary, their work benefits from cross-fertilization in both knowledge of rhetorical analysis and the writing process as well as the principles of pedagogic practice, as this volume illustrates.

One of my major concerns with regard to the practice and functions of writing provision—or support—is how it is viewed in the wider circulation of institutional discourse (see also Turner 2011a). In particular, I see institutional perceptions of those areas dealing with writing pedagogy as a perennial source of tension. While collaboration with individual academic departments, or even individual academics such as PhD supervisors, may be good, there exists in the institutional background a climate of nonunderstanding or routine misconstruals of what those dealing with student writing actually do. One particular bone of contention, and source of tension, that I focus on in this chapter is the simplistic reduction of writing issues to that of proofreading. Here, I draw on my own experience and research into perspectives on proofreading as well as wider illustrations from professional listserv posts, which reveal the sense of exasperation fueled by the persistence of assumptions that writing practitioners act as proofreaders. Such an assumption not only denies the professional and pedagogic expertise of writing practitioners, it slides over the situated reality of individual writers and their struggles, and gets in the way of more conceptually robust conversations about the internationalization of universities and what that means for the internationalization of English.

TENSIONS AROUND PROOFREADING

The following email sent to me is typical of the institutional climate around proofreading in the United Kingdom:

> I am a psychology PhD student in the final phase of writing my thesis. I have upgraded and submitted my paper once and been asked to do major corrections on my paper, and feel that it would be helpful to also have an editor check my writing. I was told by my supervisors that you offer such services in your department. I am due to re-submit in June and would be entirely grateful if you can let me know if you offer such services, or if you don't who can possibly assist me with this.

I replied that we did not offer editing services, but if the student sent me around ten pages from her thesis, and if she chose a section that she felt she had particular difficulty with, I would see her for an hour in the following week (I was being mindful of her timescale here, having received the email after the middle of May). I also mentioned that problematic issues often recurred and that she would be able to apply what she learned from our discussion of this section to other parts of the thesis. The reply I got back from the student was terse, saying that she only wanted proofreading.

Behind the specific attitude of this individual student is the widely held notion of "writing up" the research. This notion suggests that the writing serves a purely instrumental function and is not an integral part of the knowledge production process. The assumption seems to be that once the research has been done, the writing will simply take care of itself. Such an assumption runs counter to the knowledge and expertise of writing practitioners and researchers, who are only too well aware of the rhetorical role of the writing itself in shaping texts and, indeed, producing knowledge. Paul Rogers and Olivia Walling, for example, state that the historical perspective they have taken in their research reveals writing to be "an active participant in the creation of knowledge" (Rogers and Walling 2011, 260).

Unfortunately however, the "writing up" assumption is institutionally widespread and, as a result, makes it a more difficult task to relay a better institutional understanding of what writing practitioners actually do. It leaves the central writing process of re-writing or re-drafting out of the account, and thereby ignores much of the writing practitioner's expertise. Rowena Murray (2005) encapsulates well this expertise and the framing behind it when she talks about the "contradictory" aspect of revision in the writing process, whereby "writing involves both deciding in advance what to say and discovering what you want to say as you make choices about how to say it" (137). In other words, thoughts are seldom completely clear before they are expressed and more finely crafted in writing. A further implication is that writing is an important part of the learning process, and successful crafting in the mold that is best suited to the task at hand is in itself an intellectually demanding task.

As the conventional notion of "proofreading" relates to finalizing the writing process, it aligns with a mechanistic understanding of "writing up." It is therefore easily wielded institutionally as a solution to problems with written English. However, this glib institutional understanding of proofreading does not sit well with writing practitioners and is a source of perennial tension, as recurring discussions on the UK-based BALEAP[1] listserv for EAP practitioners as well as the European-based EATAW[2] listserv for writing center practitioners show. This tension is also longstanding, going back to Steven North's (1984) landmark article on the purpose of writing centers, which he characterized as a "place for learning" and defiantly not a "proofreading-shop-in-the-basement." In the following section, I identify some of the strategies that UK language centers take in the light of institutional and student demands for proofreading, as well as the pedagogic principles that it militates against.

PRIORITIZING LEARNING

In one BALEAP listserv discussion, in the Autumn 2007 term, a total of thirty-three postings from twenty-eight UK institutions were made on the topic of what to do about the demand for proofreading. The topic had been brought up prior to 2007 and has also recurred since then in 2011, 2014, and 2015, but the 2007 discussion was particularly extensive, and I noted the range of positions taken and attitudes shown.

That discussion began because a particular center had been asked to provide a proofreading service and wanted to know whether others did so, and, if so, how they organized the service. In the responses, there were ultimately three approaches to the issue, usually expressed in a tone of exasperation. One, from an earlier BALEAP discussion in 2006, voiced a position of outright defiance, a position which was also echoed in later discussions. The poster stated, "I would say that, as EAP lecturers, we should NOT proofread" (BALEAP post 2006). This position has its justification in pedagogic principles. In general, EAP practitioners, indeed writing specialists as a whole, see their role as developing the academic writing abilities of their students, perhaps helping them to understand the requirements of a specific genre, or to make clear in a specific section of text what it is that they want to say. Students who hand over their work to proofreaders in effect circumvent this developmental process, denying the opportunity to learn for themselves. This pedagogic attitude is explicit in the following two posts:

Proofreading does not help students improve their English and it might prevent them from improving it. (BALEAP listserv, 2007)

Proofreading does not aim to improve students' communicative ability. In fact, it hides any lack of ability. (BALEAP listserv, 2007)

The second approach by language centers to the issue of providing proofreading, according to the listserv responses, may be seen as an arms-length policy, whereby a center keeps a register of proofreaders and points students in their direction when proofreading is requested. The proofreaders on such a register are often also part-time EAP or writing tutors, and the additional boost to such part-time workers' finances is often stated as a beneficial side effect of such a policy. Once introduced, the negotiation over time, payment, and the kind of work the proofreader will undertake is between the proofreader and the student. This practice is also justified because it absolves the language center of responsibility for any issues of academic integrity. There was a sense of ethical unease about this practice, with many seeing it as "a gray area" but one that responded to a demand.

The third approach noted was to try to accommodate specific institutional demands, such as to facilitate PhD completion rates, as one language center respondent explained: "We also oversee an academic copy editing service, a pay service, which we set up at the request of the Graduate Faculty three years ago. It was seen as a means to address delays in PhD completions due to theses being returned as a result of poor English." Guidelines were set up for this pay service as follows, according to the respondent: "The service was set up with quite strict guidelines for use: tutors would be restricted in what they did, concentrating on 'surface' grammatical features in order to make texts more readable, and students would only be able to use the service once supervisors were happy with the content."

However, and perhaps predictably, this system did not work out as planned, as the language center respondent also reported: "Some of the guidelines are broken—for instance [the pay service] is commonly used by master's students, and rarely through referral from [discipline-based] tutors. Also, as we all know, the limits ('stick to grammatical tweaking') are not practical." As this post indicates, the boundary line between what constitutes the conventional notion of proofreading, which might comprise "grammatical tweaking," and more substantive textual intervention is becoming blurred. This blurring raises larger issues of ethics and academic integrity, which also featured on the listserv discussions.

TEXTUAL INTERVENTION AND ISSUES OF ACADEMIC INTEGRITY

While issues of academic integrity do not form part of the formal remit of language centers, they tend to slip in in a rather underhanded way through the innocuous-sounding expectation of proofreading. The feeling of having the role of ethical arbiter foisted upon them is clear from the following BALEAP post: "A lot of supervisors here have sent students to see the learning advisors/EAP tutors and, without explicitly saying so, create an expectation that we are going to proofread these dissertations. This allows them to give the ethical issues a body swerve and pass the problem on to someone else" (BALEAP listserv, 2007).

In their research into the views of students and others acting as proofreaders, Nigel Harwood, Liz Austin, and Rosemary Macaulay found that they also frequently had ethical misgivings about what it was they were doing, as the texts they were reading needed more than proofreading in its conventional sense (Harwood, Austin, and Macaulay 2009, 2010). For example, one proofreader felt that intervening at the level of structure or argumentation was unethical (175). Another felt that accepting students whose language proficiency was too low was also an ethical issue: "I don't think the university should be accepting students with that level of English. I think it's very unfair because they have an expectation that they are at a level that they can cope with the work and then they suddenly find that they aren't. . . . If there are so many corrections that they can't produce a piece of work on their own it's a waste of time to them" (58).

Awareness of the ethical issues is not restricted to writing practitioners. One Australian faculty member has drawn attention to the difficulties of drawing the boundaries of supervisor intervention in student texts. He outlines the issue as follows:

> It is often the case that the NESB (Non-English-Speaking Background) student may not be capable of editing and polishing the text of the final draft to bring it to submission standard. Who then is responsible for this task? And in performing it, is an ethical boundary crossed which signifies that the final product is no longer solely the student's own work? If the supervisor assumes this responsibility, not only is he or she taking on a very onerous and time-consuming task, normally one well beyond that required with research students from English speaking backgrounds, but the supervisor may be guilty, at least in part, of writing the thesis for the student. (Knight 1999, 97–98)

This quote illustrates the issues of ethics and responsibility around PhD writing as well as point to the aporia for the student, who "may not be capable of editing and polishing the text of the final draft to bring it to submission standard." This is yet another issue, which the institutional deployment of proofreading as a solution skates over, or indeed masks. Institutional policy makers need to recognize the reality of international Englishes, acknowledge the extent to which they can differ from the ideal of pristine prose, and agree to levels of functional acceptability as well as to levels of language expertise which individual students can realistically attain. In other words, this means moving away from the assumption that "a single standardized form of English, based on metropolitan British or American English, should be the model for all non-native learners of English" (Leung and Street 2014, 24).

INTERNATIONAL ENGLISH IN THE INTERNATIONAL UNIVERSITY

It is well understood by English Language Teaching (ELT) professionals, applied linguists, and writing practitioners that L2 writers will not convey the voice of a native speaker. The problem is rather the assumption that they should. In her overview of second language learning research, for example, Diane Larsen-Freeman (1991) concluded that "for most adult learners, complete mastery of the L2 may be impossible" (337). Chris Thaiss and Terry Myers Zawacki discuss and report on the varying attitudes toward "alternative" versions of English and rhetorical organization, including "international Englishes" that they encountered among academics across the disciplines (Thaiss and Zawacki 2006; see also Zawacki and Habib 2014 on the question of faculty dispositions toward language difference). The field of ELF (English as a Lingua Franca) highlights "tolerance for variation, and a focus on mutual cooperation and intelligibility" (Rubdy and Saraceni 2006, 12). This is of course much easier in spoken interaction than in writing where the ambient multi-modality of such interactions, with gestures, facial expressions, tone of voice and so on, all help with "mutual cooperation." However, Rani Rubdy and Mario Saraceni (2006) also suggest that "variation from the norm" in lingua franca communication is itself likely to be "the norm," and such diversification could also apply to writing. Given the fact that there are globally more non-native users of English than there are native speakers (Crystal 1997; Graddol 2001), Barbara Seidlhofer (2005) makes the point that "English is being shaped at least as much by its non-native speakers as by its native speakers" (339).

In their advocacy of a "translingual approach," Bruce Horner et al. (2011) suggest "that deviations from dominant expectations need not be errors; that conformity need not be automatically advisable; and that writers' purposes and readers' conventional expectations are neither fixed nor unified" (301). In another publication, Bruce Horner, Samantha Necamp, and Christiane Donahue characterize the "translingual model" as rejecting monolingualism as well as an additive understanding of multilingualism, and emphasizing instead "working across languages" (Horner, Necamp, and Donahue 2011, 270). In similar vein, Joan Mullin, Carol Haviland, and Amy Zenger note how students at the transnational American University Beirut perceive differences of rhetorical style and are themselves led to question the normative values of being succinct and direct in English, as opposed to, for example, being more elaborate, as in French and Arabic (Mullin, Haviland, and Zenger 2014).

There are, then, different theoretical strands from second language acquisition, ELF studies, and writing research that seek to move the focus from a reliance on traditional normative standards to a more flexible and internationalized approach. While these theoretical insights signal a need for change, alongside the fact that the use of English internationally is accelerating language change and diversification anyway, the situation is one of uncertainty; it is difficult for writing practitioners as institutional intermediaries, as it were, to take a principled stance for change when there is pressure on students to complete their doctoral studies on time and institutional and individual academic reputations are at stake. Given my own awareness of and intellectual sympathy with the theoretical landscape, as well as my experience of the widespread demand for proofreading, which I felt acted as a barrier to a wider institutional understanding of the issues, I undertook some research into the differing perspectives on proofreading held by academics, students, and EAP practitioners. Some of the research outcomes are discussed in the following section.

THROUGH THE PRISM OF PROOFREADING

The research project was entitled "Perspectives on Proofreading"[3] and looked at how proofreading was conceptualized by different stakeholders in higher education. The research included conducting semi-structured interviews with seven professors, representing the humanities, fine arts, and the social sciences; ten small focus groups with post-graduate students from the same disciplinary groups, which included both home and international students; four semi-structured interviews with PhD students, three of whom were international; and a focus group with practitioners of English for Academic Purposes. Questions included what was understood by the notion of proofreading, what role it fulfilled, whether it was deemed educational or not, and what the research participants felt about the growing commercial practice of individuals offering their services as "proofreaders" to international students in particular. The three stakeholder groups—professors, students, EAP practitioners—had distinctly differing views (see also Turner 2011b), which I outline in the following brief syntheses.

The discipline-based academics were convergent on the need for conventionally "correct," well written academic prose, where proofreading, if done by others, was not particularly problematized but seen as broadly supportive of the learning process.

The students revealed strongly affective concerns around writing. They were anxious about getting it right and about communicating their ideas effectively to their intended audience. They were angry at perceived inequalities whereby those who paid proofreaders to go over their work received better marks. They lacked confidence in their abilities with English, and those who used external proofreaders were disappointed that they did not meet expectations of how their texts would be improved. In general, there was also a despairing awareness that the process of writing/re-writing/proofreading was never-ending.

As with the listserv posts, the EAP practitioners were concerned to distance their professional role from that of proofreading. They were unconvinced that there were any educational benefits to the students from having their work proofread. They were concerned about the ethics of proofreading, not only in terms of where the boundaries lay with regard to what constituted rewriting, but also in terms of inequity with regard to those students who could not afford to pay for proofreading services. In addition to those educational and ethical concerns, there was also a sense that by being associated with the role of proofreader, their professional integrity was being dented, and their expertise was not being given enough institutional recognition. As one EAP practitioner in the focus group put it, echoing Steven North's (1984) dismissal of the proofreading role: "We should be working with students to highlight weak areas that need to be improved and giving them examples of how to improve it, but we certainly shouldn't be going through crossing every 't' and dotting every 'i'. I absolutely don't think that is our job" (author's data).

In the next section, I will look more closely at some of the views of the academics I interviewed, and in particular at the discourse in which they expressed those views. I will then go on to discuss how their views are of interest to the pedagogic debate of macro- versus micro-level textual concerns.

PROOFREADING, IRRITATION, AND THE MICRO-LEVEL OF TEXTUAL PRODUCTION

As mentioned above, the academics that I interviewed from the humanities, social sciences, and fine art disciplines generally saw proofreading as a good thing. It was seen as being helpful to the student and bringing positive benefits to the reader. What was striking was the discourse of irritation they expressed about having to read texts with errors in them. This was not restricted to international students, but applied to all students. One said, "I would see proofreading as being about making sure that all those irritating minor errors are expunged from the text."

The word "expunged" in particular signals the weight of importance attached to getting rid of linguistic and typographic errors. The effect on the reader's motivation was also apparent when another professor talked of "nagging issues of presentation that, as it were, dampen the enthusiasm." The notion of "distracting" in the following excerpt from a third professor has similar negative connotations, and marks the important distinction for the discipline-based reader between content—"the larger argument"—and form: "I think that the problem with text, which is full of those kinds of proofreading errors, they are so distracting that it makes it very difficult to read the larger argument."

One professor expanded further on the topic, focusing specifically on PhD level work, and the differing attitudes of supervisors. He made a distinction between content and language as follows: "We as a group of people in this department are quite keen on encouraging high standards of writing. But . . . if you look at the supervisors, there is a definite difference between those who want to get the big things right and are not so worried about the minutiae of language issues, whether the verb agrees with the whatever it is . . . and those who want it to be, you know, perfect."

However, the distinction he made between supervisors' attitudes was not left open; he took the issue one step further to the role of the external examiner, and here the micro-level issues loomed larger. The issue was that even if supervisors did not require "absolutely immaculate English" then the external examiner would, he said. "If the examiners want absolutely immaculate English then it will get picked up somewhere. It generally gets picked up somewhere. There definitely isn't a consensus that you can get away with all this stuff, that it doesn't matter. So somewhere along the line someone is going to blow the whistle on it." The strong ethico-legal discourse here, albeit expressed in idiomatic English "get away with" and "blow the whistle," shows the strength of feeling around errors or the need for "immaculate English." It seemed that while he was aware of others allowing non-immaculate English, for him not accepting anything other than "immaculate English" was the only academically acceptable route.

Proofreading in such a climate of expectation plays the role of remedying any textual shortcomings and thereby maintaining institutional order. I have made the point elsewhere (Turner 2015) that institutional reputations are tied up with the acceptability of the writing in PhD theses. The example I gave in that piece came from an academic who indicated that spelling mistakes in a student's thesis also meant bad supervision, which, in turn, was felt to have implications for the academic's reputation, and by extension that of the institution. The politics of proofreading therefore go beyond the textual and the ethical; it is deeply implicated in the western cultural ideology around the importance of pristine prose.

MACRO- VERSUS MICRO-LEVEL CONCERNS

These academics' views point to a stark contrast with the predominant focus of writing practitioners on macro-level textual concerns. It is routine in most traditions of writing pedagogy to work with a notional hierarchy, that is, to attend to structural issues, or the shape of the writing as a whole, first. However, as the editors of this volume suggest in their prospectus, the "privileging of whole-text over more local concerns" has become an issue for debate. The importance of "correctness" at the micro-level of text is clearly shown in my data above, and possibly suggests the need for writing practitioners to pay greater attention to the micro-level, if nothing else, in the interests of facilitating good collegial relations, that is, obliquely supporting the needs of academic readers, who do not want to stumble over errors.

John Bean (2001) exemplifies the assumption in writing practitioners' pedagogic discourse of a "hierarchy of concerns," whereby clarity of thought and the organization of ideas come before "mechanical features" such as spelling and sentence construction. While this hierarchy makes sense in many instances, the use of the term "mechanical features," especially in contexts of L2 writing, minimizes the intellectual effort required to fit individual sentences into the larger whole. Bean may have had L1 writers predominantly in mind, but in L2 practitioner discourse the hierarchization of structure over language is also prevalent. The often heard talk of "surface features" is another expression that diminishes what can be the substantive language work involved in that "surface," which suggests a minor, quibbling, grammatical point that can be relegated to work after the organization of ideas is sorted out, or ignored altogether.

Arguably, the professional reluctance to be concerned with form at the micro-level is a reaction against historically prevalent notions that school writing was only about correct sentence level grammar. However as priorities in writing pedagogy have shifted, it is possible that the baby has been thrown out with the bath water. My argument here is not to reverse the hierarchy nor to deny important advances as more analytically sophisticated approaches to different aspects of the writing process have progressed, including the socially important dimension of writer identity and voice, but rather to develop a greater awareness of the need for attention to both macro- and micro-levels and to situate both within the perspective of the writer and the audience. I have previously argued for language issues, such as grammatical and lexical choices, to be given more weight (Turner 2004) and reiterate that concern here. To illustrate further what I mean, in the following section, I look at the case of an international PhD student I worked with extensively on a one-to-one basis.

INTELLECTUAL RIGOR, SUPERVISOR EXPECTATIONS, AND MICRO-LEVEL ATTENTION TO WRITING

The student I worked with was providing a psychoanalytic treatment of two artists' work at the same time as she was critiquing the politically charged atmosphere of South Korea in the 1980s. Her subject matter was therefore theoretically complex, as was her own analysis. There was no doubt that she knew what she was talking about, as she could always explain to me extremely fluently what she meant. Also, if I suggested a specific re-formulation, she was able to critique it and say whether it captured what she wanted to say or not. This disparity between expressive fluency in conversation or dialogue and writing is not unusual, but stood out for this student as her writing was often difficult to understand. One of her supervisors had suggested that her writing needed a bit of "smoothing" and my interpretation of this was that it was, like the use of the term "proofreading" in general, a euphemism. While it confirmed that her supervisors recognized that she was a capable student, and that her analysis was her own original contribution to knowledge, it underestimated the role of competence in language expertise in getting the right message across. Linguistic expertise was glossed over, something that was left to the final editing or proofreading stage. The student too, initially, did not fully acknowledge the effort that she needed to expend in improving her flexibility in the use of English. She saw it as a technicality, as if a proofreading exercise was something necessary but tedious.

She would say things like "I don't enjoy these editing matters" or "it's just editing issue." My point here is not to belabor or valorize the importance of grammar or word choice, but to recognize the intellectual hard labor of the language work involved in the nuanced analysis expected at the higher levels of academic achievement.

In my focus on the following excerpt, I emphasize both the complexity and rigor of her analysis, and its difficulties for the reader. I point up some linguistic comparisons from two highly differing linguistic systems, to show that the issue is not only a question of L2 expertise in English. The vignette also illustrates the underrated complexity and increasingly common occurrence of PhD writing, which has to combine the three elements of working in a theoretical discourse learned in English, working with empirical data in another language, in this case Korean, and bringing the thesis together in the preferred western cultural organization of academic discourse and argumentation. The textual excerpt is as follows:

> As is said earlier, the realm of the aesthetic Oh and Lim's works provides an affective space of expansion of our cognitive capacity. It is what is achieved through the artist's preservation of the unsaid and altering the culminated state and the matter of trauma which exited in sub-mind of Korean 1980s into space of art.

On the one hand, at the structural level, the beginning of the excerpt shows a good understanding of meta-discursive signaling. Referring back to points already made is common and necessary in extended writing such as in PhD theses. On the other hand, referring back usually requires encapsulating and re-stating the point in a different way. Such reformulation is linguistically complex. It is not amenable simply to cutting and pasting, but entails paraphrasing and fitting similar conceptual content into different sentence structures and often different word choices. In the above excerpt, the verb "provides" is confusing. It appears to refer back to a previously discussed "realm of the aesthetic" but also projects forward to an interpretation of this aesthetic, in other words, what it "provides" for the viewer. These two perspectives need clarifying for the reader, perhaps with the insertion of a relative clause joining the aesthetic to the work of the two artists Oh and Lim: "the realm of the aesthetic, which Oh and Lim's work provides. . . ." What is then required is a different expression relating to the effect of the work, perhaps using the semantics of "expansion" as a verb, for example, "expands our cognitive capacity. . . ." Such changes in lexis, grammar and syntax are not slight, especially when the linguistic system of the L1 is taken into account. For example, the Korean language does not have relative pronouns, word classes or prepositions as they exist in English (see Thompson 1987).

The density of the second sentence also needs to be unpacked and separate points identified. Part of my discussion with the student revolved around the word "exited," which I assumed was a typo, where the "s" was missing. I was guided to this interpretation by the preposition "in," which followed it. However, she also wanted to convey a sense of transfer from the Korean sub-conscious as it were, into the space of art, so the semantics of "exit," as in moving out of one domain into another, was indeed relevant.

The multiple interpretations available from this one short extract highlight the scope of the need for attention to micro-level issues of language use. They are by no means "surface" or "mechanical" issues, easily put right by a spot of proofreading. In this case, the detail of word choice or grammatical construction is important for reasons of conceptual clarity and semantic nuance, as well as textual cohesion and coherence. Especially at the level of PhD writing, and perhaps especially in the humanities and social sciences, there is a need for sophisticated control over and flexibility in the use of English. I do not think writing practitioners should shy away from this, but they must be prepared to take the time to unpack the sophisticated meanings embedded in an excerpt like the above and to show the student how it can be reworked. Pedagogically, this includes both a preparedness to interpret and have the interpretation sanctioned by the student, and a willingness to produce text or a construction that the student can use in a re-working. The requirement for such an analytical commitment on the part of the writing tutor also suggests that, in the case of peer tutoring, such tutors should themselves have an understanding of graduate-level work and ideally also be familiar with the moves and conventions of the discipline or similar disciplinary area.

The process outlined here is painstaking and time consuming. It is also more directive than is the norm in writing practitioner practice, but it ultimately benefits both the student in providing insight into the use of English and the supervisor in facilitating the desired "smooth" read. (For further discussion of directive tutoring approaches for English L2 students, see Cox, this volume.)

RUFFLING THE SMOOTH READ

While academics prefer a smooth read, unencumbered by writing errors, and I have suggested that good collegial relations between discipline-based academics and writing practitioners may be a side effect of paying greater attention to the micro-level of writing, this strategy is not clear-cut, but is rather a case of treading a fine line. On the one hand, in order to give priority to a student's argumentation, it is necessary to help the student use English to do so. On the other hand, there is a need also to break with the culturally habituated expectation of a smooth read. Given the multiplicity of international voices in English, there is a case for the L2 inflected voice in writing, just as happens naturally in spoken English. There needs to be some accommodation toward the L2 inflected voice, even if this means some discomfort or *irritation* for the reader as in my above examples from faculty members. When the meaning is clear, even if the expression is not quite as the reader her or himself would put it, there is no need to make changes. I give the following examples of two separate sentences from a PhD thesis, where, in my opinion, unnecessary changes were made by a reader. The original phrases where changes were made are in italics:

1. It seems that the idea of an ordinary English lesson for students is teacher-centered.
2. Such conceptualizations of English lead to a merely skill-focused English training.

Sentence one was changed to "*students' idea of . . .*" and in sentence two, the indefinite article *a* before "merely skills focused" was deleted. While there will be instances where the use of the definite or indefinite article causes uncertainty of meaning, this was not the case here and the change seems irrelevant.

CONCLUSION

The role of the writing practitioner as arbiter of where to make micro-level changes is precarious. It can only be done in careful interaction with the student, so preferably in one-to-one sessions and only on small sections of text. However, what is perhaps even more necessary is for the writing practitioner's perspective, and advocacy of the international student's perspective, to be more widely available institutionally. In this chapter, I have focused on the institutional undervaluing of linguistic and writing expertise by reducing it to something akin to proofreading. Proofreading can also be seen as a process of cultural sanitization, making all texts conform to acknowledged standards. The writing practitioner has to combat the meaning of proofreading as it is used institutionally, which means engaging with the issues it raises, while at the same time resisting its threat to writing pedagogy.

The relevance of the international student's written voice in an increasingly internationalized higher education should put the writing practitioner's perspective, conceptual knowledge, and practical experience center stage. However, this perspective is not always recognized, and the writing practitioner's voice is often not loud enough in institutional terms. There are no easy answers as to how this situation can be improved, but the more that experiences, strategies, and policies are shared and distributed, as in this volume, the better the chances are of building confidence in this institutionally political project.

NOTES

1. The British Association of Lecturers in English for Academic Purposes.
2. European Association of Teachers of Academic Writing.
3. This project was supported by a British Academy grant, (SG-46939).

REFERENCES

Aitchison, Claire, and Alison Lee. 2006. "Research Writing: Problems and Pedagogies." *Teaching in Higher Education* 11 (3): 265–78. https://doi.org/10.1080/13562510600680574.

Bean, J. C. 2001. *Engaging Ideas: The Professor's Guide to Writing, Critical Thinking, and Active Learning in the Classroom*. San Francisco, CA: Jossey Bass.

Benesch, Sarah. 2001. *Critical English for Academic Purposes: Theory, Politics, and Practice*. Mahwah, NJ: Lawrence Erlbaum Associates.

Bourdieu, Pierre, and Jean-Claude Passeron. 1994. "Introduction: Language and Relationship to Language in the Teaching Situation." In *Academic Discourse: Linguistic Misunderstanding and Professorial Power*, ed. Pierre Bourdieu, Jean-Claude Passeron, and Monique de Saint Martin, trans. Richard Teese., 1–34. Cambridge, UK: Polity Press.

Crystal, David. 1997. *English as a Global Language*. Cambridge: Cambridge University Press.

Dudley-Evans, Tony, and Maggie-Jo St. John. 1998. *Developments in English for Specific Purposes: A Multidisciplinary Approach*. Cambridge: Cambridge University Press.

Graddol, David. 2001. "English in the Future." In *Analysing English in a Global Context*, ed. Ann Burns and Caroline Coffin, 26–37. London: Routledge.

Harwood, Nigel, Liz Austin, and Rosemary Macaulay. 2009. "Proofreading in a UK University: Proofreaders' Beliefs, Practices, and Experiences." *Journal of Second Language Writing* 18 (3): 166–190. https://doi.org/10.1016/j.jslw.2009.05.002.

Harwood, Nigel, Liz Austin, and Rosemary Macaulay. 2010. "Ethics and Integrity in Proofreading: Findings from an Interview-based Study." *English for Specific Purposes* 29 (1): 54–67. https://doi.org/10.1016/j.esp.2009.08.004.

Horner, Bruce, Min-Zhan Lu, Jacqueline J. Royster, and John Trimbur. 2011. "OPINION: Language Difference in Writing: Toward a Translingual Approach." *College English* 73 (3): 299–318.

Horner, Bruce, Susan Necamp, and Christiane Donahue. 2011. "Toward a Multilingual Composition Scholarship: From English Only to a Translingual Norm." *College Composition and Communication* 63 (2): 269–300.

Kamler, Barbara, and Pat Thomson. 2006. *Helping Doctoral Students Write: Pedagogies for Supervision*. London: Routledge.

Knight, Nick. 1999. "Responsibilities and Limits in the Supervision of NESB Research Students in the Social Sciences." In *Supervising Postgraduates from Non-English-Speaking Backgrounds*, ed. Yoni Ryan and Ortrun Zuber-Skerritt, 93–100. Maidenhead, UK: The Society for Research into Higher Education and Open University Press.

Larsen-Freeman, Diane. 1991. "Second Language Acquisition Research: Staking out the Territory." *TESOL Quarterly* 25 (2): 315–50. https://doi.org/10.2307/3587466.

Leung, Constant, and Brian Street, eds. 2014. *The Routledge Companion to English Studies*. London: Routledge.

Mullin, Joan, Carole P. Haviland, and Amy Zenger. 2014. "Import/Export Work? Using Cross-Cultural Theories to Rethink Englishes, Identities, and Genres in Writing Centers." In *Reworking English in Rhetoric and Composition: Global Interrogations, Local Interventions*, ed. Bruce Horner and Karen Kopelson, 150–65. Carbondale: Southern Illinois University Press.

Murray, Rowena. 2005. *Writing for Academic Journals*. Maidenhead, UK: Open University Press.

North, Steven. 1984. "The Idea of a Writing Center." *College English* 46 (5): 433–46. https://doi.org/10.2307/377047.

Paltridge, Brian. 2002. "Thesis and Dissertation Writing: An Examination of Published Advice and Actual Practice." *English for Specific Purposes* 21: 125–43. https://doi.org/10.1016/S0889-4906(00)00025-9.

Paltridge, Brian, and Sue Starfield. 2007. *Thesis and Dissertation Writing in a Second Language: A Handbook for Supervisors*. London: Routledge.

Rogers, Paul, and Olivia Walling. 2011. "Writing and Knowledge Making: Insights from an Historical Perspective." In *Writing in Knowledge Societies*, ed. Doreen Starke-Meyerring, Anthony Paré, Natasha Artemeva, Miriam Horne, and Larissa Youssoubova, 259–73. Fort Collins, CO: The WAC Clearinghouse/Parlor Press. https://wac.colostate.edu/books/perspectives.cfm.

Rubdy, Rani, and Mario Saraceni, eds. 2006. *English in the World: Global Rules, Global Roles*. London, New York: Continuum.

Seidlhofer, Barbara. 2005. "English as a Lingua Franca." *ELT Journal* 59 (4): 339–41. https://doi.org/10.1093/elt/cci064.

Thompson, Ian. 1987. "Japanese Speakers (Includes Broad Similarities with Korean)." In *Learner English*, ed. Michael Swan and Bernard Smith, 296–309. Cambridge: Cambridge University Press.

Swales, John. M. 1985. *Episodes in ESP*. Oxford: Pergamon Institute of English.

Swales, John M., and Christine B. Feak. 2012. *Academic Writing for Graduate Students*. 3rd ed. Ann Arbor: The University of Michigan Press. https://doi.org/10.3998/mpub.2173936.

Thaiss, Chris, and Terry M. Zawacki. 2006. *Engaged Writers and Dynamic Disciplines: Research on the Academic Writing Life*. Portsmouth, NH: Boynton/Cook Heinemann Press.

Turner, Joan. 2004. "Language as Academic Purpose." *Journal of English for Academic Purposes* 3 (2): 95–109. https://doi.org/10.1016/S1475-1585(03)00054-7.

Turner, Joan. 2011a. *Language in the Academy. Cultural Reflexivity and Intercultural Dynamics*. Bristol, UK: Multilingual Matters.

Turner, Joan. 2011b. "Re-Writing Writing in Higher Education: The Contested Spaces of Proofreading." *Studies in Higher Education* 36 (4): 427–40. https://doi.org/10.1080/03075071003671786.

Turner, Joan. 2015. "The Symbolic Economy of Research Literacies: The Role of 'Writtenness' in the PhD Thesis." In *Research Literacies and Writing Pedagogies for Masters and Doctoral Writers*, ed. Cecile Badenhorst and Cally Guérin, 205–20. Studies in Writing Series. Amsterdam: Brill Publishing. https://doi.org/10.1163/9789004304338_012.

Zawacki, Terry Myers, and Anna Sophia Habib. 2014. "Negotiating 'Errors' in L2 Writing: Faculty Dispositions and Language Difference." In *WAC and Second-Language Writers:*

Research towards Linguistically and Culturally Inclusive Programs and Practices, ed. Terry Myers Zawacki and Michelle Cox, 183–210. Fort Collins, CO: The WAC Clearinghouse and Parlor Press; http://wac.colostate.edu/books/l2/chapter7.pdf.

PART II

Reshaping Our Pedagogies and Practices

5
INTAKE AND ORIENTATION
The Role of Initial Writing Center Consultations with Graduate Students

Patrick S. Lawrence, Molly Tetreault, and Thomas Deans

In this chapter we describe how two well-established public university writing centers have come to require intake consultations to manage increasing demand for graduate support and meet the distinct needs of graduate writers. When graduate students come to either center for the first time, they are required to meet with a member of our staff who works with them to discuss their needs and goals, orient them to our philosophy, and match them with a tutor. Beyond describing why and how we require these meetings, we draw on surveys of and interviews with graduate student clients to assess the effectiveness of these sessions and gauge attitudes toward the intake policy mandate.

While individualized tutoring is the mode of writing support that writing centers most commonly offer to graduate students (Caplan and Cox 2016), prefacing such tutoring with a required meeting is, as far as we know, unique to our two universities. Our intake consultations typically run twenty minutes and cover four priorities: getting to know the writer and their project; alerting them to the range of services available in our centers and on our campuses; providing an overview of the writing center's resources and approach to conferencing; and finally, if one-to-one tutorials are deemed a good fit, matching the writer with a tutor and scheduling an appropriate number of appointments based on the length and complexity of their project. The administrator then logs notes in an online scheduling and recordkeeping system so that the assigned tutor gets a preview of the person coming their way, along with any relevant contextual information. These records also help when the effectiveness of tutoring sessions needs to be assessed down the road. We do all this in the spirit of writing center pedagogy—that is, by building rapport, posing questions, and engaging in reflective discussion.

While we see these required intake consultations as occasions for dialogue, advising, and orientation, one might certainly wonder (and we have been eager to discover) if they erode writing centers' typical commitment to open access. After all, why insert a narrow gate that only graduate students must squeeze through while undergraduates can continue to walk in or sign up freely? Some graduate students might even perceive the requirement as a form of rationing or as a signal that they aren't quite welcome. For several years we have weighed these concerns against the benefits of requiring intake consultations, and in this chapter we ask these questions anew, adding the voices of graduate writers to our own observations. We begin with brief histories of how our centers arrived at this policy and how the consultations align with our writing center philosophies. We then report on feedback from graduate writers, which on the whole has been quite positive, and on why we will continue our intake consultations.

UNIVERSITY OF NEW HAMPSHIRE (UNH) BACKGROUND

The main campus of UNH has about two thousand graduate students, and intake consultations were instituted in 2010 in the midst of a surge in demand for graduate conferences that triggered concerns about resource allocation. Some graduate students came in hoping to work through multiple chapters of a thesis during a single fifty-minute conference. Others sought out the center as a proofreading service. Underlying these patterns, we suspected, was a misconception among many graduate students about the center's philosophy and approach. At the same time, the writing center had been grappling with longstanding questions about the effectiveness of graduate tutorials. Graduate students were meeting with undergraduate writing assistants, who often left conferences worried that they had given poor or inaccurate advice to the writer. Because graduate students often arrived with much longer documents and unrealistic expectations, the staff felt stressed and disappointed that writers were not meeting their goals. And even when writers returned for multiple sessions to continue with the same project, they often signed up with different tutors due to scheduling demands. This meant explaining their research and writing goals anew, which consumed valuable session time and sometimes led to confusion. Talinn Phillips (2016) has documented these very same graduate student critiques of writing centers more generally (see also Powers and Nelson 1995 in regard to second language graduate writers). It was amid these concerns, which were amplified by the fact that increases in graduate traffic were limiting the center's availability to undergraduates (the population the writing center was originally established to serve), that the idea for the intake consultation emerged.

Intake meetings at UNH are conducted by the director of the Writing Center. Graduate students looking for only one or two appointments are not required to have a consultation, but those seeking support for a project such as a master's thesis or doctoral dissertation must. The number of intake consultations per year is modest: in 2015–2016, UNH conducted ten.

UNIVERSITY OF CONNECTICUT (UCONN) BACKGROUND

UConn's main campus has nearly seven thousand masters and doctoral students, although like UNH, its writing center was founded to serve the much larger undergraduate population. In an attempt to grapple with many of the same concerns about the effectiveness of graduate support as UNH, by 2012 the center had expanded its outreach to graduate students, most notably by developing five-week graduate writing seminars, monthly writing retreats, stand-alone workshops, and dissertation retreats (for an overview of our graduate services, see Reardon, Deans, and Maykel 2016). As that portfolio of services was being refined, the center continued to offer individualized graduate tutorials on the same model as undergraduate tutorials, although staff and administrators noticed that the tutorial system was not accounting for the length and complexity of graduate projects in much the same ways as UNH had. In addition, a large percentage of those who sought support were international doctoral students in the sciences who had little experience with writing centers or other kinds of US-style tutoring services. And, again much as at UNH, UConn started experiencing a rapid increase in demand for both graduate and undergraduate tutoring, straining capacity and stressing tutors. Given these converging factors, the administrative team opted to follow the suggestion of a staff member who had formerly worked at UNH to pilot the graduate intake requirement in 2013 and implement it fully in 2014.

At UConn the Coordinator for Graduate Writing Support (typically a doctoral student on an assistantship) meets with every graduate student who comes to our writing center. If graduate students sign up for tutorials directly, they are welcomed and can complete a first tutorial but are then directed to meet with the Coordinator before scheduling more sessions. In 2015–2016, UConn conducted fifty-seven intake consultations.

INTAKE CONSULTATIONS AND WRITING CENTER PHILOSOPHY

For each center, a driving exigency for creating the intake policy was to manage increasing demand for graduate tutorials in a climate of limited resources, and we have been largely successful in achieving that goal: shortly after the policy was instituted at each school, the number of sessions for graduate students went down, and since then has plateaued to a manageable level. We believe that such decreases in traffic have been accompanied by enhancements in quality—both the quality of tutorials as well as the quality of overall writing support, which now includes the intake consultation itself and referrals to resources beyond tutorials.

Both our centers are rooted in the widely held tenet that all students can benefit from collaborating on their writing in a spirit of conversation (Bruffee 1984). A key manifestation of that philosophy is a welcoming ethos, an open invitation for all writers to come in for appointments or drop-ins at any stage in the writing process. Yet, as noted above, steady increases in demand at both of our centers were already squeezing access for both undergraduates and graduates, putting that open door ethos in jeopardy. By requiring intake consultations, our intention was not to restrict access but instead to manage it more deliberately—indeed, we wanted to promote access that operated in a spirit more of education than of competition.

That spirit of education involves looking beyond the text to the whole person. Both our centers emphasize writing as a recursive process, as a social practice, and as complex "text work/identity work" (Kamler and Thomson 2006, 508). This orientation differs from the common *write the research up* mentality that Barbara Kamler and Pat Thomson identify as "obliterat[ing]" the "complexity" of the research writing process for graduate students, which can "mislead students about what is entailed" in writing during graduate school (3). A second motivation for the intake consultation emerged, then, as a means of helping graduate writers begin to understand the complexities of research writing through conferencing. Furthermore, as Jerry Wellington (2010) indicates in his study of graduate student writers, the *write it up after thinking it out* mentality is one source of negative feelings—such as anxiety, fear, and isolation—among graduate students (146). Through the intake consultation, the coordinator helps writers understand how tutorials might help them, and, in doing so, speaks to some of their writing-related anxieties. In fact, the intake consultation begins to introduce an explicit vocabulary for both writing and the writing process, something many doctoral students desire but may not get in their home departments (Rogers, Zawacki, and Baker 2016).

As noted earlier, we discuss with writers the range of additional resources available in our respective centers and universities, which positions writers as traveling an arc of development rather than participating in a set of "fix-it"-oriented tutoring sessions. Such conversations are especially helpful for graduate students who feel isolated or are unaware of resources across campus. By honestly articulating both the affordances and limitations of support at our respective institutions, we aim to reduce at least some of the fragmentation so common to graduate writing support (Caplan and Cox 2016, 38–39). We quite literally put a human face to this problem and in doing so move toward a solution. And while fragmentation cannot be remedied in a twenty-minute conversation, by departing from our earlier *laissez faire* practice of having graduate students sign up for tutorials directly and instead orienting them to the writing center and offering a customized set of referrals, we think we are moving closer to the integrated approach that Steve Simpson (2016) envisions as "a more holistic set of resources supporting graduate students from start to finish" (9).

In the context of our long-term efforts to remedy those larger concerns about resources, access, and isolation, we also want to get some near-term work done in these intake consultations, that is, to match the writer with a tutor (if tutoring proves most appropriate). This, too, needs to be done with attention to our guiding philosophies and within the constraints of our individual centers. At both institutions, we understand that writing expertise involves several kinds of knowledge, among them process knowledge, rhetorical knowledge, genre knowledge, subject matter knowledge, and discourse community knowledge (Beaufort 2007), and we do our best to address these areas broadly. For example, we recognize the benefits of matching writers and tutors by discipline as a means of providing more effective support (Dinitz and Harrington 2013). UConn has a good number of disciplines represented among its tutors and therefore is often able to pair graduate writers with graduate tutors in similar academic fields. UNH graduate tutors are generally PhD candidates in composition studies with far fewer than UConn coming from across the disciplines. While we understand and appreciate shared genre knowledge as an important factor in tutorial outcomes (e.g., see Autry and Carter 2015 on the genre-driven approach they have taken at North Carolina State), neither of our centers has moved in that direction. Rather, our philosophy at both centers has been more keyed to the process approaches for a variety of reasons.

Although we may prioritize the process knowledge in Beaufort's schema over genre knowledge in our sessions, we do train our staffs to be aware of the disciplinary differences in genres and conventions, and, especially at UConn, if they desire, undergraduate writers can self-select a tutor with a similar major. With graduate students, however, the intake meeting offers an opportunity to be more intentional in matching client and tutor expertise. Nonetheless, because both centers have limited graduate staff and can't plan for every contingency, we think it makes sense to focus our efforts to a larger degree on helping graduate writers become more aware of and reflective about their research and writing processes, including their approaches to genre and teacher directives, which will in turn help them, we believe, to manage the longer projects they're typically working on. The intake consultation, then, offers the opportunity to explain (even if briefly) our matching strategies in light of our focus on writing as a process and our staffing realities. This explanation can help to offset reservations a writer might have about working with a tutor in another field.

The UNH and UConn intake consultation systems have been operating in parallel, with each aware of what the other has been doing; however, there has not been any explicit coordination or collaboration across institutions. While anecdotal evidence tells us that our two systems are working fairly well, by reflecting on them in tandem and by examining feedback from graduate writers at both institutions who completed surveys and interviews, we can now more confidently recommend our practices to others.

INVESTIGATING THE POLICY AND THE PRACTICE

In the spring and summer of 2016, the UNH and UConn centers collaborated on the design of an online survey and set of interview questions to investigate the effectiveness of the intake consultations and graduate students' perceptions of the policy. We invited participation from graduate writers who came for consultations during the 2015–2016 academic year and the fall of 2016. Although we conducted our investigations separately, we subsequently shared survey responses and transcripts in order to analyze them in tandem.

The survey included the questions below followed by Likert scales to register degrees of agreement or disagreement (or convenience/inconvenience, effectiveness/lack of effectiveness, etc.):

1. Did the requirement to meet with a writing center administrator make you less likely or more likely to use the writing center?

2. How convenient did you find meeting with the writing center administrator?

3. How productive or effective did you find the time spent in the intake meeting?
4. How clearly did the writing center administrator explain the writing center's policies?
5. If you were paired with a tutor, do you think the writing conferences were less effective or more effective than if you had scheduled them on your own without meeting with the writing center administrator?

Respondents could also comment further if they wanted to elaborate on their response. The number of participants was small, just fifteen total, in large part because the scale of the intake system is modest at both institutions.

We also invited graduate writers to participate in twenty-minute interviews loosely structured around a set of additional questions that allowed them to expand on the issues raised in the survey and reflect on how the consultations shaped their perceptions of our centers. We conducted five such interviews at UConn and three at UNH. While eight is a relatively small number, we found the interviews added depth to the survey responses and, along with the survey itself, enabled us to examine our assumptions about the effectiveness of the intake consultation and assess how the requirement affected writers' attitudes about our centers' accessibility for graduate writers. Of course, regarding the latter, we don't have feedback from those who might have been steered away from our centers because of the requirement, but we were able to gather some useful insights on how to promote access and counteract any negative impressions. In the following sections, we will describe what we learned from the surveys and interviews.

EFFECTIVENESS OF THE INTAKE CONSULTATIONS

The results of the survey suggested that our initial consultations are effective, with 85 percent of participants rating the meetings they experienced as productive (64% mostly productive; 21% very productive). These numbers were reassuring and encourage us to continue with the policy, but it was the interviews that gave us a more nuanced sense of just *how* the consultations were effective, even as they alerted us to some shortcomings. We'll begin by discussing the shortcomings, since these have to do with how effectively the policy is being conveyed and how it might need to be adjusted for early and late-career writers rather than with the effectiveness of the consultation itself.

Shortcomings Interviewees Noted

One shortcoming two interviewees identified is that the policy—including its purpose—could be conveyed more effectively. As one interviewee at UConn pointed out, while the rationale for the policy and instructions for arranging an intake consultation are laid out clearly on the writing center website, he nonetheless signed up for a tutorial on his own, during which his tutor referred him to the graduate coordinator. It was at this point that he first became aware of the policy. He blamed himself for not knowing the rule, but his experience indicates that we are not reaching all graduate writers through the methods we're using, no matter how extensive they are. We know, for example, that online policy statements, the customized banner announcement that appears on the WCOnline portal login pages at both centers, fliers, listserv postings, and signs are only marginally effective at reaching diverse and often fragmented graduate populations. We also know that we need to supplement those efforts by creating awareness through student networks and personal encounters, which we try to do by sending writing center representatives to new graduate student orientations, teaching and training workshops for graduate assistants and faculty, open houses, resource fairs, and so on. Publicizing the policy, then, is an ongoing effort.

Another shortcoming of the policy voiced by two different interviewees was their sense that early-career graduate students might need intake consultations more than later-career graduate students, and thus a one-size-fits-all policy might be inappropriate. Writers who are less familiar with graduate study in general and with writing resources offered at their institution in particular, they speculated, would likely benefit more from a one-on-one orientation meeting. While this may often be the case, at both of our centers we have certainly encountered students at the dissertation stage who were unaware of writing support resources beyond tutoring and who benefitted from our referrals to those resources. We believe, then, that it is valuable to offer intake consultations to writers at all stages. As with a writing tutorial, an intake consultation often begins by assessing the extent to which certain kinds of support are most helpful and by overcoming any writer apprehension about the process. This can involve frustration with the intake requirement, especially if the writer feels confident they can navigate the university's resources without help.

These perceived shortcomings, however, were far outweighed by praise for the process, and our analysis of survey comments and interview responses suggested that the policy is effective in three important ways: it allows for greater understanding of writing center philosophy and practices, it reduces anxiety, and achieves better tutor matches.

Greater Understanding of Writing Center Philosophy and Practices

All of the graduate students we interviewed indicated that the intake consultation helped them understand the writing center's philosophy and our conference practices in some way. As one writer put it, the coordinator "gives you the rules of the game." Another interviewee found the intake consultations "help people transition into understanding what the meetings [with a tutor] are like." In particular, she mentioned the helpful advice about what to bring to her first conference. More than just appreciating learning about the nuts-and-bolts of tutorials, though, she also felt that the intake consultation clarified the writing center's overall philosophy. "I was just impressed by how it was a holistic approach," she said. "It's not just the writing part. They get the process." This insight about the value of emphasizing process, a key component of our approach to writing, led her to a better understanding of how writing and the writing center fit into her graduate life and career beyond the single tutorial. At the end of the interview, she echoed this goal, remarking, "I really like that the writing center knows that [writing a master's thesis is] a life thing. It's not just writing it down. It's scheduling your life correctly and making sure that you stay sane through the whole thing. That's what I needed."

Another interviewee stressed that the one-to-one nature of the intake meeting was very important and that it mirrors the individual attention within writing center tutorials. As he put it, "When you meet one-to-one and personalize the meeting, it works very well for the student. As opposed to calling you on the phone or emailing, the face-to-face intake and orientation puts a name to the face of the student and then I get to know you folks as well. It's important for us to get to know one another as a student and writing center." By "getting to know each other," the possibilities for the conference also became clearer to him; consequently, he saw the intake consultation as a process of working together to come up with a "game plan" for how he would proceed through tutorials and who would assist him. This understanding of the practical aspects of tutorials led him to see the center as being "on the same page about what my goals and needs are," which would, in turn, facilitate a productive first tutorial for him. "I knew," he said, "that we'd be able to work towards my end goal for a certain piece but also work on tweaking my writing."

In contrast, when asked during interviews if the intake consultations had an effect on the tutorials that followed it, some interviewees initially felt it hadn't, but we discerned from their later comments that the meeting actually did influence the way they interpreted the goals and purpose of a session. For example, one interviewee said in response to a later question, "I think what's so important is when you communicate a policy to someone that relates to them, then it becomes way more clear." Through the intake consultation, she said that she found out that she could be matched with a graduate tutor and that she subsequently found the match helpful. In general, when the interviewees reflected on the purposes and benefits of the intake consultation in response to our series of questions, we could see that the consultation had shaped in some meaningful ways their understanding of the center's process-based philosophy and tutoring practices and, we might surmise, that this understanding may have, in turn, led to a more effective tutorial.

Reduced Anxiety

For graduate students, writing is but one of many "invisible struggles" (Casanave 2016), but it is the one that the intake consultations can coax into the open for discussion. Several interviewees said that the consultation helped ease their anxieties about writing. Indeed, for one writer, her anxieties consumed most of the interview time. She described coming into the writing center overwhelmed, stressed, and close to tears, and she appreciated how the consultation spoke to these affective dimensions of writing. "I guess it was calming to have someone from the outside, to have someone say that it was going to be okay," she said. "This [kind of anxiety] happens all the time. So knowing it was a normal experience for people to be freaking out about [a thesis], I guess that's what calmed me down, having someone [say to me], 'People come in here all the time for this stuff, and we can help you.'"

It's worth noting that the "we can help you" message this graduate student heard in the intake consultation came through an explanation of the writing center's approach and the process of putting together a plan for her writing conferences, not just through verbal assurances. After hearing how tutorial sessions work and why, this student began to feel that she would, in fact, be helped. She gained a better sense of how she might use the writing center, which helped ease her anxiety. Similarly, another interviewee explained, "My intake meeting gave me confidence I was going to be able to meet my goals. In the intake meeting, I was able to see *here's* where I go for help." In addition, gaining an awareness of the writing support services available to them both within and outside of the writing center—and being offered referrals to those services—helped give the graduate writers at both UNH and UConn the sense that there is a range of support that stretches across their institution. Having a sense that their concerns about writing are shared by others and that writing support is available, can ease that sense of isolation that thesis and dissertation writers often experience once they are no longer taking classes and talking regularly to peers and teachers.

Better Tutor Matches

Among the most immediate goals for the intake consultation is matching each writer with a tutor whose expertise, personality, and schedule will be a productive fit. According to our surveys, only one person indicated that the matching was a little less effective than if they'd scheduled their own tutorials, and, while a third of survey respondents indicated they saw no effect or had no opinion about the success of the tutor matching process, a majority reported that the consultation led to more effective tutorials (26% a little more effective; 33% much more effective). The interviews echoed the survey responses, and so we are confident that, overall, we are doing well matching writers and tutors. However, the interviews also helped us to understand some of the nuances around our matching system that we needed to recognize when we explained the benefits to clients.

Some interviewees, for example, expressed skepticism about the possibility of ensuring a good match even when we'd learned more about the writer's project and goals. The interpersonal dynamics of a session are complex and the factors affecting its success can be hard to anticipate in advance. One interviewee said she was disappointed in the match: "I didn't feel the person was very engaged. I felt that they were just kind of there, not really connected, and they weren't listening to anything that I was saying. So I don't know if it's just trial and error to find that match." As she suggests, the complexities have as much to do with "personality and personal needs and learning style" as with field and schedule overlaps, and these might need to be monitored and revised as the scheduled course of tutoring progresses. Similarly, while two interviewees were pleased with the match, they indicated they would like to have "gotten more people's opinion," by working with a variety of tutors. These two points suggest that we need to check in with writers about their progress so that we can assess whether to adjust a match after several sessions, and that we need to communicate the willingness to make adjustments in the intake consultation. Even writers who might perceive our tutor selection process as deliberate and thoughtful—as we hope they will—might not be willing to question whether a match is right for them, so we should encourage them to take control in this initial stage of the process.

Mirroring the survey results, however, the majority of our interviewees recognized and appreciated our writer-tutor matching process and outcomes, as we noted. One student said, for example, that, after listening to her describe her project, the intake coordinator "told me about a few people [who might be a good match]. He said there's this person and there's that person, and this is what that person does and here's what this person does. And we both collaboratively decided that [the tutor chosen] would be the best fit for me." Another student said she hadn't known that the writing center employed graduate tutors, and, while she felt that undergraduates had been able to help her to some extent in the past, she later realized that being matched with a graduate tutor was the better move for her current work. Even when one interviewee wondered if graduate students needed to be matched with a particular graduate tutor, she seemed to answer this question for herself, articulating one of our reasons for the matching procedure: "If you're going to [tutoring with] all these different people," she said, "you can't really track development in your writing." Consistency, she speculated, allows for "see[ing] growth."

ATTITUDES TOWARD INTAKE POLICY AND PERCEPTIONS OF THE WRITING CENTER

The evidence that our intake consultations are effective for those who experience them is heartening. However, as we reflected on our practices, we also worried about how the intake policy might be shaping attitudes toward our centers or potentially inhibiting access. Might it, as we speculated in our introduction, make us seem unwelcoming or discourage graduate students from making first contact? In our surveys, one in five respondents reported that in fact they were less likely to use the writing center because of the intake consultation requirement (7% much less likely; 13% a little less likely). However, 27 percent rated the required meeting as having no effect, and a majority reported that it made them more likely to use the center (40% a little more likely; 13% much more likely). And working against the assumption that graduate students would find the intake consultation an unwelcome burden in already busy lives, over 70 percent of survey respondents reported that the meeting was "convenient" or "very convenient." Perhaps it is no surprise, then, that when we asked interviewees whether they recommended we keep, eliminate, or change the current policy, most endorsed maintaining the policy as is. Our analysis of the open-ended questions in the interview transcripts revealed two common themes that give shape and specificity to this generally positive response and indicate how the policy has had an impact on attitudes toward our centers: first, the graduate students viewed the meetings as a worthwhile investment of their time; and second, the meetings led to their perceiving the writing center with an enhanced sense of professionalism.

Time Well Invested

"[Graduate] students don't have a lot of time," one doctoral student told us. "They don't want to waste time." And yet she perceived the intake meeting as "a wise thing to do" and strongly endorsed maintaining the requirement. Our writing centers envisioned the intake consultation as an upfront investment of time designed to better allocate resources, and our interviewees described it in similar terms. As one interviewee explained, "I think you need to spend time on assessing a problem. I was willing to put that time in to save me time in the end." Another interviewee saw the entire process as more efficient than trying to navigate policies and scheduling on his own. "It's like one-stop shopping," he said, "I could sit down and schedule meetings with you and know how I'd fit everything in. All that was accomplished in one time frame, one visit. So it's very convenient, very efficient, even explaining when you'll be closed between semesters so that I know." Another said, "Some may view those [intake] sessions as a wasted step. I look at [them] as being cognizant of the limited time that grad student[s] have for such projects and to make the best of the time." Another explained that going through the intake process is "a good gut check for whether it's worth what might be a big time commitment" to attend tutorials. One student even said that she would have been fine with finding out that the center would not be able to help her. "I'd rather have done the intake session and found out that this is not a good setup for me," she said, "or [found out] yes this is [a good setup], and go from there." Finding out that tutoring wouldn't work at the outset, she explained, would allow her to seek out other resources, whether on campus or through a professional editor.

In addition to figuring out if tutoring would be a good fit for them, interviewees also said they appreciated help with setting up appointments and figuring out how to best fit conferencing into their schedules.

For example, one interviewee said that the intake meeting helped her to quickly and efficiently grasp whom she would work with, when her appointments would be, and what to expect—what she aptly called "all the information." A number of interviewees said that negotiating how many appointments they would need helped them plan their writing schedules, which they found especially valuable in balancing graduate studies and careers. As one student explained, the planning aspect of the intake meeting allowed him to figure out "how I was going to fit in sessions between my course schedule, work schedule, and my army schedule." He emphasized that the intake meeting was "efficient" and prompted him to plan more intentionally.

Enhanced Sense of Professionalism
Although we did not ask any questions about perceptions of the professionalism of the center, we were surprised that all of our interviewees indicated that the intake meeting increased their impression of the writing center's professionalism, although not all used that exact term. This sense of professionalism seemed due in part to the fact that there was a person of authority tasked with guiding tutor selection, scheduling appointments, and tending to other aspects of the process, which, in turn, gave them the sense that the center was serious and careful, that we were deliberate in allocating our resources. As one international student put it, "I just feel like after the meeting that [the center] is very organized, like not just come here and make an appointment, but organized." Another international student emphasized that the intake consultation led him to see that "the writing center is very organized," and he appreciated that someone was keeping an eye on operations and "how to best help students." Professionalism is not something we had in mind when designing our policies, but, for our interviewees, the professionalism communicated by the intake consultation turned out to be particularly appealing. Heather Blain Vorhies's (2015) research likewise affirms that graduate students, whose identities are bound up in their transition from student to professional scholar, especially value a sense of professionalism in a writing center.

We believe that this sense emerged in part because of the customized tutor matching, what one interviewee called "a more professional approach to the process rather than off-the-cuff" appointments. The persona of the coordinator/director leading the intake meeting seemed like an even more important aspect of this perception. One student described the person conducting the intake session as "an expert looking at you from 10,000 feet . . . and knowing his staff." Another remarked, "The attention to detail on the writing center and [director's] part is great." We even found that one interviewee who was dissatisfied with her tutor match nonetheless felt that meeting with the director "makes you feel like there's some sort of organization and coordination that goes along with the program, that you're not just randomly dropping in and making appointments here or there. So there's someone who is overseeing the overall needs of the student." While the interviewees seemed to understand that not everything will go smoothly all the time, they appreciated knowing "who was in charge." Such responses speak to a desire for direct lines of communication and accountability, something that can mitigate some of the isolation and fragmentation we noted earlier as symptomatic of the graduate experience.

CONCLUSIONS

In light of what we have heard from our interviewees, we plan to stick with our intake policy, albeit with a few modifications designed to address shortcomings, which we detail below. We can also more confidently recommend the intake approach to others, although any decisions others make about how to implement such a policy should account for the possibility of decreasing access in some ways while improving it in others (as well as for the potential shift in the allocation of resources from tutorials to intake consultations that may be required, a point we have not discussed in this chapter). One modification we will make involves being more strategic in our public messaging by including insights from our surveys and interviews. In future emails and social media posts (as well as at in-person events) we can refer to the time saving benefits of intake sessions and highlight how our services are tailored to the lives of busy graduate students. Even more vital than sharpening our message is reaching our constituency. We still find that many graduate students are not aware of our policies even though we advertise them in a number of ways throughout the year. Graduate student turnover and the very kinds of community fragmentation that our policies are intended to mitigate mean that disconnects will likely persist at some level. Given that, we know we will have to account for partial awareness and do our best to catch new graduate writers on the scheduler or at their initial tutorial to let them know about the policy.

In another modification, we can also be more explicit in inviting graduate clients to get back in touch with the coordinator/director if they feel a different tutor match or course of action might be better.

Two of our interviewees revealed that their tutor matches were suboptimal, and even though they still appreciated the intake process overall, neither got back in touch to register their concerns. Ironically, the enhanced sense of professionalism (and authority) that results from the intake consultation might give the graduate writers the sense that they are not as free to change their plan or request reassignment.

Others looking to extrapolate from our experience can learn from the modifications we've made or plan to make, but questions of context and resources, as well as the paradox of access, no doubt loom larger. Our policies were created in response to specific exigencies at our universities: rising demand for graduate tutorials at a time of flat budgets and surging undergraduate demand. We speculated (and now know) that an intake policy can reduce the number of graduate student writers who receive individualized tutoring. Meanwhile we wanted to remain true to the promise of access that has long been a hallmark of writing centers, to keep the door wide open for students who have been discouraged by past gatekeepers or who simply need writing support as they encounter more challenging rhetorical situations. In our way of thinking about this paradox, the inefficient use of tutoring resources we were seeing translated into a kind of limitation on access. When our schedules were squeezed by market forces rather than managed by a thoughtful administrator, we were not optimally serving writers or keeping true to our mission. Yes, we now see fewer graduate students in tutorials, but our doors are still open—even if in a different way—inviting students into a wider and more deliberate range of writing support.

REFERENCES

Autry, Meagan Kittle, and Michael Carter. 2015. "Unblocking Occluded Genres in Graduate Writing." *Composition Forum* 31. http://compositionforum.com/issue/31/north-carolina-state.php.

Beaufort, Anne. 2007. *College Writing and Beyond: A New Framework for University Writing Instruction.* Logan: Utah State University Press.

Bruffee, Kenneth A. 1984. "Collaborative Learning and the 'Conversation of Mankind.'" *College English* 46 (7): 635–52. https://doi.org/10.2307/376924.

Caplan, Nigel A., and Michelle Cox. 2016. "The State of Graduate Communication Support: Results of an International Survey." In *Supporting Graduate Writers: Research, Curriculum, and Program Design,* ed. Steve Simpson, Nigel A. Caplan, Michelle Cox, and Talinn Phillips, 22–51. Ann Arbor: University of Michigan Press.

Casanave, Christine Pearson. 2016. "What Advisors Need to Know about the Invisible 'Real-Life' Struggles of Doctoral Dissertation Writers." In *Supporting Graduate Writers: Research, Curriculum, and Program Design,* ed. Steve Simpson, Nigel A. Caplan, Michelle Cox, and Talinn Phillips, 97–116. Ann Arbor: University of Michigan Press.

Dinitz, Sue, and Susanmarie Harrington. 2013. "The Role of Disciplinary Expertise in Shaping Writing Tutorials." *Writing Center Journal* 33 (2): 73–98.

Kamler, Barbara, and Pat Thomson. 2006. *Helping Doctoral Students Write: Pedagogies for Supervision.* New York: Routledge.

Phillips, Talinn. 2016. "Writing Center Support for Graduate Students: An Integrated Model." In *Supporting Graduate Writers: Research, Curriculum, and Program Design*, ed. Steve Simpson, Nigel A. Caplan, Michelle Cox, and Talinn Phillips, 159–70. Ann Arbor: University of Michigan Press.

Powers, Judith K, and Jane V. Nelson. 1995. "L2 Writers and the Writing Center: A National Survey of Writing Center Conferencing at Graduate Institutions." *Journal of Second Language Writing* 4 (2): 113–38. https://doi.org/10.1016/1060-3743(95)90003-9.

Reardon, Kristina, Thomas Deans, and Cheryl Maykel. 2016. "Finding a Room of Their Own: Programming Time and Space for Graduate Student Writing." *WLN: A Journal of Writing Center Scholarship* 40 (5–6): 10–17.

Rogers, Paul M., Terry Myers Zawacki, and Sarah E. Baker. 2016. "Uncovering Challenges and Pedagogical Complications in Dissertation Writing and Supervisory Practices: A Multimethod Study of Doctoral Students and Advisors." In *Supporting Graduate Writers: Research, Curriculum, and Program Design*, ed. Steve Simpson, Nigel A. Caplan, Michelle Cox, and Talinn Phillips, 52–77. Ann Arbor: University of Michigan Press.

Simpson, Steve. 2016. "Introduction: New Frontiers in Graduate Writing Support and Program Design." In *Supporting Graduate Writers: Research, Curriculum, and Program Design*, ed. Steve Simpson, Nigel A. Caplan, Michelle Cox, and Talinn Phillips, 1–20. Ann Arbor: University of Michigan Press. https://doi.org/10.3998/mpub.8772400.

Vorhies, Heather Blain. 2015. "Building Professional Scholars: The Writing Center at the Graduate Level." *Writing Lab Newsletter* 39 (5–6): 6–9.

Wellington, Jerry. 2010. "More Than a Matter of Cognition: An Exploration of Affective Writing Problems of Post-Graduate Students and Their Possible Solutions." *Teaching in Higher Education* 15 (2): 135–50. https://doi.org/10.1080/13562511003619961.

6
HYBRID CONSULTATIONS FOR GRADUATE STUDENTS
How Pre-Reading Can Help Address Graduate Students' Needs

Elena Kallestinova

A 2014 survey conducted by the Consortium on Graduate Communication revealed that the 197 universities that responded each provide graduate students with one or more of the following kinds of writing support: consultations, classes, and/or workshops. Out of all the services listed on the survey as provided by graduate writing programs and centers, individual writing consultations are the most frequently offered, with 87.8 percent of the programs reporting that they provide this kind of tutorial support (Caplan and Cox 2016). The types of consultations offered by graduate writing programs range from synchronous sessions, including in-person appointments, video conferences, and phone discussions, to online chats and asynchronous e-tutorials. During a synchronous consultation, the consultant meets face-to-face (in person or using video/audio platforms) and reads the student's draft at the beginning of the session. On the other hand, a typical asynchronous consultation allows students to submit their drafts and receive comments online with no discussion involved.

Both synchronous and asynchronous consultations exhibit inherent advantages and weaknesses and might be excellent venues for specific tutoring situations. That said, however, writing center research over the last two decades has shown that graduate students experience unique writing needs based on the lengthier, discipline-specific projects they typically bring to a session (Casanave and Hubbard 1992; Farrell 1994; Powers 1995; Pemberton 2002; Phillips 2008). The question at stake for writing centers, then, is what types of individual writing consultations might best respond to the needs of the graduate student population. For example, asynchronous e-tutorials are convenient for students conducting fieldwork, spending a fellowship year in a different university, or studying long-distance where the internet connection is unstable. At the same

DOI: 10.7330/9781607327516.c006

time, however, asynchronous tutorials reduce the vital rapport between the consultant and the writer, do not allow for a dialogue through which the student can make discoveries in response to consultants' questions, and do not provide an emotional aspect in their support of graduate writers. Traditional in-person sessions, on the other hand, allow consultants to initiate a dialogue about the draft and establish rapport with the student, but do not encourage graduate students to bring long discipline-specific papers or dissertation chapters, which would take an entire session to read and understand. Describing her center's in-person thirty-minute sessions, Judith Powers (1995) acknowledged, "More often than we liked to admit, we were unable to assist thesis and dissertation writers in substantive ways because we could not understand their material or disciplines well enough to be sure we would help them locate 'real' problems, give them good advice or reinforce good solutions" (13).

To respond to the shortcomings of asynchronous and synchronous tutorial types and to complement the advantages of e-tutoring with the possibility of discussing the paper with a tutor, some writing centers have implemented a version that merges the two types, but that is conducted entirely online without face-to-face interaction. During these consultations, students submit their paper via an online tutoring service, the consultant spends some time preparing comments, and then sends the response to the writer and follows up with an online chat where they discuss some comments or remaining issues. Although the online chats provide space for questions and discussions, they are not ideal communication platforms. Frequently, the communication flow during online chats depends on the typing speed of the consultant and the writer—if the typing speed of one party is slow, it creates gaps that impede the discussion. Moreover, the discussion hinges on the consultant's and student's clarity of thinking and their ability to explain their thoughts in writing—if one party is unclear, the discussion might result in a misunderstanding. Online chats, then, are less than ideal communication platforms for discussions about writing, particularly when papers are lengthy.

In this chapter, I discuss another type of blended consultation, a combination of an asynchronous and traditional face-to-face conference, a hybrid format I claim is optimal in addressing the needs of graduate writers. This format, which pairs the face-to-face consultation with pre-reading, allows graduate consultants to receive the students' work in advance, prepare their feedback before the consultation, and discuss the students' writing during an in-person session. Going forward, I use the term "hybrid consultation" to refer to this pre-reading plus face-to-face consultation format. Using data collected from hybrid and regular face-to-face consultations at Yale University and analyzing data from the undergraduate writing program at the same institution, I argue that a hybrid consultation that allows for prior tutor preparation and face-to-face discussion is the best match for working with advanced graduate students' longer projects.

HYBRID CONSULTATIONS IN THE GRADUATE WRITING LAB

To explain how these hybrid consultations work, I provide an overview of the tutoring program at the Graduate Writing Lab (GWL) at Yale University. The by-appointment-only center was established in 2008 to offer individual consultations to students in the Graduate School of Arts and Sciences, but it has recently expanded to provide consultations to twelve professional schools and now serves approximately seven thousand students. Using the WCOnline scheduling platform, the GWL provides an option for graduate students to bring their draft to the in-person session or send it to the consultant for pre-reading before the in-person appointment; they also indicate the length of the session they desire. For shorter drafts, less than ten double-spaced pages, writers can send the draft at least twenty-four hours in advance; if the draft is longer than ten pages, the writer is asked to send it at least forty-eight hours in advance. The drafts that graduate students upload are expected to be within the range of twenty double-spaced pages. After receiving students' drafts, writing consultants pre-read them and prepare their questions and comments for the in-person session, which is mandatory for all consultations.[1]

Graduate writing consultants are restricted in the time they can spend on pre-reading a draft for a consultation: this time cannot exceed the length of the scheduled in-person session with the student. If a student schedules a thirty-minute appointment, the consultant can pre-read for thirty minutes only. The students and the consultants are provided clear guidelines for the length of the appointment and the time allowed for preparation, neither of which may exceed one hour per appointment. During their pre-reading time, consultants read the draft and prepare their questions and comments, focusing on higher order concerns but marking consistent lower order concerns if necessary. This time allows consultants to read the draft one or two times, adding comments and planning appropriate feedback. Even though writing consultants are usually graduate students with a few years of experience in graduate-level writing, grantsmanship, publishing, and teaching, they come to the writing center with different levels of confidence and preparedness to give feedback. The limit on pre-reading time signals to the consultants that they need to be productive and efficient. Some of them might struggle with how to plan and use their preparation time during the first week or two, but, with training and practice, most of them learn to handle this task quickly.

In hybrid consultations, the conversation between the consultant and the student begins before the face-to-face session opens. The WCOnline appointment scheduling form, customized to our program needs, contains a question asking clients to explain what they would like to focus on during the face-to-face session. Many students use this space to signal the stage of their writing process and the issues they anticipate needing to address during the session. Consultants use these comments to direct their feedback toward the needs of the clients. In addition, to establish a better rapport, consultants send a reminder email message to the client a day before the appointments and confirm that the written work has been received. This reminder allows consultants to initiate a dialogue with the client even before they meet face-to-face, creating a smooth transition to the consultation and avoiding an awkward initial encounter with new clients.

During the session, the consultant and the client negotiate the agenda and begin their conversation following the format of a regular in-person session. With the hybrid format, consultants can usually better plan the session since they are more familiar with the student's draft and have their tentative agenda at hand. After each appointment, writing consultants submit their electronic client report form using WCOnline. This report elicits information about the length of the appointment, the time spent pre-reading for the appointment, the length of the draft (in double-spaced pages), and the type of documents discussed at the session. Along with the details about the appointment, the client report form asks about the most important higher and lower order concerns discussed in the session. The client report form, once submitted, prompts WCOnline to send the client a link to a customized survey that asks them to evaluate the session; the software then aggregates the report forms and the survey responses.

Hybrid consultations have been a popular option for graduate students since they were implemented in 2008. At the same time, these consultations are more expensive because the consultants are compensated not only for the time of their in-person meetings, but also for the time they spend preparing for the sessions and emailing graduate students to establish rapport. To understand whether hybrid consultations are indeed an effective model and are worth the extra investment, I raised two questions: are they better than traditional in-person sessions, and are they more suitable for graduate students compared to undergraduate students? To address these questions, I conducted a systematic inquiry that examined the length of the drafts that graduate students bring to these sessions, the genres of these drafts, and the kinds of issues addressed in these sessions. I also compared hybrid consultations with regular in-person sessions with respect to higher order concerns (HOCs) addressed and client and consultant preferences. In the following sections of this chapter, I analyze the data to show why I consider hybrid consultations optimal for graduate students' needs.

EVALUATING THE HYBRID CONSULTATION FORMAT

To learn whether the hybrid consultations we have instituted are more productive for working with graduate students than other modes, I consider data from four sources: three years of GWL appointment data, appointment data from the Yale College Writing Center (for comparative purposes), a survey of graduate writing consultants, and anonymous client evaluations—all of which I describe in detail below.

Graduate Writing Lab Appointment Data

To evaluate how graduate students use regular and hybrid consultations, what types of writing they bring to consultations, and what types of HOCs are discussed in the sessions, I collected data on individual consultations at the GWL, using the appointment report and client report function of our scheduling software. I analyzed consultations over a period of three academic years: 2012–2013, 2013–2014, and 2014–2015. In total, 2,492 consultations were analyzed and coded as regular or hybrid. If clients provided a draft before the in-person appointment, and the consultant pre-read the draft before the session, the consultation was counted as hybrid. If students chose not to provide a draft before the appointment or if they sent it too late for pre-reading, the consultation was counted as a regular session. To compare the content of regular and hybrid consultations, I analyzed the type of documents and the category of HOCs discussed in the sessions.

Yale College Appointment Data

To examine whether undergraduate students differ from graduate students in their use of hybrid and regular sessions, I analyzed the consultation data provided by the Yale College Writing Center (YCWC), which offers writing resources for just under six thousand undergraduate students. The YCWC offers two types of tutoring appointments: residential college tutoring and a drop-in service. Residential college tutoring is similar to the graduate writing consultation format since the scheduling for these sessions is conducted through WCOnline with the same reporting functions. Moreover, residential college tutors, similar to graduate writing consultants, encourage students to submit their drafts in advance, that is, to use the hybrid model, since many college tutors find this model more efficient for working with their students. After each consultation, residential college tutors report the time they spent on pre-reading for each session. The drop-in service for undergraduate students permits only regular in-person sessions, and these sessions are not included in the study.[2]

To investigate how undergraduate students use hybrid consultations (as compared with graduate students), I analyzed 12,265 hybrid consultations with undergraduate students conducted during academic years 2012–2013, 2013–2014, and 2014–2015. Specifically, I considered the number of total sessions, the number of sessions for which tutors did pre-reading, the length of sessions, and the length of time spent pre-reading. Using Graph Pad Prism 6, I compared the statistical difference between the two sets of data, as shown in the Results section.

Writing Consultant Surveys

To understand how writing consultants working with graduate students feel about pre-reading compared to in-session reading, I created and conducted an online survey asking about the preferences of the consultant regarding how they read drafts for hybrid and regular sessions. The survey consisted of seven questions targeted to the study and was distributed to fifteen writing consultants who work in the GWL; fourteen responded to the survey. The participating consultants had worked in the GWL from one to forty-five months before taking this survey, averaging 19.6 months per consultant. The diverse educational background of the consultants (six from the humanities, three from the social sciences, two from the natural sciences, and three from the physical sciences) provides a multidisciplinary perspective on consulting with graduate student writers.

Anonymous Client Evaluation Surveys

To evaluate graduate students' satisfaction with hybrid and regular consultations, I analyzed 396 anonymous post-consultation evaluation surveys from academic year 2015–2016. These surveys were sent to graduate students within twenty-four to forty-eight hours after they attended a writing consultation at the GWL. The surveys represent 37 percent of the consultations (396 out of 1,054), a high response rate for an anonymous survey. The surveys ask when the student sent the draft to the consultant, what the length of the draft was, and whether the writing consultant pre-read the draft before the in-person session. These questions allowed me to code students' responses as "hybrid" or "regular" session surveys. The students were also asked, on a scale of one to four, to evaluate the quality of the feedback that they received during their consultation and the usefulness of their consultation. All students' answers were coded as "completely satisfied" and "not completely satisfied" and analyzed using Graph Pad Prism 6.

DIFFERENCES BETWEEN IN-PERSON AND HYBRID CONSULTATIONS

To understand the advantages of hybrid consultations for graduate writers, I examined whether graduate students chose hybrid or regular sessions, what types of drafts were considered during these two types of sessions, which format writing consultants preferred, and how these two models were evaluated by writers through post-consultation surveys. In the following subsections, I present the answers to these questions based on evidence from the GWL.

Hybrid versus Regular Consultations with Graduate and Undergraduate Students

The analysis of writing consultations from 2012 to 2015 shows that graduate students preferred hybrid consultations when they were offered a choice between a hybrid and in-person session (see figure 6.1).

Even though the students were given the choice of scheduling hybrid or in-person sessions, hybrid consultations were much more popular. During this three-year period, the number of regular in-person consultations held annually did not exceed 10 percent and varied between 7.18 and 9.87 percent of all consultations. Moreover, graduate students selected hybrid consultations much more frequently than undergraduate students did, as demonstrated in figure 6.2.

Indeed, graduate students chose hybrid sessions 91.3 percent of the time on average (2,275 out of 2,492 consultations) compared to 60.7 percent for undergraduate students (7,447 out of 12,265 consultations). Based on Fisher's test, this difference is statistically significant for each year analyzed in this study ($p < 0.0001$).

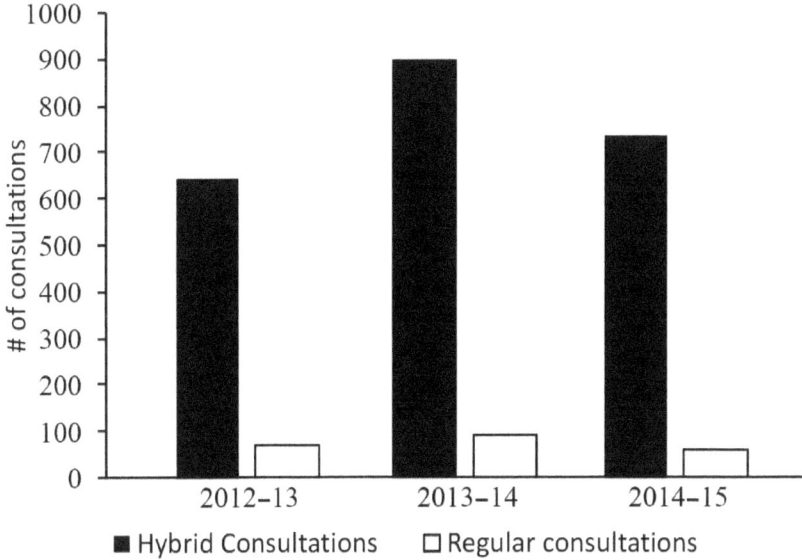

Figure 6.1. The distribution of hybrid and regular consultations with graduate students.

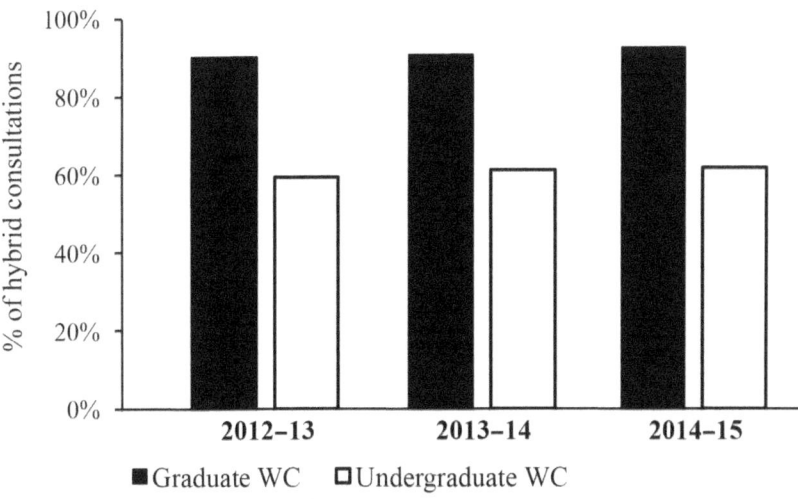

Figure 6.2. Use of hybrid consultations by graduate and undergraduate students.

Preparation Time for Consultations

To understand the types of work that graduate students bring to consultations and the time spent by consultants to prepare for the consultations, I analyzed the types and length of drafts discussed during hybrid

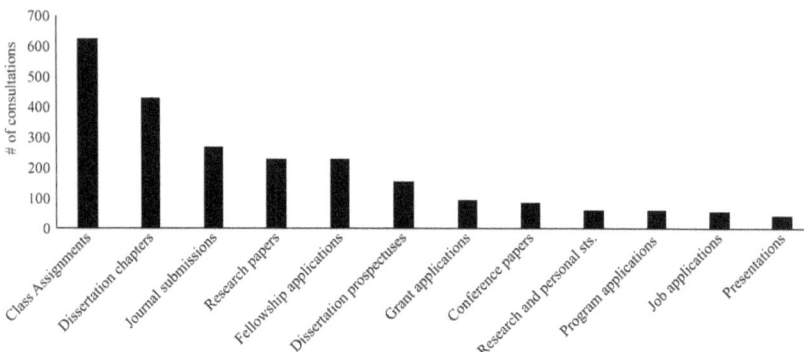

Figure 6.3. Academic genres discussed during graduate writing consultations.

and regular consultations. The data collected from 2012 to 2015 reveal that writing consultants pre-read drafts from more than twenty different genres of academic writing. The most frequent genres discussed during consultations are listed in figure 6.3.

The top twelve genres that graduate students brought to the GWL constituted 94 percent of all appointments (2,344 out of 2,492). The category brought in most frequently was that of class assignments, which included literature reviews, response papers, term papers, book reviews, book summaries, transcripts of interviews, and translations, among others.[3] Genres of writing brought in less frequently included research and personal statements, applications for doctoral and professional schools, job applications, and presentations. The rest of the genres, not included in the figure, were abstracts, qualifying papers, book reviews, essays, encyclopedia entries, Institutional Review Board applications, blogs, articles for newsletters, reports, recommendation letters, booklets, emails, practice essays, end-of-the year program reviews, and others.

The average length of the documents in each genre is displayed in figure 6.4.[4] The drafts longer than ten pages were dissertation chapters, journal submissions, research papers, qualifying exam papers, dissertation prospectuses, class assignments, and conference papers. These genres represented 74 percent of the consultations with graduate students.

Interestingly, the analysis of the number of double-spaced pages submitted for hybrid consultations and brought to regular appointments in 2012–2015 shows that graduate students sent longer drafts when choosing a hybrid appointment compared to drafts brought to in-person consultations (see figure 6.5).

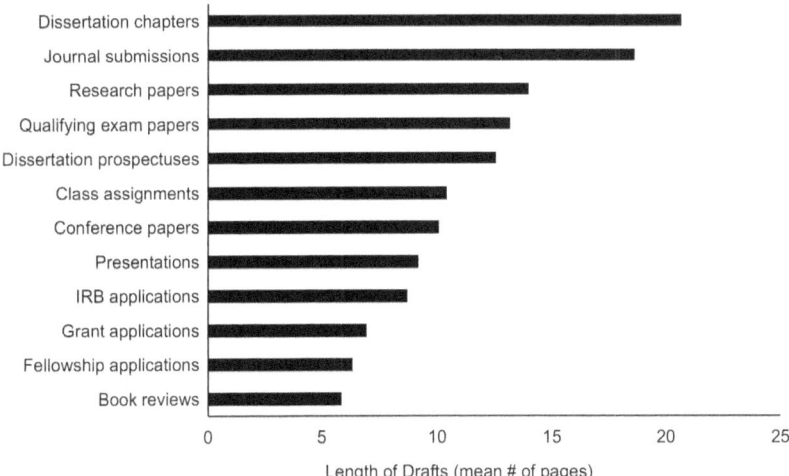

Figure 6.4. Average length of graduate students' drafts discussed during consultations.

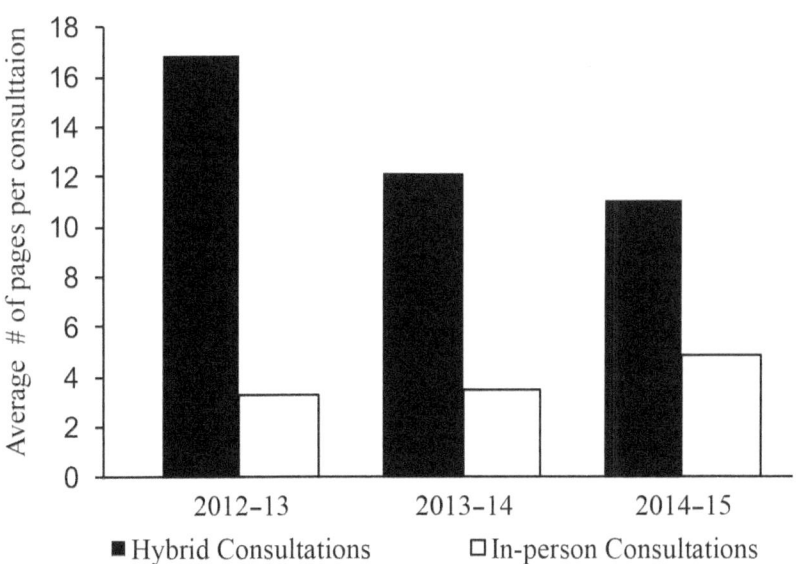

Figure 6.5. Length of graduate students' drafts in hybrid and in-person consultations.

The length of drafts averaged 13.1 pages for hybrid consultations and 3.8 pages for in-person session drafts. This difference is statistically significant ($p < 0.0001$) as shown by a non-parametric Mann–Whitney test. These results demonstrate that graduate students relied on hybrid

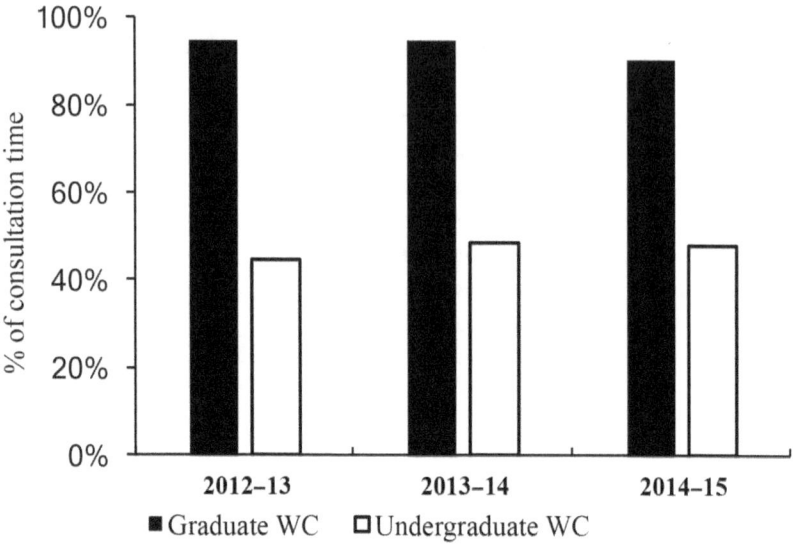

Figure 6.6. Preparation time of consultants working with graduate and undergraduate students.

consultations over in-person sessions to receive feedback on their longer graduate projects.

To show the higher importance of pre-reading for graduate students compared to undergraduate students, I analyzed the preparation time for hybrid consultations in the two centers. As can be seen in figure 6.6, consultants working with graduate students in hybrid sessions tended to spend more time on preparation compared to consultants working with undergraduate students.

The average preparation time for in-person sessions at the YCWC, which was 47 percent of the consultation time, is significantly lower than the preparation time at the GWL, which was 93.2 percent of the consultation time ($p < 0.0001$).[5] The results support the idea that graduate and undergraduate consulting strategies should be differentiated and highlight the importance of pre-reading in graduate consultations.

Consultants Working with Graduate Students

To understand consultants' preferences regarding hybrid or regular consultations, I present the responses of the fourteen graduate writing consultants who participated in the survey. When asked whether they

Table 6.1. Writing consultants' representative comments on reading during hybrid or regular consultations.

Hybrid Sessions (with pre-reading in advance)	Regular Session (with in-session reading)
I have quiet time to read a paper at least twice, first for higher-level and then lower-level concerns.	When I have to read pieces during a session, I'll often only feel I have time to skim it and give my initial, "gut" reaction.
When I pre-read, I have time to think about the organization and structure of the writing. I also have time to take notes, which help to guide a consultation.	I always feel a little uncomfortable when I have to read drafts in front of students—it's a lot more pressure to try to thoroughly assess a written piece when someone is looking over your shoulder!
I need a "big picture" view first so that I can do the best job possible. If I do not pre-read, I waste a lot of time focusing on more minor issues, like grammar or sentence structure.	In-session reading is quick, dirty and often incomplete. Trying to develop comments on the organization or argument of a paper in 15 min with the student sitting next to you is almost impossible. Therefore, the comments and suggestions are generally on low order and grammatical errors, with higher order issues taking a back seat.
Pre-reading allows me to re-read sections if I need to, think over the logical flow more thoroughly, and even look up terminology or the prompt (e.g., for fellowship applications that I'm unfamiliar with) if necessary.	Without pre-reading, I find myself trying to give the student as much as I can during our meeting, which means that we sometimes talk too much about "writing lessons" or that I am stuffing as much insight as I can into the discussion.
It takes a while for me to diagnose the core or recurring issues in a student's piece. Sometimes it even takes a while to discern a writer's argument (or the lack thereof).	I feel under pressure from a student waiting for me to read, and I feel like the time is not being used efficiently.
I am far more likely to make the session helpful and satisfying if I have read the draft in advance and had time to think about it and prepare a strategy for the session.	With in-session reading, I find sessions can be very hit and miss, and for me the unpredictability and lack of control makes those sessions more difficult.

found it easier or more difficult to consult with students when they pre-read their writing in advance, all participants chose the pre-reading option, as shown in their comments in table 6.1.

These representative comments show that graduate consultants expressed a strong partiality for hybrid consultations. They stated that hybrid consultations make the process of working with graduate students less stressful and more structured, satisfying, and efficient. They noted that unless graduate students come to brainstorm ideas, to receive a "first-impression" reaction, or to talk about "writing lessons," a consultant cannot effectively address higher order concerns in students' drafts without preparation.

When asked if they prefer a quiet or social place to accomplish pre-reading for their consultation, 100 percent of the graduate writing consultants reported that they need a quiet space. Most of the consultants (thirteen out of fourteen) listed "home" as the most common place to accomplish their pre-reading. Five out of eleven included "office" as a common location; four people named "library," and one person added "a computer lab." They identified in their comments that they need a quiet space to concentrate, to focus without distraction, to keep sustained attention, and to read aloud if needed. Some of them noted that talking, music, or background noise easily causes distractions with this type of mental work.

In these surveys, then, graduate writing consultants expressed a strong preference for hybrid consultations, the model that allows them to accomplish pre-reading in advance. At the same time, they revealed serious concerns about the efficiency and quality of their work when they read a draft during an in-person session.

Feedback during Hybrid and In-Person Sessions

To evaluate whether and how feedback during hybrid consultations differs from that provided during in-person consultations, I analyzed HOCs that graduate writing consultants identified in 1,780 appointments (1,633 hybrid and 147 regular) during 2013–2014 and 2014–2015. The statistical analysis of HOCs revealed a difference between hybrid consultations and regular appointments (see table 6.2).

As shown in table 6.2, the HOCs addressed in hybrid and regular consultations differed significantly in four categories: development, coherence/flow, voice/tone, and clarity of ideas. The four categories with statistically significant values are presented in figure 6.7.

Consultants consistently identified problems with coherence/flow and clarity of ideas as more prevalent during hybrid consultations than during regular consultations. At the same time, issues relating to development and voice/tone appeared more frequently during regular consultations.

The question of why coherence/flow and clarity of ideas are more common with hybrid sessions while development and voice/tone are more frequent comments in regular sessions is worthy of additional study. The complex, multilayered, and overlapping nature of these concepts can obscure the picture. One possible explanation is that development and tone/style problems are easier to spot in a draft than coherence/flow and clarity of ideas. Indeed, consultants identify development as the primary concern when they notice that the writer does not provide evidence for a particular point or presents underdeveloped

Table 6.2. Frequency of different HOC discussions during in-person and hybrid consultations.

HOCs, 2013–2015	In-person, n = 147	Hybrid, n = 1,633	Chi-square, df	P value	Stat. Significance
N/a	5.4%	3.9%	0.9188, 1	0.3378	ns
Thesis	6.1%	3.2%	3.392, 1	0.0655	ns
Focus	5.4%	5.3%	0.01208, 1	0.9125	ns
Argument	12.9%	12.5%	0.03301, 1	0.8558	ns
Development	15.0%	9.4%	4.773, 1	0.0289	*
Structure and Organization	27.9%	23.3%	1.666, 1	0.1968	ns
Coherence/ Flow	6.8%	16.5%	9.469, 1	0.0021	**
Voice and Tone	9.5%	4.3%	8.370, 1	0.0038	**
Clarity of Ideas	8.8%	20.1%	10.80, 1	0.0010	**
Other	2.0%	1.5%	0.3067, 1	0.5797	ns

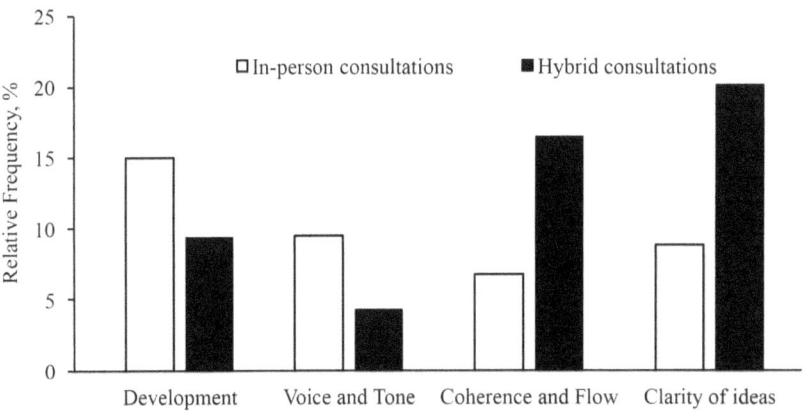

Figure 6.7. Comparison of HOCs addressed in in-person and hybrid consultations.

argumentation to support an idea. This problem is not difficult to recognize from a first reading, when a consultant sees that details, explanations, and examples that should support the argument or the thesis are missing. Similarly, consultants detect inappropriate tone and style—the inner voice of the piece—almost effortlessly when they start reading a draft and match the voice and tone with the audience expectations, the type of the document, and the writer's rhetorical goals.

On the other hand, coherence/flow and clarity of ideas may require additional effort to identify and explain to the writer. For example, in a passage where all sentences are clear and meaningful, the paragraph might feel clumsy, disjointed, and murky if the coherence of the sentences and flow of ideas are broken. Consultants might notice the existence of a problem, but they have to exert extra effort and read the troublesome passage a few times to be able to correctly identify the problem. Coherence and flow are even harder to diagnose in longer documents where missing links and broken flow are dispersed across numerous pages of text. In those cases, only careful and uninterrupted multiple readings may bear fruit. Addressing the clarity of ideas, like noticing coherence and flow, requires extra effort from consultants. Frequently, when reading a condensed or complicated text, the reader may be unsure of whether the lack of understanding comes from a lack of clarity on the part of the writer or inattentive reading on the part of the reader. To make sure that the reason is unclear writing, the consultant may need to re-read the text several times. Given that hybrid consultations allow consultants the luxury of uninterrupted multiple readings, it is not surprising that coherence/flow and clarity of ideas surface as more frequent when consultants are given time to read in advance. At the same time, during regular sessions where consultants are more stressed and hurried, development of ideas and style/tone are the more commonly addressed issues.

Graduate Students' Evaluations of Hybrid and Regular Consultations

To determine whether graduate students are better satisfied with hybrid versus regular consultations, I considered post-consultation surveys for 2015–2016. In 396 surveys received through WCOnline during one academic year, graduate students reported strong satisfaction (99.2%) with their consultations and the feedback they receive. When the feedback was broken into regular versus hybrid consultations, clients' demonstrated higher satisfaction rates with hybrid consultations than with regular sessions (see figure 6.8).

The results show that students found consultants' feedback from hybrid consultations more helpful than that from regular sessions. This difference is statistically significant, as supported by Fisher's two-tailed statistical analysis ($p = 0.0373$). Similar results were found when students were asked to evaluate the usefulness of their consultation overall, as demonstrated in figure 6.9.

Similar to the previous finding, a higher satisfaction rate with hybrid consultations is supported by Fisher's statistical test ($p = 0.0222$),

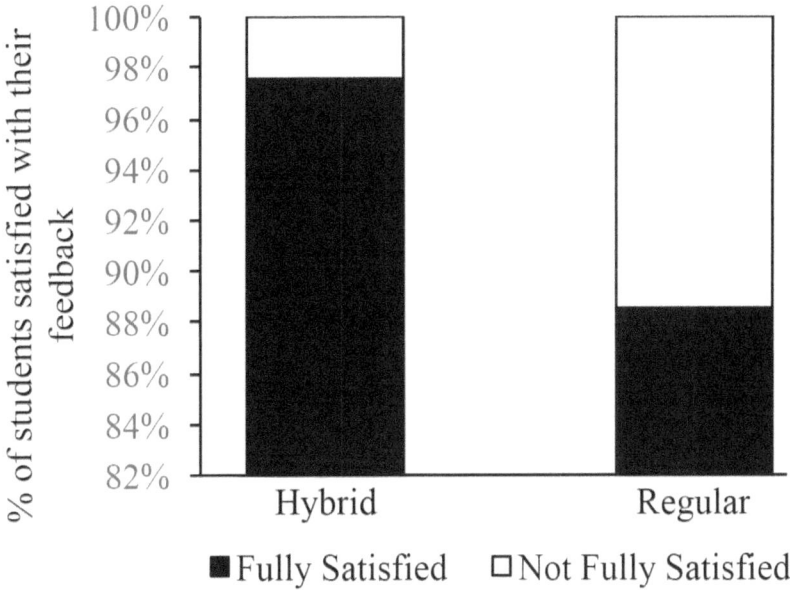

Figure 6.8. Graduate students' responses to the post-consultation survey question "Did the consultant provide helpful feedback?"

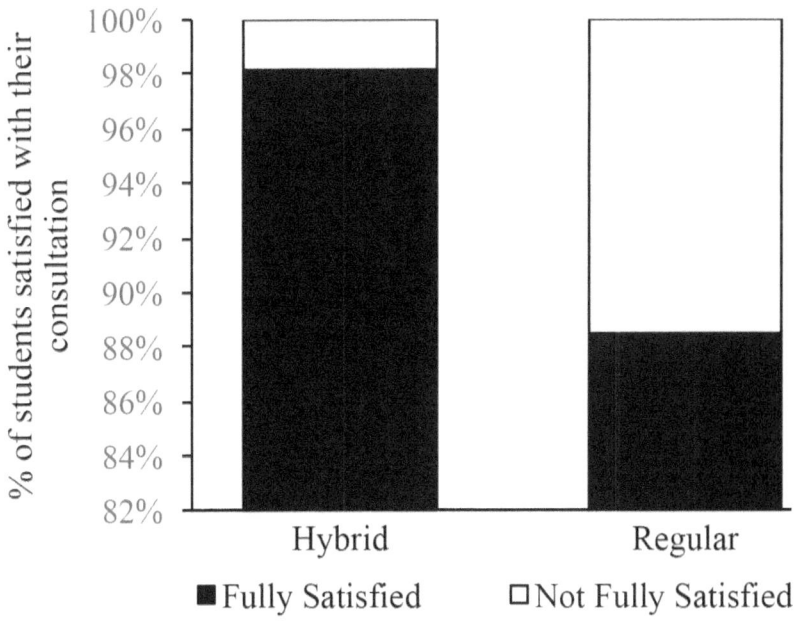

Figure 6.9. Graduate students' responses to the post-consultation survey question "Did you find your consultation useful?"

showing that the difference is significant. Although students' drafts varied in length and complexity and sometimes had to be split to be discussed through several sessions, many students found it very useful when consultants provided feedback tailored toward their complete draft; as one survey participant wrote: "I appreciate that the consultant had read through my entire paper in advance and came prepared with feedback and areas in which I needed to better clarify. She provided me with a neutral, outsider perspective to my topic." In addition, many graduate students appreciated that consultants were able to contribute useful suggestions that could improve their drafts; one participant remarked that "the consultant's comments were thorough, precise, and accurate. After our meetings I always have a lot to work on, which is of course the best thing I could ask for. It is clear that the consultant puts in a lot of effort with her work and it is extremely appreciated." Moreover, graduate student writers valued feedback when they recognized that the feedback would have a long-term impact on their writing skills, as illustrated in this observation: "The consultant provided great feedback both on my writing and the organization of the chapter. She was really great at explaining certain rules to me, which I had never realized before. I am definitely going to keep that in mind while writing my other chapters."

Overall, graduate students highly valued the hybrid sessions where consultants read their draft in advance and demonstrated familiarity with their writing. They especially appreciated feedback on the overall structure of their piece, coupled with specific suggestions to improve the quality of their written work on different levels. This feedback allowed them, they told us, to improve not only their draft, but also their writing skills in general.

INTERPRETING THE PREFERENCE FOR HYBRID CONSULTATIONS

In this study, both graduate writers and consultants demonstrated a strong preference for hybrid consultations over regular sessions. The graduate writers' predilection for hybrid consultations is not surprising. First, the format of a hybrid consultation allows them to submit and discuss a longer draft. Graduate students bring significantly longer drafts to hybrid sessions (13.1 pages) compared to regular sessions (3.8 pages), almost certainly because they understand that, in a format that allows for pre-reading, the consultant has time to read their work carefully and to discuss it thoughtfully in the session.

Another reason for graduate students' preference for hybrid consultations may come from the emotional dimension of receiving feedback on their writing. Graduate students, especially relatively novice academic writers, experience strong apprehension when their written work is being read and evaluated, and they try to avoid situations in which their draft is read in their presence. In Rosemary Caffarella and Bruce Barnett's study asking doctoral students to receive feedback from others and reflect on the experience, they were surprised to learn how emotional the process of receiving feedback was. They discovered that common descriptors of what doctoral students experienced immediately before and during receiving feedback were "anxiety," "apprehension," "frustration," "anger," and even "intellectual striptease" (Caffarella and Barnett 2000, 46–47). That graduate students take criticism so personally is not unexpected. As Caffarella and Barnett (2000) explain, "graduate students, and most professionals, are judged on what they write. With the stakes so high regarding their writing ability, it is not surprising that graduate students are so emotionally invested in how their work is critiqued" (49). Just as in Caffarella and Barnett's study, graduate writers in GWL sessions may feel nervous and anxious when their work is being read and thus prefer the hybrid consultations that allow them to avoid in-session reading.[6]

Like the graduate student writers, writing consultants strongly preferred hybrid consultations. Their discomfort with in-person consultations that do not provide time for preparation stems primarily from the genres that graduate students work on and the discipline-specific language of those drafts. As our writing center data show, consultants work with a range of genres of various lengths and complexity. Many genres of academic writing, especially papers written on topics unfamiliar to consultants, are likely to be challenging for accurate text comprehension, especially when the consultant is provided the opportunity to read a draft only once. During in-person sessions, consultants tend to limit themselves to reading a draft once while the writer is waiting. Indeed, given a good reading rate of three hundred words per minute, it takes a consultant between ten and twenty minutes to read ten to twenty double-spaced pages of text only once. With hybrid consultations, this challenging task becomes possible because writing consultants can take extra time for a second read and can choose the time and the conditions for reading and preparing feedback.

The mode and conditions under which writing consultants conduct their reading play an important role in comprehension. The level of reading comprehension is much higher when consultants silently pre-read without distractions. A number of studies have reported that rates of reading comprehension depend on the mode of reading. For example, Betty Holmes (1985) in "The Effect of Four Different Modes of

Reading on Comprehension" compared reading comprehension during silent reading, oral reading with an audience present, and silent reading following someone else who is reading the text orally.[7] Her empirical study with forty-eight adult college students revealed that silent reading yields superior reading comprehension compared to the other options. Indeed, the loss of comprehension in the "oral reading to audience" condition was triggered by the reader's unconscious desire to perform well, which caused the reader to focus more on correct pronunciation, intonation, expression, and greater fluency than on understanding of the text. At the same time, the poor performance in the "silent reading with listening mode" condition resulted primarily from the students' distraction at the slow speaking speed with which the text was read aloud, and the specifics of the reader's pronunciation (Holmes 1985, 583). These findings are supported by later studies showing that silent reading is faster and yields better text comprehension (van den Boer, van Bergen, and de Jong 2014; McCallum et al. 2004).

These studies have important implications for reading practices in the writing center. While reading aloud can be useful for working on short passages, this practice is not optimal for reading comprehension. Silent reading provides a better alternative, but to be effective, this reading practice calls for a specific kind of environment. A number of empirical psychological studies have investigated the effect of background distractions (typical in a writing center) on reading comprehension; they show that reading comprehension decreases in conditions with background noise (Jewell 1979; Salamé and Baddeley 1982) and background speech (Martin, Wogalter, and Forlano 1988; Sörqvist, Halin, and Hygge 2010). Moreover, more recent studies show that the degree of the decreased reading comprehension correlates with personality type, with extroverts being more susceptible to distraction than introverts are (Veitch 1990; Ylias and Heaven 2003). Since pre-reading a paper during in-person consultations rarely happens without distractions, background noise, or background speech in the writing center, hybrid consultations present an attractive alternative. Not surprisingly, all writing consultants who participated in the survey revealed a strong preference for pre-reading in quiet locations (at home, in an office, library, or computer lab) where focused reading and sustained concentration are possible. During hybrid consultations, when consultants choose those locations that work best for them, they can perform pre-reading with higher accuracy, deeper comprehension, and better outcomes, the latter as shown by stronger clients' evaluations.

Furthermore, the discipline-specific nature of texts discussed in graduate consultations adds complexity to the process. What graduate students need most is a consultation with an educated reader who comprehends ideas presented in the draft. At the same time, each draft encompasses years of experience in the field and a strong disciplinary background. For writing consultants, who in most cases lack a research background in the subfield of the writer, each draft is a venture into a new world of terminology, disciplinary conventions, rhetorical constraints, and complicated ideas. To be able to participate in a conversation with the writer, the educated reader should, first, understand the ideas presented in the draft. Then, the reader is expected to critically evaluate the text with a keen eye for HOCs and other problems that appear consistently in the text. Moreover, the reader needs to prioritize and structure the feedback to build a productive discussion during the session. Last but not least, the reader should establish a rapport with the writer and gain the writer's confidence that the feedback provided is valuable and authoritative. Given the difficulty and length of graduate students' drafts, it would be naïve to expect that a peer reader could accomplish all these tasks during an in-person consultation without preparation. The hybrid model provides a strong advantage to writing consultants by not only giving them extra time to read, but also by allowing them to process and think about the ideas between the time of pre-reading and the time of the consultation. For all of these reasons, many writing consultants prefer to conduct pre-reading before their consultations. At the same time, graduate clients eagerly choose hybrid consultations to save time, avoid anxiety when their paper is read in their presence, and receive constructive feedback on longer drafts.

NEXT STEPS

To address the distinct needs of the graduate population, writing centers or other programs may need to adjust writing consultations to allow consultants to productively work with graduate students. Offering hybrid consultations that combine pre-reading with in-person meetings is one such possible adjustment. The study presented here shows that in this graduate writing center, hybrid consultations are preferred over regular sessions by graduate students, who choose them more frequently than undergraduate students, and by writing consultants, who express a strong partiality toward hybrid consultations. The research on reading comprehension suggests that this preference is likely to extend beyond the specific writing center discussed in this chapter.

Although hybrid consultations are more expensive to administer since they add pre-reading to the time of regular sessions, the additional expenses are warranted, if we believe that participants' satisfaction orients to the quality of the reading, dialogue, and learning that take place in such a consultation. Writing center administrators will also benefit from a hybrid model that helps to ensure high-quality work from their staff and positive student evaluations. By setting appropriate writing center policy and consultation instructions, the hybrid consultation model is a rewarding investment.

NOTES

1. The Graduate Writing Lab requires that all students who schedule consultations come to the in-person session to meet with the writing consultant to discuss the draft. Although pre-reading allows consultants time and space to familiarize themselves with the writer's work, prepare questions, and identify positive aspects and areas for improvement, it cannot replace the session. For those students who cannot come in-person, the Graduate Writing Lab offers remote face-to-face meetings by Zoom, Skype, or WCOnline.
2. The format of the drop-in service is very different from the format of graduate writing consultations and residential college tutoring. First, the drop-in service is offered to undergraduate students only and does not have an analogous service for graduate students. Second, drop-in sessions do not accommodate pre-reading, in contrast to graduate consultations. Third, they allow writing partners to meet with clients without a time limit. Since writing partners in the drop-in service can pre-read or discuss the paper for as long as they need, these sessions are difficult to compare with graduate or residential college sessions that are time-bound. Because these undergraduate drop-in consultations are inherently different from the graduate consultations, they are not relevant for this study.
3. Of course "class assignments" do not constitute a single genre of writing. Although this category is the most common category of writing for undergraduate consultations as well, the actual genres and their lengths vary. While most undergraduate class assignments include essays, short research papers, or lab reports, graduate students' class assignments include longer seminar and research papers.
4. Figure 6.3 lists the most frequent twelve genres, and figure 6.4 exhibits the drafts by their length. Three types of drafts appear in figure 6.3 but not in figure 6.4; these include research and personal statements, program applications, and job applications; their average length is five pages or fewer.
5. The difference in preparation time between undergraduate and graduate students was related to the length of the documents brought to the sessions. Since the data on the length of the documents pre-read by Yale College Writing Center consultants was not collected, the preparation time was the second good predictor of the difference in the length of the documents, assuming that the average reading speed of consultants in both centers was the same.
6. This argument is relevant for undergraduate students as well, and might explain why many undergraduate students, when given the option of a hybrid consultation, take advantage of this consultation model. However, undergraduate consultations, with their shorter drafts, can generally be efficient when offered as in-person sessions.
7. Holmes (1985) analyzed a fourth mode of reading, oral reading without an audience. The results of the study, however, did not reveal any significant difference

in reading comprehension between reading orally to oneself and reading silently. Since reading orally to oneself is not a common practice in the writing center, I do not include this mode in the discussion.

REFERENCES

Caffarella, Rosemary S, and Bruce G. Barnett. 2000. "Teaching Doctoral Students to Become Scholarly Writers: The Importance of Giving and Receiving Critiques." *Studies in Higher Education* 25 (1): 39–52. https://doi.org/10.1080/030750700116000.

Caplan, Nigel, and Michelle Cox. 2016. "The State of Graduate Communication Support: What Do We Know? What Do We Need to Know?" In *Supporting Graduate Students: Research, Curriculum, and Program Design*, ed. Steve Simpson, Nigel A. Caplan, Michelle Cox, and Talinn Phillips, 310. Ann Arbor: University of Michigan Press.

Casanave, Christine Pearson, and Philip Hubbard. 1992. "The Writing Assignments and Writing Problems of Doctoral Students: Faculty Perceptions, Pedagogical Issues, and Needed Research." *English for Specific Purposes* 11 (1): 33–49. https://doi.org/10.1016/0889-4906(92)90005-U.

Farrell, John Thomas. 1994. "Some of the Challenges to Writing Centers Posed by Graduate Students." *Writing Lab Newsletter* 18 (6): 3–5.

Holmes, Betty C. 1985. "The Effect of Four Different Modes of Reading on Comprehension." *Reading Research Quarterly* 20 (5): 575–85. https://doi.org/10.2307/747944.

Jewell, L. R. 1979. "Effects of Noise on Reading Comprehension and Task Completion Time." PhD diss., University of Missouri-Columbia.

Martin, Randi C., Michael S. Wogalter, and Janice G. Forlano. 1988. "Reading Comprehension in the Presence of Unattended Speech and Music." *Journal of Memory and Language* 27 (4): 382–98. https://doi.org/10.1016/0749-596X(88)90063-0.

McCallum, R. Steve, Shannon Sharp, Sherry Mee Bell, and Thomas George. 2004. "Silent versus Oral Reading Comprehension and Efficiency." *Psychology in the Schools* 41 (2): 241–46. https://doi.org/10.1002/pits.10152.

Pemberton, Michael. 2002. "Working with Graduate Students." In *The Writing Center Resource Manual*, 2nd ed., ed. Bobbie Bayliss Silk, 1–5. Emmitsburg, MD: NWCA Press.

Phillips, Talinn Marie Tiller. 2008. "Examining Bridges, Expanding Boundaries, Imagining New Identities: The Writing Center as a Bridge for Second Language Graduate Writers." PhD diss., Ohio University. Proquest.

Powers, Judith. 1995. "Assisting the Graduate Thesis Writer." *Writing Center Journal* 20 (2): 13–16.

Salamé, Pierre, and Alan Baddeley. 1982. "Disruption of Short-Term Memory by Unattended Speech: Implications for the Structure of Working Memory." *Journal of Verbal Learning and Verbal Behavior* 21 (2): 150–64. https://doi.org/10.1016/S0022-5371(82)90521-7.

Sörqvist, Patrik, Niklas Halin, and Staffan Hygge. 2010. "Individual Differences in Susceptibility to the Effects of Speech on Reading Comprehension." *Applied Cognitive Psychology* 24 (1): 67–76. https://doi.org/10.1002/acp.1543.

Van den Boer, Madelon, Elsje van Bergen, and Peter F. de Jong. 2014. "Underlying Skills of Oral and Silent Reading." *Journal of Experimental Child Psychology* 128 (December): 138–51. https://doi.org/10.1016/j.jecp.2014.07.008.

Veitch, Jennifer A. 1990. "Office Noise and Illumination Effects on Reading Comprehension." *Journal of Environmental Psychology* 10 (3): 209–217. https://doi.org/10.1016/S0272-4944(05)80096-9.

Ylias, Georganne, and Patrick C.L Heaven. 2003. "The Influence of Distraction on Reading Comprehension: A Big Five Analysis." *Personality and Individual Differences* 34 (6): 1069–79. https://doi.org/10.1016/S0191-8869(02)00096-X.

7
"NOTICING" LANGUAGE IN THE WRITING CENTER
Preparing Writing Center Tutors to Support Graduate Multilingual Writers

Michelle Cox

Training writing center tutors to work with graduate student writing is in itself challenging; training them to also attend to the distinct needs that multilingual graduate students bring to the center can be a real struggle. Drawing on the context of a graduate writing center in which a set of tutors are hired and trained specifically to work with multilingual graduate writers, in this chapter I discuss an approach to tutor training that is supportive of second language writing processes, including close attention to language—both Standard Written American English and the precise use of the specialized language required for the complex, high stakes writing tasks of the students' graduate programs. I frame my discussion of attention to language with the concept of "noticing," a concept introduced by linguist Richard W. Schmidt (1990) to describe an important step in language learning and which has since been extended to inform second language writing studies.

THEORETICAL FRAMEWORK
"Noticing" was first proposed by Schmidt (1990) as playing a strong role in second language acquisition. Drawing from research in psychology on attention and memory as well as a study of his own acquisition of Brazilian Portuguese (Schmidt and Frota 1986), Schmidt argues that in order to acquire language forms (i.e., syntax, verbal constructions) from language input (i.e., hearing the language, reading the language), we must first notice those forms from that input. To test this argument, Schmidt kept a language learning journal and made monthly recordings of his conversations in Brazilian Portuguese during the five months he spent in Brazil, starting with a five-week course on the language. His co-researcher Sylvia Frota then analyzed the tapes to compare his performance on twenty-one verbal constructions, fourteen of which he was

DOI: 10.7330/9781607327516.c007

explicitly taught. They discovered that the frequency of input was less important for output (his own production of the language) than was his ability to notice the language forms in the input, as indicated by his journal entries (Schmidt and Frota 1986, 12). While Schmidt and Frota (1986) and, subsequently, Schmidt (1990) focused on the noticing process in relation to input, Merrill Swain (1995, 1998) suggested that the noticing function also plays a role in language learning during output. Swain (1995) posited that, while producing language, language learners notice the gaps in their language knowledge and are thus attuned to noticing the missing pieces of knowledge from input (159).

Together, these theories, which have come to be called the Noticing Hypothesis and Output Hypothesis, have spurred a great deal of research on second language acquisition in relation to output. Though much of the research has focused on speaking, a thread of this research has focused on writing (Cumming 1990; Swain and Lapkin 1995, 2001; Qi and Lapkin 2001; Griffin 2004; Manchón 2011). Based on an extensive review of this literature, Rosa Manchón (2011) argued that writing better facilitates the noticing process (and thus language acquisition process) than does speaking, as writing demands more attuned focus to form and presents more opportunities for reflecting on language production. Drawing on research on the relationship between language learning and writing (Swain and Lapkin 1995; Bitchener 2008; Storch 2009; Sheen 2010), Manchón argued that three approaches seem to deepen the role of noticing and move noticing from problem detection in one's own writing to understanding how to address a language problem: collaborative writing, feedback, and metatalk and reflection on drafts.

This expanded concept of noticing has important implications for the tutoring of graduate multilingual students in the writing center, as it may ease two central concerns tutors may have in relation to focusing on language: that this focus would conflict with writing center philosophy of improving the writer, not the writing (North 1984) and that this focus would conflict with the writing center goal of promoting writer agency in the tutorial session, as close attention to language would lead to copyediting rather than collaborative talk about writing (Brooks 1991). Yet when extended to a writing center context, Manchón's research indicates that focusing on language in a tutorial does not need to be conflated with copyediting; on the contrary, a writing tutorial, since it involves collaboration, meta-talk, and feedback, provides an ideal interactive space for fostering active language learning through and about writing. In other words, if the main activity of a writing center tutorial—talking about a draft—leads to improving the writer, not only the writing, then talk about language use in context, even when focused on issues that might otherwise be seen as lower order concerns (i.e., word choice, syntax, punctuation), also has the potential to improve the writer along with the writing.

The second potential writing center concern about attention to language conflicting with the goal of promoting writer agency is interesting to consider given that learner agency is central to the act of noticing. As explained by psychologist John Godolphin Bennett (1976), "unless we notice, we cannot be in a position to choose or act for ourselves" (i). Indeed, noticing—and a concern for agency—are central to writing center sessions with multilingual graduate students, the focus of this chapter, and both are part of the process when writer and tutor show each other what they notice in a draft and then work together to identify solutions to the potential problems they've identified. For instance, either the writing center tutor or multilingual graduate writer may notice a textual feature or rhetorical approach that varies from conventional academic English or from the specialized discourses and genre conventions valued in the discipline. Together they investigate the issue, each drawing on their respective areas of knowledge and array of strategies, with the writer responsible for making decisions about any changes to the text. The goal of this noticing and negotiating process is for the writer to gain greater awareness of and control over her own text, outcomes valued in writing center practice even as the focus of the session is on language concerns (also see Shapiro et al. 2016, for a discussion of agency in relation to multilingual writing support and pedagogy).

In this chapter, I draw on this theoretical framework to discuss the role of attention to language when tutoring multilingual graduate writing. I first describe how multilingual graduate writers attend to language throughout the writing process, and then focus on elements of this process that I have found to be most important and effective for tutors to support during sessions: analysis of mentor texts (sample texts drawn from the students' fields) for discipline-specific genre and language learning, attention to some of the key features of academic English (i.e., such as language used to express writer responsibility and stance-taking), and attention to sentence-level issues (i.e., lexical, grammatical, and syntactic issues). I then discuss how tutors may prioritize among these elements and other features of the text during a session, and how they can maintain a focus on learning, even when attending to sentence-level issues. I end by discussing why the framework of noticing, along with strategies for addressing language concerns, meets important needs when working with these writers. But first, I describe the context from which I draw these strategies—the tutoring of multilingual graduate students within a graduate writing center at Cornell University.

THE CONTEXT: THE ELSO TUTORING PROGRAM AT CORNELL UNIVERSITY

From 1972 to 2013, all tutoring at Cornell was handled by the Writing Walk-In Service, a writing center led by the Knight Institute for Writing in the Disciplines. Increased demand by graduate student writers and changes in how multilingual students were supported by the university prompted the creation of a separate tutoring service for graduate students in 2013, the Graduate Writing Service (GWS), also led by the Knight Institute. In 2014, I was hired by the Graduate School to launch a writing and speaking support program for international graduate students—the English Language Support Office (ELSO), housed by the Knight Institute. When I was hired, the GWS director asked my office to also offer tutoring services, as her tutors are not trained to support the language needs of multilingual students and because focusing on sentence level issues is seen as pushing up against the program's policy of not providing copy-editing. That year, one of the ELSO lecturers had a course release to provide ten weekly hours of tutoring to multilingual graduate students. It quickly became apparent that these hours were insufficient. Not only were there waitlists for the ELSO consultant's hours, but the demand spilled over to the Writing Walk-In Service and GWS. In fact, in fall of 2014, the Writing Walk-In Service reported that 90 percent of its sessions with graduate writers were focused on multilingual writing issues and the GWS reported that 88 percent of its clients used English as an additional language. In fall of 2015, I hired four graduate students as peer tutors, selected based on their interest in and experience working with international multilingual students, openness to learning about second language acquisition, and interest in working with both holistic issues and sentence-level issues in student writing. In addition, all of the tutors I hired were multilingual and/or had international experience, giving them insight into the strengths and challenges of multilingual international graduate students. Together, these tutors provided twenty-four hours of tutoring a week with sessions lasting from thirty minutes to an hour. As demand was still unmet as indicated by waitlists, high utilization rates, and three-week waits for appointments, in Spring 2016, I hired two more tutors, bringing the tutoring focused on writing up to thirty-seven hours a week, including five weekly hours of tutoring focused on pronunciation.

It is also important to understand how tutoring multilingual graduate students fits into the broader picture of multilingual writing and speaking support at Cornell. In addition to this tutoring program, ELSO offers multilingual graduate students a set of credit-bearing seven-week courses on topics related to writing and speaking (all of which are tailored to the writing and speaking contexts of graduate school), a workshop series on writing and speaking, a conversation program, and, started in Spring 2016, a facilitated writing groups program. In the tutoring program, as in all of the ELSO initiatives, we think hard about the kinds of writing and language knowledge graduate students already have, the kinds of writing and rhetorical knowledge faculty may assume students have (based on the US education system and tacit conventions of US academic writing), and the complexities of writing and speaking at the graduate level that all students need to negotiate.

Unlike the GWS, on our tutoring program website we do not include a statement about having a policy against copy-editing, as we've learned that multilingual graduate students often interpret this statement to mean that the tutors will not work with them on sentence-level language issues. Instead, we fold a focus on language into a description of what a tutorial may focus on, stating that "tutors may help writers to get started on writing projects and presentations, revise drafts for structure and organization, identify and discuss issues related to grammar, word choice, syntax, and expression, [and] gain insight into linguistic, stylistic, and rhetorical conventions of writing and presentations in US academic settings" (English Language Support Office 2015). Though we offer to work with students on invention, revision, and rhetorical issues, many of our tutees express a desire to work on language-related issues. The ways in which tutors learn to "notice" these issues with the graduate writer will be the focus of the remainder of this chapter.

NOTICING THE PLACE OF LANGUAGE DURING THE WRITING PROCESS

In our appointment form, we ask students to tell us their goals for the tutorial session. In the fall of 2015, 190 of the 252 forms (75.4%) included a response to this question, and, of these, 124 (65.3%) made a reference to language-oriented goals, such as "proofreading," "polishing English," "identify[ing] patterns of error," and "improving weaknesses in language." Not surprisingly, then, in their Fall 2015 tutoring notes, tutors reported that they addressed language issues in 133 (65.9%) of the sessions, mentioning the following language-related areas of focus:

verb tense, subject/verb agreement, articles, prepositions, word choice, flow, signposting, wordiness, syntax, and clarity.

Clearly, multilingual students have few opportunities to sit side-by-side with a fluent English user and go through a text line-by-line, gaining insight into what this reader notices, learning strategies for making decisions about revisions, and having the opportunity to ask questions about English language use. What can be learned from this experience moves beyond what is often possible in a writing course or English language course, or from receiving comments from an instructor in the student's discipline, as this experience brings together skills and knowledge learned in each of these contexts, and brings them to bear on an authentic text.

And yet writing center tutors are often trained to think of attention to language as coming at the end of a writing process, as part of lower-order concerns and final editing. They often hold off on focusing on language issues until the writer is nearing the final draft, feeling that it is ineffective and inefficient to polish a sentence or paragraph when the writer is still in the midst of invention or revision. However, as I indicate in table 7.1 below, for many multilingual writers, attention to language occurs throughout the processes of inventing, revising, and editing. Moreover, their strategies for working through these processes may include analyzing the language of mentor texts (texts selected by the student to serve as models) and seeking language-focused feedback from readers at every step.

So, for example, during the invention stage, multilingual writers may be noticing "beautiful English" as they read texts in their field, capturing words, phrases, and sentence structures for use in their own writing, while also analyzing these mentor texts for genre conventions (Cox 2010). During revision, multilingual writers may seek feedback on expression and may return to the mentor texts to mine them further for particular kinds of language use related to rhetorical style (Leki 1995). During editing, multilingual writers may seek feedback on language accuracy, as well as answers to particular questions related to language (Goldstein 2005), which they may also attempt to answer by using online corpora (i.e., Corpus of Contemporary American English) (Swales 2006).

NOTICING THE PLACE OF LANGUAGE DURING THE TUTORING PROCESS

In tutor training, I share the table below with tutors to discuss why it can be effective to consider language during a session with a multilingual

Table 7.1. Second Language Writing Processes

	Invention	Revision	Editing
What this phase includes	Reading and note-taking, collecting and analyzing data, creating a plan, brainstorming, writing new prose (first draft material)	Reorganizing an existing draft or parts of a draft; further developing ideas; further developing the draft in relation to the audience; identifying gaps	Fine-tuning the formatting and citation style; editing at the sentence-level
Common strategies for L1 writers	Free-writing, mind-mapping, talking through ideas with others, outlining; focusing on developing ideas and concepts rather than fine-tuning language; starting with parts of the draft that are easiest to write and attempting other chunks later in the process	Seeking readers for feedback on the overall logic and development; using strategies like reverse outlining to analyze the structure of a draft; allowing for a cooling off period before revising	Seeking readers for feedback on style; reading a draft out loud; allowing for a cooling off period; checking for syntactic and punctuation issues that have been pointed out by readers or editors in the past
Additional strategies used by L2 writers	Writing in the L1; analyzing several samples of the genre ("mentor texts") to understand the overall structure and development as well as the ideas used; keeping a language journal that includes disciplinary discourse, sentence templates, linking terms, and other instances of "beautiful English"	Seeking readers for feedback on expression (whether all sentences communicate the intended message); reverse outlining a sample text to compare to own draft; color-coding features of writer-responsible text or stance-taking language (in a sample text and own draft); analyzing the rhetorical moves used in mentor texts	Seeking readers for feedback on word choice, grammar, usage, syntax, and punctuation; analyzing a mentor text to answer specific language questions (e.g., verb tense patterns, usage of passive voice, variations in how particular ideas are expressed in the writer's discipline); using an online corpus to answer language questions (e.g., preposition use, article use, frequency of particular words)

writer at different points in the writing process. The table also allows me to focus on aspects of second language writing processes with which the tutors may be less familiar, particularly analysis of mentor texts, use of features of writer-responsible text, and use of stance-taking language, each of which I discuss next.

Noticing the Role of Mentor Texts

Analysis of a "mentor text"—a sample text identified by the writer—may come up at any stage of the writing process for different purposes.

Mentor text analysis is a long-used pedagogy in second language writing instruction (e.g., see how mentor text analysis is referred to throughout John Swales and Chris Feak's popular textbook on graduate writing, *Academic Writing for Graduate Students, 3rd ed.* 2012). Multilingual graduate student writers may use mentor text analysis because the strategy was introduced to them in a course or they may have come to this strategy on their own (see Cox 2010). It is important for tutors to be aware of mentor text analysis, so that they can better understand writing processes used by the students; be in a better position to help students answer discipline-specific questions about genre, discourse, style, usage, and rhetorical choices; and guide students in using mentor text analysis effectively, as this strategy can lead to mimicry or even plagiarism.

During tutor training, I devote a weekly training session to mentor text analysis. I ask the tutors to bring a journal article from their field to serve as a mentor text, as well as to share this article with the group electronically. I then present an assignment used in one of our multilingual graduate writing courses, which provides students with a list of forty-six questions on genre conventions, rhetorical situation, structure/organization, and style/discourse/language to answer through mentor text analysis. The tutors work through these questions, using a mentor text from their field. We then compare the strategies we came up with for answering the questions, as well as the answers themselves, in order to compare and contrast disciplinary conventions. The tutor then has a host of strategies available to share with tutees when questions come up during sessions, such as "how long should an introduction to a journal article be?" or "how should an argument in a discussion section be organized?" For the former question, the tutor might share with the student a strategy comparing the introduction lengths from articles from the same journal, the journal to which the student plans to submit the draft, or comparing introduction lengths from the same type of article—that is, meta-analysis, theoretical, research. Strategies for approaching the latter question might involve analyzing whether an author has positioned claims at the beginning or end of paragraphs or doing a reverse outline to see how the writer has advanced an argument.

Noticing Features of Writer-Responsible Text

In the United States, much academic writing is "writer-responsible" in that the burden for clear communication falls mainly on the writer, rather than the reader (Hinds 1987). Techniques for crafting writer-responsible text include signposting with forecasting statements, topic sentences, and conjunctive adverbs, and creating cohesion through the old-to-new information sentence pattern and demonstrative pronouns. It's important to share with writing center tutors how and when these techniques are used because when cohesive features are missing from the graduate student's text, readers may feel disoriented and unsure of how to navigate or make sense of the text. As one faculty member commented to me, student papers missing these cohesive elements tend to come across as "word salad." A student in one of my graduate classes told me that mere weeks after she learned about creating writer-responsible texts and started using forecasting and cohesive techniques in her drafts, her advisor commented that her writing had "matured." In fact, I think that creating writer-responsible texts is even more important for clear communication than many other aspects of usage and grammar. If a reader is able to follow the organization and flow of a text, they are often able to read past some issues at the sentence level.

To introduce tutors to the different features of writing-responsible texts, I present to them a handout I crafted that defines writer responsibility and presents approaches for signposting and for creating cohesion, drawing examples from two graduate writing textbooks: *Writing Science: How to Write Papers that Get Cited and Proposals that Get Funded* (Schimel 2012) and *Academic Writing for Graduate Students* (Swales and Feak 2012). (This handout is also available to multilingual graduate students through our program Blackboard site and is used in our courses.) I then ask the tutors to examine a section of a journal article from their field, marking all uses of writer-responsible text. The tutors were surprised to see the prevalence of this type of language, which they've read past many times but had never noticed. I also share with the tutors online resources they may find useful during a session, such as online handouts listing linking words developed by universities (i.e., the useful handout created by Massey University Centre for Teaching and Learning (n.d.), "Signpost Words and Phrases," available online, along with websites that pull examples of signposting language from corpora, such as the *University of Manchester Academic Phrasebank* [Morely 2017]). During a session, these resources might be used to introduce tutees to language options, followed by a discussion of the differences among the options and what might be most effective for the text's rhetorical context.

Noticing Stance-Taking Language

Like using signposting to construct a writer-responsible text, stance-taking language is a key feature of US academic style that is also often unnoticed by tutors until pointed out. As defined by Zak Lancaster (2011), stance-taking language refers to "phrase and clause level wordings that operate to construct an authorial presence in the text and to negotiate meanings with the anticipated reader and other participants in the discourse" (para. 6). Lancaster analyzed four undergraduate multilingual writers' papers for an upper-level economics course to examine how the students' use of stance-taking language related to evaluative comments and grades given by the instructor. In Lancaster's study, the instructor interpreted the student papers that were at times missing or misusing stance-taking language as "not very 'complex' or 'sophisticated' in their argumentation." In contrast, the instructor praised the student papers that effectively used stance-taking language as "'clearly written' and 'well-reasoned,' display[ing] an awareness of 'the big picture'" (para. 30). As these comments indicate, the ways in which students use stance-taking language have implications for how readers perceive their writing and critical thinking skills. The nuanced authorial stances students were expected to compose in this upper-level writing-in-the-disciplines (WID) course would be even more valued in academic and professional contexts in which multilingual graduate students write.

As Lancaster has pointed out, faculty expectations for use of stance-taking language "often remain implicit" as they are "not discussed explicitly in class" or even in faculty comments on student papers (para. 55), but raising awareness of stance-taking language among student writers can allow them to gain more control over these features so important to academic writing. To introduce stance-taking language to tutors, I present to them a simplified version of Lancaster's framework combined with examples drawn from Swales and Feak (2012) in a handout that they can also use during tutoring sessions. The handout includes definitions and examples of hedges, boosters, attitude markers, engagement markers, self-mentions, and evaluative adjectives, as well as approaches to moderating a claim, using distancing to indicate stance, and softening generalizations (see also Lancaster 2014). With that framework, we examine a text that we have already read as part of tutor training, identifying the sections in which stance-taking language is most often used and the different types being used, and we discuss the effect of this language on the reader. In the next training session, I ask the tutors to analyze articles from their fields, an important step as stance-taking language varies according to disciplines and rhetorical contexts.

After the tutors have practiced analyzing stance-taking language, we go on to discuss strategies for addressing stance-taking language with multilingual graduate writers, which include sharing with the tutees the stance-taking instructional materials (we have found that graduate writers appreciate having access to theoretical frameworks rather than just how-to advice), assessing the effectiveness of stance-taking language in a student's draft, and working with the student to analyze a mentor text. As with the language of writer-responsible text, the goal is both to raise awareness of this type of language in the writer's field and to help the writer have more control over this use of language in their own writing.

Noticing Lexical, Grammatical, and Syntactic Issues

While knowing how to effectively use mentor texts during the writing process, construct writer-responsible texts, and use stance-taking language are all important for crafting effective graduate-level writing, multilingual graduate students often also want to work on lexical, grammatical, and syntactic issues in their writing. The stakes of graduate writing are high, and thus students care deeply about how their writing is represented to their many audiences, which include dissertation supervisors and committees, seminar instructors, editorial boards of journals, hiring committees, and grant selection committees. Further, research has shown that advanced language learners are able to turn their attention to language accuracy once a certain level of fluency is achieved (Takeuchi 2003). Thus, in terms of graduate students' language development, it is appropriate for tutors to notice and help students to fine-tune their use of lexical, grammatical, and syntactic forms in texts.

To train tutors in working on these kinds of sentence-level issues, I introduce resources that can help them better identify and work through problems that are often prevalent in graduate writing, such as how to handle long sentences that indicate complexity of thought but that may be structurally awkward or incorrect or how to determine when active or passive voice is appropriate. For some training sessions, tutors bring sentences from tutee's texts that they feel present an interesting syntactic or grammatical problem, and we work through the problems as a group. For questions related to lexical issues, such as the use of discipline-specific vocabulary or phrases, I introduce tutors to online corpora. Several are available, including:

- University of Manchester Phrasebank (Morely 2017)
- The Michigan Corpus of Upper-Level Student Papers (MICUSP) (2009)
- The Corpus of Contemporary American English (COCA) (Davies 2008)
- Word and Phrase Info (Davies 2012)

It is well worth using tutor-training time to familiarize tutors with these resources. In Nigel Caplan's (2012) excellent chapter on collocation and corpus searching in *Grammar Choices for Graduate and Professional Writers*, he offers a set of exercises that are useful for this purpose as they lead students through the use of MICUSP and COCA. I spend a training session trying out Caplan's exercises with the tutors and then talking about how we might make use of the corpora during tutoring sessions. The tutors have found corpora especially useful for instances when questions about language come up that neither the tutor nor tutee know the answer to, such as whether a certain technical phrase takes an article or how commonly used a certain reporting verb may be in scientific writing.

I also introduce tutors to a process for focusing on these sentence-level issues. I recommend that tutors start a session with both the writer and the tutor commenting on what they each notice in a draft. For instance, the tutor and tutee can both read copies of a certain section simultaneously, each highlighting language they notice as inaccurate or ineffective, and identifying areas each feels unsure of or has questions about. Then, the tutor and tutee can work line-by-line, moving through issues by drawing on the tutor and tutee's areas of knowledge, as well as turning to handbooks or corpora. In the ELSO program, we see this as a co-inquiry approach, with both the tutor and tutee posing questions and together discovering answers.

With this explanation of strategies for mentor text analysis, noticing and tutoring for key aspects of academic style (writer-responsible text and stance-taking language), and noticing and tutoring for lexical, grammatical, and syntactic features of graduate students texts, I next discuss how to help tutors prioritize among these aspects of the text while keeping the focus on learning during a session.

PRIORITIZING DURING A SESSION

How much time should one spent on the stylistic, lexical, grammatical, usage, and syntactic issues in student writing? How can a tutor decide which of these issues to prioritize during a session? Here is what I tell my ELSO tutors:

- Focus on expression first. Do all of the sentences communicate? (If the discourse is outside your area of knowledge, you may focus on the ability to follow the connections among ideas within and between sentences.) Are there sentences that are more syntactically tangled than others? Chances are these are spots where the writer had difficulty expressing a complex idea. When you come across these sentences, ask the writer what they wanted to say. Listen, and take notes, and then read the notes to the writer. The writer can then gauge whether the notes communicate the message or if they need to try to explain the idea again. To check whether a text is communicating the intended message, try "Say back" (Elbow and Belanoff 1999): tell the writer what you see as the main idea of a draft or a paragraph. The writer can then gauge how effectively they communicated. You might also begin a session by asking the writer if there are any areas where they felt a point wasn't fully expressed and start with those areas.

- Once the draft communicates the writer's ideas effectively, prioritize as you would for any student writer, giving feedback appropriate to the stage of the writing process and level of concern.
- If the tutee is not yet at the polishing stage but wants the tutor to go through the draft line-by-line, I recommend following the tutee's lead. It may be that the writer relies on peers or professors in their field for other kinds of feedback, and thus wants to dedicate this time to language support.
- When moving line-by-line, focus on concerns related to syntax and word choice first, as these tend to interrupt communication more than concerns related to word form, verb tense, articles, prepositions, and punctuation. If there are many concerns related to syntax and word choice, spend the majority of your time focusing on these (you may even simply correct word form, verb tense, articles, and prepositions as you read as a gift to the writer).
- If syntactic and word choice concerns are not heavily present, it is worth spending time on issues related to word form, verb tense, articles, and prepositions. These features of the text may not seem as important, but when writers feel that they can better notice and control these areas of grammar, they feel more confident as English users and writers. Further, paying particular attention to these concerns in relation to how language is used in the student's field will increase their control over these specialized discourses.

Of course, the top priority is student learning. In the next section, I discuss how to ensure that learning is the main outcome of any session.

KEEPING THE FOCUS ON LEARNING

One widely held concern about focusing on language in sessions is that students (and faculty and administrators) will misunderstand the educational mission of the writing center. Indeed, in the ELSO tutoring appointment forms, some of tutees' goals for the sessions were expressed so succinctly that it would appear that they were expecting the tutor to copy-edit. For example, in response to the question, "What do you hope to accomplish in this session," some students answered "proofing," "expression check," and "grammar error correction." However, some of the longer entries showed that many of the students are seeking to build their language awareness and writing knowledge:

- I wish to read through the materials and check if there are any errors in grammar or unclear expressions.
- To read and understand patterns of errors in writing, and to get a sense of what are the common mistakes.
- The goal will be to identify patterns of errors in grammar or usage in order to develop effective strategies for line-editing.
- To be able to improve the project, and identify my mistakes, learn, and improve upon my writing skills.
- I hope to receive advice about the organization, clarity of the paper as well as corrections of grammar mistakes.
- Get feedback on some of my common errors in writing and how to address them.

Returning to the point I made in my introduction about noticing language in a session being very different from copyediting, I would argue that these students, along with many others, were hoping for an educational experience that moves past copyediting, as evidenced by the fact that we don't actually see many misunderstandings about our purpose during tutoring sessions. Of the over one hundred international graduate students and post-docs who used our tutoring services this semester, only one seemed to expect copy-editing, signaled by the fact that he wanted to drop off his paper with the tutor and pick it up later, as the tutor reported to me. All of the other tutees expected to take part in the session, a sign that they wanted to learn how to improve their writing.

Further, these students were choosing the tutoring service over copy-editing services, though the Graduate School, the Graduate Writing Service, and English Language Support Office each distributes lists of local private editors. One might see the students' choice of ELSO as purely a financial decision since these private services are costly, but the email inquiries I receive from students suggest otherwise, such as this query I received from an Indonesian graduate student:

> I have been writing drafts of my application essay, but writing in English is very challenging for me. I do not feel that the essays I've written convey my thoughts as well as I think it could be. When I look for help, what I found are people who either writes the essay for you, or who offers to edit the essay, something that is *not* what I have in mind. I am looking for someone who would constructively criticize my essay based on what I am trying to say. [. . .] I would like to meet and talk to someone about my interest, why I am applying and learn how I can write a strong essay.

As this student so eloquently expresses, many graduate writers are seeking learning opportunities for furthering their English language development. Thus, it's critical to introduce tutors to strategies for conducting sentence-level oriented sessions while also keeping the focus on learning.

To see how tutors were handling these kinds of sessions and where learning might be happening, I combed through tutoring reports where they jot down strategies that were effective during the session (so we can all learn from one another) and identified the following ways they are paying attention to writing at the sentence level while, at the same time, teaching the writer how to find and address for themselves problem areas in the writing:

- Use, and teach the writer to use, resources that support language learning during the session so that the writer can continue to use these resources on their own.
- Make explicit the strategies you use to find areas that may require editing and think out loud as you try to figure out how to address an issue.
- Explain the structural, syntactic, or grammatical problem and show the writer how to fix it. For instance, for lack of subject/verb agreement, show the student how *you* pull out the subject and verb from a long sentence.
- During the session, do not to rush through a draft, but allow time for the tutee to ask questions about English language use.
- At the end of the session, ask the writer to summarize issues identified during the session and plan out next steps.
- At the end of the session, highlight sentences that have issues similar to those focused on during the session, so that the tutee can work on these on their own.

These approaches integrate tutoring on writing with a focus on language, thus effectively supporting multilingual graduate students as both English language users and writers.

CONCLUSION

Writing centers can have powerfully transformative effects on the academic lives of multilingual graduate students when tutors are trained not only to support these novice scholars as writers but also as language users. The concept of noticing provides both justification for and approaches to focusing on academic style and sentence-level issues while also maintaining student agency and keeping the focus of a session on learning. By attending to both writing and language in the writing center, tutors become advocates for multilingual graduate students, empowering them to more effectively meet the demands of the complex and high-stakes writing tasks they face, thereby allowing them to make their voices heard in their departments, fields, and professions.

REFERENCES

Bennett, John Godolphin. 1976. *Noticing.* Vol. 2 of The Sherborne Theme Talks Series. Sherborne, UK: Coombe Springs Press.

Bitchener, John. 2008. "Evidence in Support of Written Corrective Feedback." *Journal of Second Language Writing* 17 (2): 102–118. https://doi.org/10.1016/j.jslw.2007.11.004.

Brooks, Jeff. 1991. "Minimalist Tutoring: Making Students Do All the Work." *Writing Lab Newsletter* 15:1–4.

Caplan, Nigel. 2012. *Grammar Choices for Graduate and Professional Students.* Ann Arbor: University of Michigan Press. https://doi.org/10.3998/mpub.4322525.

Cox, Michelle. 2010. "Identity, Second Language Writers, and the Learning of Workplace Writing." In *Reinventing Identities in Second Language Writing,* ed. Michelle Cox, Jay Jordan, Christina Ortmeier-Hooper, and Gwen G. Schwartz, 75–95. Urbana, IL: National Council of Teachers of English.

Cumming, Alister. 1990. "Metalinguistic and Ideational Thinking in Second Language Composing." *Written Communication* 7 (4): 482–511. https://doi.org/10.1177/0741088390007004003.

Davies, Mark. 2008. The Corpus of Contemporary American English (COCA). https://corpus.byu.edu/coca/.

Davies, Mark. 2012. Word and Phrase Info. https://www.wordandphrase.info.

Elbow, Peter, and Pat Belanoff. 1999. *Sharing and Responding.* 3rd ed. Columbus, OH: McGraw-Hill.

English Language Support Office. 2018. "ELSO Tutoring." Cornell English Language Support Office Website. https://knight.as.cornell.edu/elso-tutoring.

Goldstein, Lynn M. 2005. *Teacher Written Commentary in Second Language Writing Classrooms. The Michigan Series on Teaching Multilingual Writers.* Ann Arbor: University of Michigan Press. https://doi.org/10.3998/mpub.6737.

Griffin, Robert B. 2004. "The Output Hypothesis Revisited: An Examination of Noticing and Its Relationship to L2 Development in Writing." PhD diss., Indiana University. Retrieved from University of Michigan, Order No. DA3162237.

Hinds, John. 1987. "Reader versus Writer Responsibility: A New Topology." In *Writing across Languages: Analyses of L2 Text,* ed. Ulla Connor and Robert B. Kaplan, 141–52. Reading, MA: Addison Wesley Publishing Company.

Lancaster, Zak. 2011. "Interpersonal Stance in L1 and L2 Students' Argumentative Writing in Economics: Implications for Faculty Development in WAC/WID Programs." *Across the Disciplines* 8 (4). http://wac.colostate.edu/atd/ell/lancaster.cfm.

Lancaster, Zak. 2014. "Making Stance Explicit for Second Language Writers in the Disciplines: What Faculty Need to Know about the Language of Stancetaking." In *WAC and Second-Language Writing: Research Towards Linguistically and Culturally Inclusive Programs and Practices,* ed. Terry Myers Zawacki and Michelle Cox, 269–98. Fort Collins, CO: The WAC Clearinghouse and Parlor Press. https://wac.colostate.edu/books/l2/.

Leki, Ilona. 1995. "Coping Strategies of ESL Students in Writing Tasks Across the Curriculum." *TESOL Quarterly* 29 (2): 235–260. https://doi.org/10.2307/3587624.

Manchón, Rosa M. 2011. "Writing to Learn the Language: Issues in Theory and Research." In *Learning-to-Write and Writing-to-Learn in an Additional Language,* ed. Rosa M. Manchón, 61–82. Amsterdam: John Benjamins Publishing Company. https://doi.org/10.1075/lllt.31.07man.

Massey University Centre for Teaching and Learning. n.d. "Signpost Words and Phrases." http://owll.massey.ac.nz/pdf/studyup-essays-2-handout.pdf.

Michigan Corpus of Upper-Level Student Papers (MICUSP). 2009. Ann Arbor: The Regents of the University of Michigan. http://www.elicorpora.info.

Morely, John. 2017. University of Manchester Phrasebank. http://www.phrasebank.manchester.ac.uk.

North, Stephen. 1984. "The Idea of a Writing Center." *College English* 46 (5): 433–446. https://doi.org/10.2307/377047.

Qi, Donald S., and Sharon Lapkin. 2001. "Exploring the Role of Noticing in a Three-Stage Second Language Writing Task." *Journal of Second Language Writing* 10 (4): 277–303. https://doi.org/10.1016/S1060-3743(01)00046-7.

Sheen, Younghee. 2010. "Differential Effects of Oral and Written Corrective Feedback in the ESL Classroom." *Studies in Second Language Acquisition* 32 (02): 203–234. https://doi.org/10.1017/S0272263109990507.

Schimel, Joshua. 2012. *Writing Science: How to Write Papers that Get Cited and Proposals that Get Funded.* New York: Oxford University Press.

Schmidt, Richard. 1990. "The Role of Consciousness in Second Language Learning." *Applied Linguistics* 11 (2): 129–158. https://doi.org/10.1093/applin/11.2.129.

Schmidt, Richard, and Sylvia Frota. 1986. "Developing Basic Conversational Ability in a Second Language: A Case Study of an Adult Learner of Portuguese." In *Talking to Learn: Conversation in Second Language Acquisition,* ed. Richard R. Day, 237–326. Rowley, MA: Newbury House.

Shapiro, Shawna, Michelle Cox, Gail Shuck, and Emily Simnitt. 2016. "Teaching for Agency: From Appreciating Linguistic Diversity to Empowering Student Writers." *Composition Studies* 14 (1): 31–52.

Storch, Neomy. 2009. "Metatalk in Pair Work Activity: Level of Engagement and Implications for Language Development." *Language Teaching Research* 11 (2): 143–59. https://doi.org/10.1177/1362168870704600.

Swain, Merrill. 1995. "Three Functions of Output in Second Language Learning." In *Principles and Practices in Applied Linguistics,* ed. Guy Cook and Barbara Seidlhofer, 125–44. Oxford: Oxford University Press.

Swain, Merrill. 1998. "Focus on Form through Conscious Reflection." In *Focus on Form in Classroom Second Language Acquisition,* ed. Catherine Doughty and Jessica Williams, 64–81. Cambridge: Cambridge University Press.

Swain, Merrill, and Sharon Lapkin. 1995. "Problems in Output and the Cognitive Processes They Generate: A Step toward Second Language Learning." *Applied Linguistics* 16 (3): 371–391. https://doi.org/10.1093/applin/16.3.371.

Swain, Merrill, and Sharon Lapkin. 2001. "Focus on Form through Collaborative Dialogue: Exploring Task Effects." In *Researching Pedagogic Tasks: Second Language Learning, Teaching, and Testing,* ed. Martin Bygate, Peter Skehan, and Merrill Swain, 99–118. London: Longman.

Swales, John M. 2006. "A Corpus-Based EAP Course for NNS Doctoral Students: Moving from Available Specialized Corpora to Self-Compiled Corpora." *English for Specific Purposes* 25 (1): 56–75. https://doi.org/10.1016/j.esp.2005.02.010.

Swales, John M., and Christine B. Feak. 2012. *Academic Writing for Graduate Students.* 3rd ed. Ann Arbor: University of Michigan Press. https://doi.org/10.3998/mpub.2173936.

Takeuchi, Osamu. 2003. "What Can We Learn from Good Foreign Language Learners? A Qualitative Study in the Japanese Foreign Language Context." *System* 31 (3): 385–392. https://doi.org/10.1016/S0346-251X(03)00049-6.

8
"NOVELTY MOVES"
Training Tutors to Engage with Technical Content

Juliann Reineke, Mary Glavan, Doug Phillips, and Joanna Wolfe

Tutors often feel intimidated by the highly technical or specialized content that characterizes graduate-level writing, particularly in fields far from their own. Take the following abstract, typical of graduate student STEM writers:

> We propose a routability-driven analytical placer that aims at distributing pins evenly. This is accomplished by including a group of pin density constraints in its mathematical formulation. Moreover, for mixed-size circuits, we adopt a scaled smoothing method to cope with fixed macro blocks. As a result, we have fewer cells overlapping with fixed blocks after global placement, implying that the optimization of the global placement solution is more accurate and that the global placement solution resembles a legal solution more. Routing solutions obtained by a commercial router show that for most benchmark circuits, better routing results can be achieved on the placement results generated by our pin density oriented placer. (Li and Koh 2013)

At first glance, many novice tutors—particularly those with humanities backgrounds—will find this abstract's technical content overwhelming. Convinced they may not be able to understand the content, these tutors may instead focus on sentence-level issues, such as fixing the parallelism problems in the fourth sentence or adding a missing comma in the last sentence. Such surface-level changes will do little to improve readers' abilities to comprehend the passage. Moreover, tutors unfamiliar with the conventions of the writers' discipline may even provide inappropriate surface-level advice (Mackiewicz 2004). What *will* improve this abstract is more clearly articulating the problems the writers' work is addressing and more explicitly connecting these problems to the proposed technological innovations. This abstract thus represents a central dilemma for writing centers working with graduate students: how to address highly specialized content while also providing discipline-appropriate advice on writing conventions.

DOI: 10.7330/9781607327516.c008

One way writing centers are approaching this problem is by reimagining the role of the tutor as a type of peer advisor, an approach based on the assumption that discipline knowledge is essential for a content-driven session. As Judith Powers (1995) notes, "Working with unfamiliar material and conventions, often in highly technical contexts, [tutors] are unlikely to be able either to frame questions that will help the student 'discover' solutions to their problems or, more important, recognize 'good' solutions when they appear and reinforce them" (14–15). While Powers, in her writing center, elicited the needed disciplinary expertise by consulting students' faculty advisors, other practitioners have advocated training graduate students in the disciplines to be graduate writing consultants (Gillespie 2007) or assigning a "matchmaker" who would pair a graduate student tutor (or a senior undergraduate tutor in the same discipline) with the graduate student tutee (Reardon, Deans, and Maykel 2016, 16; see also Lawrence, Tetrault and Deans in this volume). Not only are such solutions logistically unwieldy for some writing centers, but as Susan Hubbuch (1988) states, it may be difficult for specialist tutors who are confident in their content knowledge to avoid co-opting sessions, thereby minimizing the writer's inventive process.

Another solution to the twin dilemma of responding to specialized content and providing discipline-appropriate guidance is to adopt a genre-based tutoring approach (Walker 1998; Clark 1999; Chanock 2007; Devet 2014; Gordon 2014; Vorhies 2015). As Bonnie Devet (2014) argues, a focus on genre can help both clients and tutors recognize that "disparate disciplines share ways of knowing" and provide tutors with strategies for working with writers and texts from fields of study different from their own (3). Genre knowledge, rather than content knowledge, can help tutors demystify academic writing for clients, thereby giving students a framework for developing thoughtful writing (Fahnestock 1993; Walker 1998; Clark 1999; Gordon 2014). However, much of the current literature on genre-based tutoring focuses on undergraduate clients (Walker 1998; Clark 1999; Chanock 2002; Clark and Hernandez 2011; Dinitz and Harrington 2014). It is not clear if a genre-based approach could help, say, an undergraduate tutor majoring in creative writing work with a text as alien as the abstract that begins this chapter. Would such a tutor be able to engage with the technical content of this abstract or provide appropriate advice without mistakenly applying genre conventions from one field incorrectly to another genre, as Jo Mackiewicz (2004) saw tutors do? Would such a tutor become too didactic and prescriptive when conveying genre knowledge (Freedman 1993, 224)? And even if this tutor provided appropriate advice, would graduate students trust what she has to say?

Our writing center attempts to prepare tutors for the demands of working with advanced graduate student writers through intensive training in what Joanna Wolfe, Barrie Olson, and Laura Wilder (2014) call Comparative Genre Analysis, or CGA. Conducting CGA, students (tutors, writers) carefully compare and contrast the conventions of a genre they are already conversant in with those of other, less familiar genres. Analyzing genres this way, tutors and writers develop a greater understanding of how both genres function. CGA requires readers to attend to unexpected similarities as well as differences across genres and to connect the features they observe to the values and needs of the discourse communities they support. As a tutor training method, CGA prepares tutors to work with genres from multiple academic disciplines without having to master the conventions of those genres.

One way of seeing *similarities* across disciplines is through the use of rhetorical *topoi*. As Wolfe, Olson, and Wilder (2014) argue, even while dramatic differences can appear in the organization and style of academic writing in different disciplines, most academic writing shares common *topoi*—or recurrent lines of argument. For example, Wolfe, Olson, and Wilder identify how variations of the "pattern + interpretation" *topos* are common not just in literary studies, but also in history, engineering, business, and psychology. One common academic *topos* that we find particularly useful, not only for training tutors in CGA but also for use with graduate writers, is John Swales's (1990) Create a Research Space (CARS) model for describing the moves academic writers use in research article introductions. Swales found these moves— "establishing a territory," "establishing a niche," and "occupying the niche" (141)—to be used across disciplines; they represent one way of *doing and writing* (Carter 2007) that helps writers announce the value of their work by "staking a novelty claim" (Kaufer and Geisler 1989, 301).

To tackle tough technical writing in their sessions with graduate students, our tutors learn an adaptation of Swales's (1990) *topos* that we call "the novelty moves." The term "novelty" helps us emphasize that these moves are not arbitrary but support a key value common to most, if not all, academic discourse communities: that of creating *new* knowledge. Our "novelty moves" adaptation differs from Swales's three-part CARS model in two ways. First, we divide Swales's first move, "establishing a territory," into two separate moves: "explain the significance" and "describe the status quo," since we found that tutors tended to intuitively describe the first move in these terms. We use the phrase "describe the status quo" to help writers in applied disciplines—where the research contribution might consist of *building* rather than *studying* something new—see how the novelty moves apply to their work. Finally, we revised Swales's terminology to avoid the word "niche," which we found that English L2 speakers had difficulty translating, and instead use the phrases "create a gap" and "fill the gap" to describe the last two moves. Our revisions of Swales's terms make them easier for a wide range of writers to comprehend quickly and apply to their own work.

While the use of Swales's (1990) model is not unique to our center, nor to graduate writing instruction (Kuteeva and Negretti 2016), what is innovative is the training our tutors receive to enable them to use these moves as a question-generating heuristic instead of a prescriptive template. Our tutors begin by identifying relatively simple and straightforward iterations of the novelty moves and then practice identifying them in a range of genres and meta-genres (Carter 2007) such as abstracts, literature reviews, proposals, problem/solution papers, and artistic statements, working to see the similarities as well as understand the reasons for the differences. For instance, tutors come to observe that the "status quo" and "create a gap" moves are typically combined when the gap is a well-recognized problem, as is often the case in applied disciplines such as engineering, or that "significance" is often implied in theoretical disciplines such as history, where the project contributes by advancing an approach or perspective within the field but may not solve problems like projects in the applied sciences.

We have substantial evidence that, as a whole, our tutors are successful in meeting the needs of graduate student writers. We serve 429 graduate students per year, roughly 60 percent of our clientele. Each year since our center opened in 2012, our graduate student appointments have nearly tripled. Of the approximately 104 PhD students who made an appointment at our writing center in 2016, over 55 percent returned for multiple appointments, which strongly indicates that they feel the sessions are worth their time. These writers have won awards, published papers, and passed exams. They have acknowledged our tutors' support in articles and dissertations. We have also heard praise from their advisors expressing appreciation over how much their students' writing has improved.

However, this success is not easily achieved. Our center has the luxury of being able to invest considerable time and effort into tutor training. Our tutors take an intensive, semester-long practicum for credit that prepares them to tutor in our center. Moreover, most tutors work for approximately four weeks in our center before they begin tutoring independently. In this time, they observe sessions, participate in mock tutoring with experienced supervisors, and complete a range of activities, which we describe in more detail below. Even with this well-scaffolded training, however, we have tutors who shy away from engaging with difficult technical content and instead provide surface-level organizational suggestions and mechanical corrections.[1] In our experience, just providing tutors with knowledge about the novelty moves is insufficient to prepare them to engage with the technically complex projects and confident graduate researchers we see in our center.

But what exactly do tutors need to understand or be able to do in order to use their genre knowledge to help advanced graduate writers with technically dense projects? How do our tutors perceive their own learning process and how do they define their emerging mastery in being able to apply the novelty moves? Learning the answers to these questions will help us better understand the challenges involved in implementing genre-based tutoring and enable us to more precisely define the kinds of knowledge accomplished tutors have and that novices may lack.

We are also interested in exploring how the challenges of working with graduate researchers influence how our tutors perceive their role as peer collaborators when they are faced with the unfamiliar and highly specialized technical texts our graduate writers bring to the GCC. As Pemberton (this volume) and others (e.g., Phillips 2013) have noted, the relationship between graduate writers and tutors can be fraught with concerns about expertise, authority, and disciplinarity. These concerns are inevitably exacerbated when undergraduate tutors work with advanced PhD students. Yet, some of our best tutors are undergraduates. How do our tutors handle these issues of expertise and authority when working with advanced writers from disciplines different from their own? How do our tutors perceive their role in working with these students?

In the sections below, we provide a model for genre-based tutor training by first describing the training we provide our tutors and focusing on the elements that support tutors' use of the novelty moves. Next, we describe the results of interviews with twelve of our experienced and successful tutors. We asked these tutors about their experiences learning to apply the novelty moves to complex, technical projects in order to draw conclusions about what it means to expertly apply genre knowledge in a writing center. We also asked how this genre-based training affects tutors' perceptions of their role as collaborators in the writing center. In particular, we were interested in learning how tutors use their rhetorical knowledge and genre expertise to engage with specialized content and collaborate with clients in the inventive process.

PREPARING TUTORS TO USE A NOVELTY MOVES APPROACH

Carnegie Mellon is a private Research I technical university serving a graduate student population of approximately seven thousand, who represent just over half of the university's total enrollment. More than half of these graduate students are from STEM fields such as mechanical engineering, computer science, and robotics.[2] Our writing center, the Global Communication Center, was founded in 2012 and has been steadily growing. In 2015–2016, we served nearly nine hundred student writers, over 60 percent of whom were graduate students.

Our center employs twenty-five tutors, roughly a third of whom are undergraduate students.[3] While the majority of our tutors are students in the English Department, all (including undergraduates) are trained to assist graduate writers from STEM disciplines on a wide range of projects including research articles, NSF grant proposals, and PhD theses. New tutors enroll in a semester-long practicum, taught by either Joanna Wolfe, the director of the center, or Juliann Reineke, the associate director, in which tutors learn research-backed communication principles and strategies to use in consultations with writers across the disciplines who work in many genres. Prior to engaging with clients in live sessions, our tutors analyze texts from various disciplines and different meta-genres; because they encounter graduate student writers as soon as they begin tutoring, we want tutors to have ample experience working with highly specialized texts from a variety of fields before they hold actual consultations in the GCC. Furthermore, this training, as we show below, helps tutors make the crucial move from conceptual knowledge of genre to practical application. The segment of the practicum that focuses specifically on the novelty moves, outlined here, illustrates our approach overall to preparing tutors to use the genre-based pedagogies they need in order to work fruitfully with advanced graduate student writers:

- **Our handout**: we have created a concise two-page handout explaining the novelty moves with annotated examples from three different disciplines. This handout is used both to train the tutors and to inform writers in tutoring sessions. It emphasizes that the novelty moves are a flexible heuristic used in diverse academic disciplines. A copy of this handout can be found at https://www.cmu.edu/gcc/Handouts-and-Resources/index.html.
- **CGA and class discussion**: tutors practice identifying the novelty moves in a range of sample texts that span Michael Carter's (2007) four metagenres and compare their understanding of the novelty moves to that of their peers. This discussion helps tutors recognize the adaptable nature of the novelty moves.

- **Screen-Capture videos**: before tutors participate in a real tutoring session, we ask them to record a screen-capture video (we use Screencast-O-Matic,[4] free software that allows users to create videos up to fifteen minutes in length). The software captures the user's voice and records whatever is on the computer screen; videos can be published to multiple locations, such as YouTube, directly from the software. Using this application, tutors practice explaining the novelty moves to an imaginary writer and apply the novelty moves to a sample text such as the abstract that opened this chapter. The tutors then receive feedback on their videos from multiple writing center supervisors. This activity helps the practicum instructor and other supervisors determine if the tutor is struggling with theoretical knowledge, practical application, or both. We have found that all new tutors, often during the first few minutes of the video, are faced with the immediate realization that theoretical knowledge does not easily translate to clear and coherent application.
- **Mock tutoring**: applying the novelty moves in a real session can be challenging, particularly for new tutors who are still learning which questions to ask and simultaneously trying to understand a client's research. To increase the complexity of tutors' training tasks, we have them mock tutor a "client," played by a senior tutor or administrator on the writing center staff. At this stage of their training, new tutors need practice applying their understanding of these rhetorical moves: thus, mock tutoring, like creating a screen-capture video, helps tutors move along the theoretical/practical knowledge spectrum.

INTERVIEWS WITH PAST AND PRESENT TUTORS

To better understand how non-specialist tutors use their genre expertise in their sessions with graduate writers, we conducted semi-structured interviews with fourteen tutors (three undergrad, eight masters, three PhD) who have all completed a genre-based practicum and tutored at the GCC for at least one semester.[5] Two of the undergraduate tutors we interviewed are from STEM fields; all other tutors have humanities and social science backgrounds.

The ten interview questions (see appendix) ask tutors to reflect on their training with the novelty moves and discuss how they use the moves in their sessions with graduate writers. We transcribed the interviews and then analyzed the transcripts to identify segments where tutors identified challenges in applying the novelty moves, segments where they reflected on their growth or expertise in applying the novelty moves, and places where they discussed concerns about establishing trust. We then looked for commonalities in tutors' responses, allowing our categories to arise organically from the data. Finally, we examined the transcripts carefully for places where tutors described *how* they went about using the novelty moves in sessions, looking at these segments for evidence of how tutors perceived their roles in sessions.

Our interviews show that tutors rely on intensive training to gain the confidence and flexibility necessary to apply and adapt the novelty moves in sessions that contain highly technical content. Tutors see their role as inherently collaborative, even when they are faced with unfamiliar content; the novelty moves provide them with a framework for understanding complex research. Furthermore, our results show that undergraduates, even those from the humanities, can gain their clients' trust so that collaboration can take place. Ultimately, our results suggest that a well-scaffolded genre-based training can enable tutors to hold content-driven sessions with graduate students.

Challenges to Applying Genre-Based Approaches to Tutoring: Recognizing Variations and Practical Application

We start this section with what our successful tutors tellingly did *not* identify as a challenge: namely, working with technical content. Of the fourteen tutors we interviewed, only one stated that she still sometimes felt intimidated by technical content. As a whole, however, our tutors stated that their training in the novelty moves and experience identifying these moves in multiple genres gave them the confidence that they *should* be able to understand the general framework and importance of a project—even if the technical details elude them.

> SARA (MA): I did not think that it would be easy for me to work with [technical content], but now I have more confidence that if I'm reading something and it doesn't make any sense to me, it's maybe not just that I'm not an expert, it's that the paper itself does not make any sense, and the novelty moves is one of the ways that I know that.
>
> CHRIS (MA): I'm not intimidated at all [when the text is technical] and I think novelty moves are the reason why technical language doesn't intimidate me, because I should be able to read an abstract.
>
> NINA (MA): Usually I think if [the material] is highly technical, the content is their responsibility. . . . I know the general idea of where each piece of their paper fits in, but I don't necessarily need to understand all the really complex details.

These tutors illustrate a claim made in many writing center handbooks: lack of familiarity with content does not need to be a barrier in providing feedback on student writing. One of our undergraduate tutors goes so far as to define confidence as the ability to look past technical content and identify the underlying argument in a technical report. This tutor, an English professional writing major who served as a dedicated tutor and grader for an advanced Mechanical Engineering class, reflects on her experience:

> LISA (BA): Starting out, if I did experience something heavily technical, I spent way too much time trying, I tried too hard to understand it almost. . . . Now I'm much more confident. I'm tutoring that MechE course and I do not understand almost anything in that course. Like I could not do their homework or anything. But, I can at least, kind of blur my eyes, and just be like, "Okay, you're generally talking about this process and you say that this process does x, and so why?" I couldn't tell you how the process works necessarily, but seeing how they are arguing about it, I'm a little bit better at. It's definitely made me more confident, just knowing whatever technical content you're throwing at me, I can still do it.

Lisa uses the novelty moves to establish a basic understanding of the content and guide the session. Similar to other tutors, she does not let intimidating technical content result in the tutoring session devolving into a discussion of surface-level issues.

In contrast to their confidence in handling technical content, what our tutors *did* identify as a major challenge was learning to respond appropriately to variations in the novelty moves. This struggle to adapt to variation manifested in two interrelated ways. First, tutors described the challenge of understanding how the novelty moves could be applied to a range of projects—not just typical research papers. These tutors initially struggled to see how starkly different meta-genres employed the same, basic rhetorical moves. For instance, Nina describes how she had difficulty seeing how the novelty moves could be applied to non-scientific genres such as art proposals or fellowship applications:

> NINA (MA): So I would be [prepping for a session and talking to the Assistant Director] and I would say, "Well, it is like this proposal or this other thing, or maybe for an [undergraduate] grant or a fellowship." And, [the Assistant Director] would be like "Oh, you could use the novelty moves for that." And I would be like "You could? I didn't know that." So, early on in the process it is not like you have memorized what they can be used for. Because, you think "Oh, for research articles and only for scientific articles," but they are really not. . . . It took a minute to comprehend that [the novelty moves] could be used for different things. You can use them for different genres, but you have to tweak them a little bit. . . . I was kind of realizing that they had kind of a wide application [but] that took a little while. I can see why they would be helpful in different genres, but coming to that conclusion myself was difficult at first.

Second, tutors described the challenge of learning to tailor their advice in order to account for the different permutations the novelty moves might take in specific rhetorical and disciplinary contexts.

> Ross (PhD): I feel like I'm still learning them (laughing). I mean there's a level of understanding where I see the significance, the status quo, the gap. I know those definitions and can see how [the novelty moves] work together, and then there's the increasing complexity of how that actually works for all unique different types of research projects. . . . Things that I've found myself thinking about now are these kind of different instantiations of the novelty moves in different disciplines and genres and stuff. . . . I think a lot of times what people are looking for is feedback about . . . how they're doing it within a particular style or discipline . . . [and] that's taking the novelty moves to the next level.
>
> Mari (PhD): I think there are still more field specific ways of articulating novelty . . . that I needed to have been more familiar with. And it was just a matter of time.

These tutors recognize that in different disciplines and genres, these rhetorical moves are, as Ross says, instantiated differently, and that writers want feedback not only on whether the moves have been made, but also on whether they have been made in ways that are appropriate to the writers' disciplines and genres. What all of these tutors gesture toward is the considerable amount of time necessary to gain confidence when applying the novelty moves to different genres and disciplines, further reinforcing the necessity for intensive (and often lengthy) training before new tutors conduct live sessions with clients.

Overall, nine of the fourteen tutors we interviewed described learning to adapt to variations as a central challenge in their ability to apply the novelty moves. In fact, many tutors characterized their increasing flexibility in applying the novelty moves as primary evidence of their growth as a tutor:

> Lisa (BA): Having more experiences with the novelty moves [and] applying them to situations, I don't follow [them] so step by step by step. Because in a lot of cases you'll have two status quos, like "status quo" and then another "status quo" and then "gap," so I think being able to adapt them to the situation and being able to recognize when there might be that situation [that calls for adaptation]. . . . I've definitely gotten better at that.

Our tutors' emphasis on the difficulty of responding to variation in the novelty moves points to the usefulness of incorporating CGA into tutor training. For tutors working with advanced graduate students, experience with CGA can prepare them to respond to disciplinary variations and permutations in how a *topos* (such as the novelty moves) is implemented—even as they look past these variations to draw on their knowledge of the underlying rhetorical functions this *topos* should serve. Our tutors confirm what Devet (2014) notes, that CGA can help "tutors avoid panicking when students are writing a paper in a major that differs from their own field" (3).

In addition to recognizing differences and adapting to them, tutors described their evolving expertise and comfort in explaining *why* these moves exist. They describe how they learned the importance of communicating to writers not just how the novelty moves proceed but how the novelty moves reflect the values and reading practices of academic discourse communities:

> MARI (PHD): When talking about status quo, I would ask students, "Well why do you think it's important to cite other authors or other researchers in field?" And then they would explain that and then I would ask how might this be significant within [their] larger paper.
>
> PETER (PHD): What made the novelty moves clear for me had more to do with why the novelty moves actually exist. Not so much what the steps are. So, when I am explaining them, I usually start with like really ten degrees of removal. "Let's think about once this document is out there and published, how are people going to have to use it? . . . How do you read? If you pick up something off the table, how do you decide if it is something you should spend time on or not?"

Peter's growing expertise in applying the novelty moves thus consists of helping writers recognize the rationale for the line of argument created when writers use these moves. Kelly likewise learned through experience that writers could benefit not only by using the sequence of moves (or "steps," as the tutors may call them in this context) but by learning the rationale for using this *topos* in the first place:

> KELLY (MA): Something about [a research application brought in by a writer] wasn't interesting, and I realized that the novelty moves would help people see why what you are doing is interesting. And, I just remember, as I explained it to the student the reason why I was suggesting this change, they got it, why they needed the novelty moves.

In asking the writer to better explain what's interesting in the research application, Kelly echoes Peter's approach to asking why someone might choose to read the published document. Both tutors' awareness of how the novelty moves work allows them to help writers to step back from the specialized content of their research, a distancing that in turn allows the writer to envision and speak to an audience who may not immediately perceive the project's significance.

Yet, learning how to successfully recognize and respond to variations in *topoi* can be challenging. Both the interviews and our own observations of tutors-in-training, especially as they participated in activities like mock tutoring and creating screen-capture videos, show that tutors need time to develop skills in verbalizing or teaching someone else their theoretical knowledge. Jess explains how, at the start of her training, she struggled significantly with moving from what Carter (2007) refers to as "declarative or conceptual knowledge" to "procedural or process knowledge" (378):

> JESS (BS): I think what I struggled most with was, I guess, coming up with one clear way to articulate why we would use them, because when you introduce the four novelty moves you can kind of see intuitively why they would be important, but when you try to put that into words it's sometimes a little more difficult.

Jess's difficulty in articulating the rhetorical purchase that the novelty moves provide for writers—or in explaining their value differently to different writers—further points to the need for extensive training. Without the immediate, expert feedback they receive in mock tutoring or the ability to hear themselves struggle via screen-capture videos (coupled with expert feedback), novice tutors risk focusing on lower-order concerns, such as transitions between paragraphs, or genre prescriptions, such as the appropriate length of an abstract. In other words, tutors' movement from "conceptual knowledge" to "process knowledge" (Carter 2007, 378) of a *topos* is neither simple nor intuitive. While our goal is to help tutors *adapt topoi* like the novelty moves across academic disciplines, our interviews suggest that tutors need scaffolded training and support to develop both the conceptual and process knowledge needed to reach this point.

Tutors' Perceptions of Their Role as Collaborators

Perhaps the most striking finding in our interview transcripts was the extent to which tutors positioned themselves not simply as responding to graduate student writing, but as actively collaborating with writers in the process of rhetorical invention. They suggest that the novelty moves provide them with a framework for asking the right questions and helping the client generate content.

In her well-cited essay "Collaboration, Control, and the Idea of a Writing Center," Andrea Lunsford (2008 [1991]) describes a collaborative "Burkean Parlor" as the ideal of a writing center. Lunsford warns writing center practitioners, however, about the difficulty of fostering a truly collaborative environment, rightly noting that what often passes for collaboration in a tutoring environment can in reality be a masked form of control. Lunsford describes creating truly collaborative tasks as "damnably difficult" and notes that "collaborative environments and tasks must *demand* collaboration" (95; emphasis in original). She states that creating a truly collaborative environment that engages participants equally requires "careful and ongoing monitoring and evaluating of the collaboration or group process" (95) and cautions against a "pretense of democracy" in which the tutor is still the seat of authority but "is simply pretending it isn't so" (96).

Our experiences working with graduate researchers suggest that Lunsford's warnings against control masquerading as collaboration simply may not be an issue with most graduate student writers. The writers we work with are extremely invested in their projects and have a clear sense of what they want to communicate. What they often lack is a complete understanding of the rhetorical situation and the language for achieving their communicative goals. Our sessions with graduate student writers are innately collaborative because they involve higher-order problem solving and clear division of expertise—criteria that Lunsford (2008) associates with tasks that consistently call for collaboration (95). In our sessions, the writer is unquestionably the content expert. In fact, some of the comments presented above indicate that tutors explicitly locate responsibility for the content with the writer. This mutual recognition of the writer's expertise in the content domain in many ways eliminates—or at least greatly reduces—the possibility of the tutor coopting the writer's voice. Instead, tutors are able to exert their own expertise in the rhetorical domain, helping writers identify and understand the options at their disposal.

Our interviews revealed two primary ways in which this collaboration was achieved. In the first, tutors construct their role as that of an active listener who uses the novelty moves to develop and articulate an understanding of what the writer is trying to communicate. As Sara describes below, tutors adopting this role reflect back their understanding of the writers' project until the writer and tutor agree upon a mutually acceptable and understandable way of phrasing the project:

> SARA (MA): For me, the most useful thing about [the novelty moves] is that thing where you go back like "Oh, what you're telling me is this?" . . . and they're like "No, no, no, no, no" and then they finally kind of phrase it according to [the novelty moves] framework and then I'm like "Oh, of course" and they're like "Yes, exactly."

This give-and-take, where the tutor and writer work together to articulate a research narrative that is clear to the tutor without sacrificing any of the writer's intentions, characterizes many of the most successful sessions in our center. Other tutors similarly describe the benefit of questions such as "Are you saying this?" or "Wait, you're telling me . . . ?" in helping a writer "come up for air and see the bigger picture of things" (Lisa, BA). Such sessions involve the "constructive controversy" that Wolfe (2010) defines as a critical component in true collaboration.

While sometimes tutors collaborate by reflecting back their understanding of a writer's project until the writer agrees with their interpretation, at other times, tutors take on a more active questioning role, leading writers through a series of prompts and encouraging them to generate content:

> PETER (PHD): When they struggle with forming the language . . . what I have to do is feed them a question like "Tell me in one sentence what is the broadest, most general issue that your work responds to?" "Ok, tell me two or three people, how do they understand that problem or how have they talked about it before?" "What is something you think is a problem with that understanding?" We have to kind of create the sentences in that order together.
>
> MICHAEL (PHD): I can ask some novelty move type questions. "So what is the prior research?" Then having them explain it and I'm careful to take notes. Then I'll show them: "Look, here's what you have here and this is what you've told me. This really makes sense the way you've put it, and these are your own words, too."
>
> MARI (PHD): [I] prompt them to try to identify the different moves within their own paper, so maybe not necessarily in that structure or like in that sequence . . . [and we] piece it together as like a team.

In the passages above, tutors present themselves as directive as they ask questions that steer writers to develop specific kinds of content, and in their insistence that writers *should* be able to answer these questions in a way that the tutors can understand. At the same time, however, these tutors are ultimately writer-centered in that they facilitate the writers' invention of material. With the novelty moves operating not as generic prescriptions but rather as heuristics for guiding conversation, tutors and writers can construct interactions that approximate Lunsford's vision of authentic writing center collaboration.

Negotiating Expertise and Gaining Graduate Student Writers' Trust

To participate in the kinds of collaborative sessions we describe above, writers need to be able to trust their tutor's expertise. This trust is not always immediately granted. Writers often question tutors' ability to know what is expected in their discipline. They sometimes resist working with the novelty moves, claiming that their project is unique and therefore does not require these moves. Tutors describe a range of strategies for countering such resistance.

One common strategy is to cite the research behind the novelty moves as a rationale for using them. Tutors often rely on our handout to make the evidence-based case that these moves appear in genres of writing across disciplines:

> NINA (MA): I usually back it up with "This is a standard way of doing things. Research is showing that this is a useful way of doing it. These are developed from Swales, who looked at all of these different original articles and identified [that] a lot of people are using these moves because they are pretty well established." Um, that is usually my go-to way, like when someone is really resistant to a suggestion, to back it up with research.
>
> MARI (PHD): I think a lot of tutors come in contact with these kinds of situations where students become resistant, maybe perhaps . . . because they think that it's a suggestion from us personally rather than us trying to be a medium of like, you know, larger conventions. But I didn't really see it as a personal offense, I think I kind of tried to make it clear that, "Okay, well, research has shown like blah, blah, blah."

Both Nina and Mari address clients' distrust by explaining the research that grounds their use of the novelty moves. In this way, tutors are positioning themselves not as discipline experts but as rhetorical experts.

Some tutors also rely on their own personal experience using the novelty moves to establish this rhetorical expertise:

> LISA (BA): I usually try to sell [the novelty moves] as a utility tool . . . so I try to push for the—like, "you can use this anywhere," where I'm like "I've used this in proposals, I've used this literature essays, I've used this in Human-Computer Interaction [HCI] papers, like I use this everywhere."

Josie (BA) describes the most difficult aspect of working with PhD students as persuading them that "this simple template fits your really complex stuff." For tutors who see the problem from this perspective, explaining the novelty moves in the context of the writer's own project can help prevent potential resistance:

> LISA (BA): With somebody who might be less convinced, like if I think they are an expert and they might be less convinced, I usually try to incorporate their own paper [into my explanation] . . . so they can see how it can apply to them.

Even with significant training and support, many tutors encounter initial resistance from graduate student writers who have difficulty accepting that tutors without disciplinary expertise can help them improve their work. Our interviews suggest, however, that tutors can assuage their clients' reluctance by enacting a common academic move, namely, citing the research that supports their position. Further, tutors can help writers see the novelty moves taking shape in their own writing. When writers realize they have already begun to do what the tutor is suggesting, they are often more receptive to the tutor's expertise and ability to understand content and more easily accept tutors' collaborative role.

CONCLUSION

We propose that writing centers can provide advanced graduate student writers with the content-driven sessions they need, even when their work is highly specialized, and even when the tutors are not members of the writers' disciplines. Genre-informed approaches like the one described in this chapter play a key role in allowing tutors to work productively with graduate students across the university. In our study, tutors' genre expertise permitted them to see past potentially intimidating technical content and focus on how well the writing is accomplishing its goal of selling a research project as a new and worthwhile endeavor. The specific genre-based tutoring approach described in this chapter, that of using the "novelty moves" *topos* to help writers articulate the value of their work, ultimately creates a clear division of labor—where tutor and writer have well demarcated expertise—that provides for balanced collaboration in writing conferences, and that allows the tutor to support the writer in the task of rhetorical invention.

Our study also provides a close look at some of the challenges tutors encounter in implementing this genre-informed tutoring pedagogy in sessions, as well as how they meet those challenges. As tutors try out this strategy in training, they often need more than one practice session to transform an internal understanding of the novelty moves into a comprehensible external linguistic representation for an audience. Tutors also told us they may need prompting to see that the novelty moves operate across a variety of genres, and that discerning how these moves are instantiated in different disciplines and genres constitutes a more advanced kind of genre knowledge, one that takes time and practice to develop. We also learned that tutors developed a repertoire of strategies for responding to writers' resistance to exploring how the novelty moves might be relevant to their texts and projects; these strategies included discussing the values that underlie the novelty moves, citing the research that shows how widely these moves are used in the disciplines, and using the writers' own projects as a context for illustrating the benefits of describing the status quo, articulating a gap, and arguing for the significance of their scholarly work.

Our study strongly suggests that genre-informed approaches to working with advanced disciplinary writers can be highly effective. It also indicates that tutors who use these approaches develop—indeed, must develop—considerable pedagogical expertise as they work across disciplines and genres. Preparing tutors to work skillfully with these approaches, then, calls for thoughtful, well-scaffolded training that includes ample opportunities to build, practice, and deepen genre knowledge.

NOTES

1. These tutors are asked to work solely with undergraduates or do not continue in the writing center.
2. In Fall 2015, 3,630 grad students came from College of Science, College of Computer Science, and College of Engineering.
3. At present (2016–2017), the center employs nine undergraduate and sixteen graduate students.
4. Readers can find this software at https://screencast-o-matic.com/home.
5. We emailed twenty current and former tutors trained to use the novelty moves and invited them to participate in the study.

APPENDIX

Interview questions

1. Tell me about a time when you attempted to teach the novelty moves to a grad student writer at the GCC and it didn't go well. What happened? Why do you think it didn't go well? What were you thinking? What do you think the student was thinking?

2. What challenges have you encountered during those sessions? How do you recognize when it doesn't seem to be working?

3. Tell me about a time that teaching the novelty moves did go well. How can you recognize when teaching the novelty moves is going well? What happened? Why do you think it went well? What were you thinking? What do you think the student was thinking?

4. How do you introduce the novelty moves? Do you summarize them? Read them from the handout? Read over the examples?

5. Have your strategies for teaching the novelty moves changed as you've become a more experienced tutor?

6. What was the most challenging part of learning the novelty moves as a tutor?

7. Did you use Screencast-O-Matic? How so? How did it affect your ability to learn or learn to teach the novelty moves? What training activities, if any, did you feel were most helpful to you in learning/becoming comfortable with the novelty moves? Why were these helpful/unhelpful?
8. Has tutoring with the novelty moves affected your confidence in working with writers with technical projects? How comfortable do you feel tutoring students with novelty moves?
9. How does the content/technical level of the paper influence your confidence? Has tutoring with the novelty moves helped you in your own work?
10. What do you think could have better prepared you to tutor students with the novelty moves? In other words, what other types of training do you think would have most benefitted you, or what could have been done differently with current tutor training activities?

REFERENCES

Carter, Michael. 2007. "Ways of Knowing, Doing, and Writing in the Disciplines." *College Composition and Communication* 58 (3): 385–418.

Chanock, Kate. 2007. "Helping Thesis Writers to Think about Genre: What Is Prescribed, What May Be Possible." *WAC Journal* 18: 31–41.

Chanock, Kate. 2002. "How a Writing Tutor Can Help When Unfamiliar with the Content: A Case Study." *WAC Journal* 13:113–31.

Clark, Irene L. 1999. "Addressing Genre in the Writing Center." *Writing Center Journal* 20 (1): 7–32.

Clark, Irene L., and Andrea Hernandez. 2011. "Genre Awareness, Academic Argument, and Transferability." *WAC Journal* 22:65–78.

Devet, Bonnie D. 2014. "Using Metagenre and Ecocomposition to Train Writing Center Tutors for Writing in the Disciplines." *Praxis: A Writing Center Journal* 11 (2): 1–7.

Dinitz, Sue, and Susanmarie Harrington. 2014. "The Role of Disciplinary Expertise in Shaping Writing Tutorials." *Writing Center Journal* 33 (2): 73–98.

Fahnestock, Jeanne. 1993. "Genre and Rhetorical Craft." *Research in the Teaching of English* 27 (3): 265–71.

Freedman, Aviva. 1993. "Show and Tell? The Role of Explicit Teaching in the Learning of New Genres." *Research in the Teaching of English* 27 (3): 222–51.

Gillespie, Paula. 2007. "Graduate Writing Consultants for Ph.D. Programs Part 1: Using What We Know: Networking and Planning." *Writing Lab Newsletter* 32 (2): 1–6.

Gordon, Layne M.P. 2014. "Beyond Generalist vs. Specialist: Making Connections between Genre Theory and Writing Center Pedagogy." *Praxis: A Writing Center Journal* 11 (2): 1–5.

Hubbuch, Susan M. 1988. "A Tutor Needs to Know the Subject Matter to Help a Student with a Paper: __Agree __Disagree __Not Sure." *Writing Center Journal* 8 (2): 23–30.

Kaufer, David S., and Cheryl Geisler. 1989. "Novelty in Academic Writing." *Written Communication* 6 (3): 286–311. https://doi.org/10.1177/0741088389006003003.

Kuteeva, Maria, and Raffaella Negretti. 2016. "Graduate Students' Genre Knowledge and Perceived Disciplinary Practices: Creating a Research Space Across Disciplines." *English for Specific Purposes* 41:36–49. https://doi.org/10.1016/j.esp.2015.08.004.

Li, Shuai, and Cheng-Kok Koh. 2013. *An Effective Routability-driven Placer for Mixed-size Circuit Designs*. Purdue Technical Reports. West Lafayette, IN: Purdue University, School of Electrical and Computer Engineering. https://docs.lib.purdue.edu/ecetr/446/.

Lunsford, Andrea. 2008 (1991). "Collaboration, Control, and the Idea of a Writing Center?" *The Writing Center Journal* 12 (1): 3–10. Reprinted in *The Longman Guide to Writing Center Theory and Practice*, ed. Robert W. Barnett and Jacob S. Blumner, 92–99. New York: Pearson Longman, 2008.

Mackiewicz, Jo. 2004. "The Effects of Tutor Expertise in Engineering Writing: A Linguistic Analysis of Writing Tutors' Comments." *IEEE Transactions on Professional Communication* 47 (4): 316–328. https://doi.org/10.1109/TPC.2004.840485.

Phillips, Talinn. 2013. "Tutor Training and Services for Multilingual Graduate Writers: A Reconsideration." *Praxis: A Writing Center Journal* 10 (2).

Powers, Judith K. 1995. "Assisting the Graduate Thesis Writer through Faculty and Writing Center Collaboration." *Writing Lab Newsletter* 20 (2): 13–16.

Reardon, Kristina, Tom Deans, and Cheryl Maykel. 2016. "Finding a Room of Their Own: Programming Time and Space for Grad Student Writing at the UConn Writing Center." *Writing Lab Newsletter* 40 (5–6): 10–17.

Swales, John M. 1990. *Genre Analysis: English in Academic and Research Settings*. New York: Cambridge University Press.

Vorhies, Heather B. 2015. "Building Professional Scholars: The Writing Center at the Graduate Level." *Writing Lab Newsletter* 39 (5–6): 6–9.

Walker, Kristin. 1998. "The Debate over Generalist and Specialist Tutors: Genre Theory's Contribution." *Writing Center Journal* 18 (2): 27–46.

Wolfe, Joanna. 2010. *Team Writing: A Guide to Working in Groups*. Boston: Bedford-St. Martins.

Wolfe, Joanna, Barrie Olson, and Laura Wilder. 2014. "Knowing What We Know about Writing in the Disciplines: A New Approach to Teaching for Transfer in FYC." *WAC Journal* 25:42–77.

PART III

Expanding the Center

9
A CHANGE FOR THE BETTER
Writing Center/WID Partnerships to Support Graduate Writing

Laura Brady, Nathalie Singh-Corcoran, and James Holsinger

Graduate students pose a unique challenge to writing centers: their writing projects are increasingly specialized and support from department to department is idiosyncratic. For obvious reasons such as scale, scope, and methods, there is no singular way to structure a thesis or dissertation. Even when writing centers consult with dissertation advisors, advisors do not always know what they are looking for, or they may have difficulty articulating their writing advice. On the students' side, dissertation writers don't always know how to ask the right questions of their faculty advisors. As a result of all these factors, Nathalie, the director of our writing center, saw a clear need to partner with writing-in-the-disciplines (WID) initiatives being led by Laura to offer focused support to graduate students working on theses and dissertations as well as provide support for their faculty advisors. Together, the directors could examine the assumptions, expectations, and needs of graduate students and faculty advisors. We could then assess the role of general versus discipline-specific tutoring strategies for clients writing extended genres (such as theses and dissertations) to see what kinds of changes might be involved in moving from a largely undergraduate writing center to a renamed Studio that also supports advanced graduate student writers. While the partnership made sense to both directors, the question was how to initiate and manage the changes that would need to occur.

While we will describe our local situation to show the change process in our writing center, our larger goal in this chapter is to suggest a framework for change that can help writing center directors anticipate, initiate, manage, and continue their own programmatic growth—especially in terms of changes that support graduate students working on theses and dissertations (Kamler and Thomson 2014; Paré, Starke-Meyerring, and McAlpine 2011; Simpson 2012; Lee and Golde 2013).

DOI: 10.7330/9781607327516.c009

SOME LOCAL CONTEXT

Let us give you a brief background. Our undergraduate writing center was established in 2005, and it primarily served students in our first-year composition sequence. However, as general education requirements shifted to include writing, speaking, and communication across the curriculum (CAC) more broadly, our center began to offer more WAC support to undergraduate students. This new emphasis on WAC also helped us see the need for discipline-focused graduate student support as a natural extension of our center's work. When our institution became concerned with graduate-level retention and completion rates, we saw an opening for establishing a more formal and intentional WID/writing center partnership. This more formal partnership was something we had already hoped to pursue given that both the writing center and the WID initiatives shared the common goals of supporting student writing and the teaching of writing. We could also readily see how each program could inform the other by sharing data and research; to that end, we did a broad survey of WAC/WID and writing center scholarship to lend support to our efforts (already underway) to gain additional resources for both L2 (English second language) writers, another pressing need, and graduate student writers across campus.

In 2013, the Office of Graduate Education and Life gave us a small amount of pilot funding to explore ways we could expand our work to serve advanced graduate student writers specifically. With that seed money, we've built a program that continues to grow. In the pilot year (2014) alone, we saw a 21 percent increase in graduate students seeking help on theses and dissertations. Since 2014, we have focused on establishing our ethos across campus, building alliances, and assessing needs and resources. What resources did we have and what resources would we need to develop? Where else could we find support, and where might we encounter resistance? We turned to Organizational Development theory to help us answer these questions.

Organizational Development (OD) theory pays attention to when and how change occurs—episodically or continuously, proactively or reactively. In 1999, Karen Vaught-Alexander contributed a chapter to the collection *Writing Centers and Writing Across the Curriculum Programs* that drew on Organizational Development theory to create partnerships (Vaught-Alexander 1999). Her chapter includes several smart ideas about how to understand the structures, motivations, and resistance associated with change as it occurs within universities and within writing centers. OD theory explains that readiness for change is likely to vary in relation to the perceived value of the change and the situational context (Weiner 2009, 4). Is the change important or necessary? Is the change realistic and achievable given the available resources? How does the local context shape the ways in which programs develop and evolve? The following points, based in OD theory, structure the remainder of this essay but also provide change principles that we hope will help other sites analyze resources necessary to develop and sustain writing support for graduate students on their own campuses:

- Change Is Contextual: Survey the Local Environment
- Change Is Spiral: Adapt and Evolve
- Change Is Gradual: Develop Collaborative Solutions
- Change Is Strategic: Know the Available Resources
- Change Is Ongoing: Reflect and Revise (again)

CHANGE IS CONTEXTUAL: SURVEY THE LOCAL ENVIRONMENT

Were our university stakeholders—faculty and graduate students—receptive to new support for graduate writing? Before we began the pilot, we needed to understand the environment for graduate student writing on our campus. The university's strategic plan gave us an overarching goal: improve retention and completion rates. Yet the underlying issues surrounding retention and completion—the general sense that "graduate students have problems with writing"—had not been explored. We set out to uncover those issues. What was it about their writing that posed problems? And could our writing center/WID partnership help us address graduate writing concerns more effectively?

We circulated brief surveys to graduate students and faculty across the disciplines to ask if graduate tutoring would be useful. In the faculty survey, we asked respondents to identify the likelihood that they would refer advanced graduate students to a writing center for writing assistance. Twenty-six percent of the faculty from across the represented disciplines responded to the survey. Of these faculty responses, 90 percent saw the potential value of graduate writing support and said they would refer students. About 10 percent of the graduate student body responded to the survey, lower than the faculty response rate but still a representative sample of their numbers in the social sciences, sciences, and humanities. Responses were again positive: 85 percent of the responding graduate students agreed that graduate writing tutoring had potential to aid students as they moved toward completion of their degrees and said it was likely that they would seek writing assistance for projects like theses and dissertations and for general writing help.

Now we needed more specific insights. We followed the survey with in-depth interviews with advanced graduate students and faculty supervising dissertations and master's theses who represented the humanities, the sciences, and the social sciences. We interviewed a total of twelve participants (six faculty and six graduate students), asking them to describe the most common genres in their fields and to identify specific challenges facing advanced writers. We found some interesting parallels in their responses. For example, both faculty and graduate students cited literature reviews, scholarly articles, conference presentations, and grants as the most common genres, with a couple of mentions of case histories and "standards" of documentation.

One biology professor explained that advanced graduate students have difficulty "summarizing their work into a compelling story"; a psychology professor made a similar observation. A colleague from anthropology noted that graduate students have to learn how to select the scholarly studies most relevant to their own project, identify key concepts, and then use those concepts as a bridge to their own work, and that this process becomes increasingly important as advanced students work on theses or dissertations. A graduate student in Spanish recognized problems "forming a cohesive argument once completing and comprehending reading; forming an analysis without presenting it as a series of disconnected thoughts." A graduate student in geography described the dissertation genre as "hard to pin down" and noted the challenges of trying to write "something I've never done before; a brand new venture." In other words, faculty and graduate students both seem well aware of the difficulty in moving from novice to expert (see Paré, Starke-Meyerring, and McAlpine 2011).

As we reviewed the responses from both faculty and graduate students, we noticed another pattern: both groups remarked on the difficulty that graduate writers often have with the process of putting everything together and saying something new while making a sustained argument, a response consistent with the patterns that Paré, Starke-Meyerring, and McAlpine (2011) have identified: as writers advance from novice to expert, they shift roles from undergraduate "eavesdroppers" who listen in to academic conversations; to ventriloquists who, as new members of a discipline, project someone else's voice to make their own points; to "stewards of their discipline" who participate as active members the field, often through their own writing (219). A WID/writing center partnership can be particularly helpful in informing and supporting graduate student writers' development as they move through these shifting roles, as the following example demonstrates.

A graduate student in geography came to the writing center when her advisor asked her to develop a more "academic" tone in her dissertation prospectus. She brought in a sample of her writing where the faculty member had red-lined and rewritten several sentences to illustrate what he wanted from her. The advisor cut excess words but liked the overall content. Because the student is still developing her own authority as a writer, she focused on the red-lined marks and saw herself as a failed writer; she overlooked the fact that her content was solid. She saw his line edits as errors to be corrected rather than in terms of disciplinary conventions to be mastered. On his side, this faculty member knew he wanted a more "academic" tone, but did not know how to explain what he meant by that in terms of readers' expectations within this field of study. A WID/writing center partnership might help address this and other writers' concerns about how to project more authority in their work by providing a better understanding of the rhetorical moves involved in making and conveying disciplinary knowledge. Recent scholarship explains that poor doctoral writing is often tied to issues of authority; as Barbara Kamler and Pat Thomson note, it's difficult to "write as an authority when one does not feel authoritative" (Kamler and Thomson 2008, 508). "Texts and identities are formed together," they explain, "in and through writing" (508). It's hard to contribute with confidence when you are still learning what is expected in your field.

Faculty advisors like the one in the example we just offered helped us identify a niche that our partnership might fill: we could provide some principles and strategies to faculty and tutors for explaining disciplinary conventions and expectations. Some advisors clearly have a language for talking about advanced disciplinary writing with their advisees, but others do not. We were heartened to hear that some advisors teach seminars focused on writing and that others provide continuous, formative feedback on everything from course papers to theses and dissertations, but we still heard faculty who expected students at the doctoral level to already possess a certain degree of writing proficiency. And none of the graduate student respondents mentioned receiving explicit writing instruction in a course.

In other words, it seems that even when faculty think they are providing advanced disciplinary-writing instruction, the graduate students are not recognizing it as such. In fact, when graduate students mentioned their advisors or committee, they were as likely to view the committee as mercurial rather than helpful. A study by Paul Rogers, Terry Myers Zawacki, and Sarah Baker helps account for the challenges for both writers and supervisors (Rogers, Zawacki, and Baker 2016). Their study revealed that doctoral students and their supervisors look at the dissertation writing processes from very different perspectives. The disciplinary conventions are so familiar to the faculty that they are almost invisible; the students, however, are still novices who are trying to locate, name, and practice these markers (64). It's not surprising then that doctoral students desire *more* one-on-one support from their supervisors, *more* explicit instruction, and *more* specific comments (66–68). This need for explicitness suggests that as writers develop expertise, they also must develop a conscious awareness of situated rhetorical moves (Kamler and Thomson 2014; Paré 2011).

We do not have the space in this chapter to address the challenges specific to English second language (L2) graduate student writers, but we were turning our attention to their needs and that scholarship, too (Paltridge and Starfield 2007; Casanave and Li 2008; Curry and Lillis 2013; Casanave 2014; Simpson, Caplan, Cox, and Phillips 2016). We were, in sum, convinced of the need to support all graduate student writers as they became authorities in their respective fields.

We could now focus on what OD theory calls "change efficacy" (Weiner 2009) by asking: do we know what it will take to implement this change effectively; do we have the resources to implement this change effectively; and can we implement this change effectively given the situation we currently face?

CHANGE IS SPIRAL: ADAPT AND EVOLVE TO MEET LOCAL CONDITIONS

Prior to the pilot, the writing center was already supporting some graduate students on an informal basis when they would drop in to work with undergraduate peer tutors, as we noted earlier. As we reviewed the survey results and the interview transcripts, we saw the need to offer focused support for advanced students working on theses and dissertations. We did not have the space or the funds to create a specially designated center for graduate students, but we did have enough money to create two new graduate peer consultant positions dedicated to working on extended writing genres. We could also develop new training materials that emphasized theses, proposals, and dissertations. Finally, we could review and adapt existing policies and procedures for a new set of clients (e.g., graduate appointments are typically longer and we specify that we will not serve as a proxy for a dissertation or master's thesis chair). But first we had to get advanced graduate students to use the support we were offering.

It is not a secret that most graduate students feel pressure to be competent in their fields—junior members of their professional communities. The pressure to somehow already know everything often precludes asking for help, particularly from fellow graduate students. This reluctance is compounded by the misconception that a writing center is mostly a place of remediation. To take this a step further, as Elizabeth Boquet (1999) points out, many teachers and students continue to see the directive to "go to the writing center" as a "disciplinary measure" (469). Boquet surmises that most students find the writing center a "safe place," *despite* the mandate to seek writing help from their professors, but we needed to consider the possibility that many graduate students would feel some embarrassment or inadequacy in seeking specialized help with writing.

To adapt to this particular perception, we tried a simple name change from Writing Center to Writing Studio, which we hoped would thwart potentially negative associations with tutoring. The graduate peers who work in the center are not tutors but "consultants." These subtle shifts in language are also intended to signal a more collaborative exchange as we recast the writing center image to focus on graduate students' needs and actions.

To change our protocols, we re-examined our goals and approaches. What did we want to achieve with a graduate consulting studio? We hoped that increased support would help graduate students come to see writing as a way of knowing *and* doing (Carter 2007). The kinds of questions we found ourselves asking the advanced graduate students who sought help from the writing center were similar to the questions that Douglas Downs and Elizabeth Wardle describe as central to "a course about how to understand and think about writing in school and society" (Downs and Wardle 2007, 558). We recast their questions only slightly to ask graduate student writers the following during consultation sessions:

- How does [your] writing work?
- How do people [in your discipline] use writing?
- What are [your] problems related to writing and reading?
- How can [writing consultants help you solve your problems]? (558)

We try to make explicit our Studio and consultants' assumptions that "good" writing is rhetorically aware, context specific, and situated. Yet, while the consultants may ask questions like those we just listed, they may not have the expertise to address the graduate writer's responses to those questions or the disciplinary knowledge of the genres that may be invoked. For instance, if we think about the interview with the geography student who described the dissertation as "something I've never done before; a brand new venture," then the consultant may have difficulty knowing just what questions to ask next, and the writer may also not have a clear enough sense of the conventions to direct further conversation. This is the challenge in helping graduate students write and speak with more authority as they make the transition from novice to expert (Paré, Starke-Meyerring, and McAlpine 2011). As one of the faculty members noted in our preliminary survey: "If tutors do not understand scientific writing or the norms of a particular field, they are not always very helpful."

We now needed to consider whether our consultants (primarily graduate students in English) would have the knowledge and expertise necessary for providing effective feedback to peers in other disciplines, especially when the greatest demand for our services often comes from students in STEM fields.

CHANGE IS GRADUAL: DEVELOP COLLABORATIVE SOLUTIONS

The STEM faculty member we mentioned earlier who wished for consultants with disciplinary knowledge echoes recent writing center research that suggests generalist or non-expert tutors are less successful at providing global feedback than discipline-specific (a.k.a. expert) tutors. According to Sue Dinitz and Susanmarie Harrington, disciplinary expertise increases tutor effectiveness from both the faculty and student perspectives (Dinitz and Harrington 2014). In their study, they found that generalist tutors focused primarily on usage errors because they lacked the disciplinary authority to overcome a student's resistance when they tried to offer more global feedback. Whereas expert tutors were more likely to "more accurately analyze students' ideas, drafts, and input, and then push back when the students' analyses were based on a faulty understanding of writing in the discipline" (92). Dinitz and Harrington acknowledge that it may be impossible to staff a writing center with expert tutors but that staff development should place a greater emphasis on preparing tutors to work with students outside of their own majors. (See Reineke et al. in this volume for an example of such tutor preparation.)

While Dinitz and Harrington's research focuses on undergraduate peer tutors, their work resonates across contexts. Training and reflection can also improve the effectiveness of generalist graduate-student tutors. Our writing center's investment in WAC/WID initiatives has helped us start to address the challenges of cross-disciplinary training and consulting. We've adapted one such initiative from Heather Robinson and Jonathan Hall, who recognize the value of helping students understand the conventions and contexts for writing (Robinson and Hall 2013). Like Dinitz and Harrington, they note that the writing center tutor's role has too often been "limited to giving feedback as a general reader" (30). To help tutors develop the disciplinary knowledge they need to be more informed readers, Robinson and Hall advocate discipline- and assignment-specific tutoring tools, or DATTs. DATTs, collaboratively created by tutors and disciplinary faculty, "provide a breakdown of the task and the strategies used to negotiate the actual writing of the assignment" (34). They've found that their basic scaffolding of assignment description, conventions, and strategies has proven adaptable and replicable. The DATTs have several additional advantages.

- DATTs provide continuity of knowledge and process as tutors change from year to year. (38)
- They create a more active role for the tutors when the DATTs are used to set agendas for "document-led collaboration" with student writers. (39–40)
- They integrate disciplinary faculty as part of the Writing Center/Studio team. (42)

Our writing center is currently collaborating with graduate faculty to create DATTs for genres that advanced graduate writers report the most difficulty with, like the proposal or the literature review. So far, Laura and Nathalie have been the main points of contact with faculty but meet monthly with the graduate consultants to keep them involved in the conversations. The graduate consultants then develop new resources based on the faculty needs. These discipline- and task-specific resources can be used internally (at the department-level) and at the writing center.

For us, collaborative problem solving has proven an effective way to address the challenges of cross-disciplinary development and support for graduate writing. New approaches and actions lead to new insights. As organizational change theory emphasizes, "the way to change culture is not to first change how people think, but instead to start by changing how people behave—what they *do*" (Shook 2010, 66). In addition to adapting Robinson and Hall 's DATT approach to graduate genres, we now encourage interdisciplinary professional development among our consultants. In their first year, all graduate consultants complete a reading list that focuses specifically on WAC/WID, writing centers, and writing pedagogy (see the appendix for this list). Their reading, in combination with their consulting work, informs the workshops that they design and lead each term and often leads to new collaborative research projects.

Purpose: What exactly do I want to happen?
Audience: Who is reading, listening, or viewing?
Conventions: What is expected in this context?
Trouble: What could get in the way of my goals?

Figure 9.1. PACT graphic and key questions

We are also asking faculty and students across the curriculum to use a common set of questions for thinking rhetorically about the situations that shape genres. The four key questions (figure 9.1) remind writers to consider purpose, audience, conventions and trouble-shooting (PACT) for any communication.

The PACT heuristic encourages conversations around writing. As we have argued elsewhere (Brady and Singh-Corcoran 2016, 6–8), the PACT heuristic does more than encourage graduate consultants and graduate student writers to reflect on their communicative assumptions, expectations, and needs. PACT has also helped us remain mindful of our programmatic situation as we consider our goals, our audiences and alliances, institutional expectations and challenges.

We are, in other words, relying on a series of collaborative actions to change behaviors and change the culture as we develop support for graduate writing. As Claire Aitchison and Anthony Paré assert, "it takes more than one-off courses or writing retreats to create the sort of nurturing and challenging environment that develops writing abilities" (Aitchison and Paré 2012, 20). Like many graduate writing centers, we offer tutoring, workshops, a dissertation retreat, and writing groups. We are starting to collaborate with faculty. We know that we could do more—especially in terms of supporting our multilingual graduate writers. But we also want to remain aware of our limits in terms of our available resources and potentially changing conditions.

CHANGE IS STRATEGIC: KNOW THE AVAILABLE RESOURCES

Once we had established our WID/writing center partnership as necessary, important, and beneficial to strategic goals and our graduate students' progress, we needed to consider what factors would foster the success—or failure—of our partnership over time. Human and financial resources were among the first factors we considered.

In terms of human resources, our graduate writing center/WID partnership relies in part on administrative support from both the writing center director and the WAC director. This administrative support relies in turn on commitments at the department and college level to count the work in terms of each director's annual goals. Other key resources include an interdisciplinary advisory group at the college level (SpeakWrite 2015) and an established funding alliance with the university's Office of Graduate Education and Life. Our human resources fell short, however, in one key area. We needed more consultants at the outset, and we find ourselves in need of additional consultants again as we grow. In addition to recruiting graduate-level consultants, we are continually considering the budgets, spaces, professional development, and structures associated with our partnership as it develops and expands.

Almost any expansion confronts the question of financial resources. We asked for two dedicated graduate consultants for the pilot. Each would be available ten hours a week (a half-time appointment) and would be paid as part of a dedicated graduate teaching assistantship (GTA). The pilot has proved so successful that the Office of Graduate Education and Life approached us with an offer of additional financial support if we can expand our consultations. We like the continuity that a dedicated GTA assignment allows, but, as we grow, we will try adding more GTA consultants who are paid on an hourly basis. (At our university, GTAs can be compensated for an additional one-hundred hours beyond their main appointment if they are certified as making satisfactory progress toward their degrees.) Additional consultants will, we hope, allow us to add some flexibility to respond to high-demand times and to recruit beyond our traditional English pool.

We also want to be mindful of Christine Jensen Sundstrom's (2014) accounts of the success yet subsequent demise (2016) of a graduate writing program at the University of Kansas. Her cautionary tale reflects on what their program did well, pointing to strong alliances, offerings well-suited to graduate student and faculty needs, and a rhetorical-genre approach. But she also reflects on what went wrong, such as shifts in institutional vision and support structures and reduced budgets (Sundstrom 2016, 197–99). Sundstrom's analysis reminds us that the evolution of a program rarely follows a straight line. Changing conditions shape survival, variation, or extinction, so programs have to continue to reflect, revise, and adapt (Brady 2013, 11).

CHANGE IS ONGOING: REFLECT AND REVISE

While changes in administration and budget are beyond any program's control, reflective practices (such as Sundstrom's) allow writing center and WAC directors to remain mindful of their programmatic situation. Ongoing and sustainable changes rely on taking stock of existing strengths as well as needs; framing specific practical goals within the larger mission of the program and university; committing to collaborative problem solving; and practicing regular review (Reid 2003, 21; Brady 2006, 31). With the goal of continuous, ongoing change in mind, we suggest creating a map as one way to reflect and take stock. Again, we offer an example based on our program.

A concept map made us consider the overall structure of our program and goals in new ways. What and who were central? What and who were marginalized? Creating a conceptual map is consistent with Dan Melzer's (2013) call for Critical Systems Thinking (CST) as a methodology to understand, critique, and transform campus writing programs. In addition to analyzing how structures and processes relate to each other, Melzer explains that understanding these relationships can locate points of leverage where even small changes will affect the entire system: "These points of leverage are typically points in the system that have a high level of connection to multiple actors in the system, so that any change in the leverage point would affect many actors and have long-term ramifications for the entire system" (78). One such leverage point might be a negative reinforcing process that has potential to become a positive reinforcing process (90). On our campus, for example, dissatisfaction with graduate-level completion rates and a lack of systematic support for dissertation writers and their advisors offered a catalyst for positive change, prompting us to map the various relationships on our campus.

To give you a sense of our first map, imagine a series of concentric circles. We initially put the Writing Studio in the inner circle, at the center of our map, since our WID/writing center partnership began with tutoring support for advanced graduate student writers. Several actors inhabited this central Studio space: the Writing Studio director, the undergraduate peer consultants, and both undergraduate and graduate students seeking help with their writing. In the next circle, we had the English Department *and* the College of Arts and Sciences, both of which provide funding for our Studio. This circle included our department chair since the department hires and funds the position of Writing Studio director, but also our dean and a senior associate dean since the College funds the undergraduate peer consultants. This dual oversight also applies to the WAC/WID director. The WAC/WID director's position is appointed and partially funded by the dean of the college to oversee college-wide writing initiatives; the position is also subject to annual review by the department chair as a salaried faculty member in English. Beyond the Studio and the department/college levels we added two more circles to represent the Office of Graduate Education and Life and the university itself. Our institution prides itself on its Carnegie ranking as a "Highest Research Activity" doctoral institution (The Carnegie Classification of Institutions of Higher Education 2015). As a result, university administrators and the Office of Graduate Education and Life both place a high value on PhD completion rates.

As we looked at this series of circles, however, we realized that the concentric circles that placed the Studio at the center could also isolate the Studio unless we emphasized movement across circles. The *borders around* the concentric circles offered a new space to consider, especially if we wanted boundaries to be permeable rather than rigid. These border zones helped us identify points of leverage. Rather than accepting that all change at our university moved from the top down, our mapping helped us to realize that two positions had a high level of connection to multiple actors in the system: the Writing Studio director and the WAC/WID director. Both positions frequently cross borders to foster effective communication across the disciplines; both interact with students, faculty, and administrators across campus; both meet regularly as members of the composition faculty and as standing members of an interdisciplinary advisory board that is part of a communication-across-curriculum initiative (SpeakWrite 2015). By focusing on shared communication goals and faculty-student interactions, we were able to shift from a traditional spatial map that simply located where we were to a dynamic and conceptual map that would let us analyze how and why structures, roles, and assumptions influence each other.

For instance, the university's concerns over graduate writing are motivated, at least in part, by the effect that low graduate-degree completion rates have on Carnegie research rankings. If we keep our focus on these high-level concerns, we value rankings over student needs. By placing the WID/writing center partnership at the center, we shift our attention to the actors and actions that support advanced graduate student writers in small but significant ways such as new resources for working on extended graduate genres. We focus less on failure rates and more on the causes for slow completion rates; we consider the needs of novice members as they become expert in their chosen fields of study. We can also focus on feedback strategies that might help faculty bridge the gap for their students between novice and expert. That is, Melzer's application of CST to campus writing programs has helped us reflect on our WID/writing center partnership and our goals in new ways.

Periodically charting relationships and trying different components at the center will also help us clarify future plans. For instance, what might it look like to put advanced graduate students and their advisors at the center of the map? How might focusing on points of connection between them and other actors in the university system help us create new alliances? We are already thinking about how that future map might include our research librarians, the Office of International Students and Scholars, and our university's Teaching and Learning Commons (which provides teaching support and resources for faculty, graduate students, and postdoctoral fellows).

CONCLUSION

Large-scale change does not occur quickly. Organizational development theory has helped us imagine possibilities and partnerships by giving us a means to anticipate, manage and sustain change that is tailored to our local needs, opportunities, and constraints. We are mindful, however, that even carefully designed support for advanced graduate student writers can fail. Again we heed Sundstrom's cautionary tale. She reminds us that that the long-term support of graduate student writers will need "high-level administrative support and a solid financial footing," and she suggests ways in which current scholarship and coalitions can lend stability across institutional efforts to support graduate student writers (Sundstrom 2016, 204). On our campus, analyses of organizational structures and local alliances at the university, college, and department levels have (so far) helped us anticipate and mitigate threats such as recent budget cuts and upper-level administrative changes, but we need to keep attending to those alliances. And we need to keep gathering evidence. We can demonstrate increased demand through quantitative tracking and surveys; we can offer qualitative evidence through interviews with faculty and students. We need to start thinking about other data, such as assessment. Just as important, we need to follow Sundstrom's advice to develop scholarship and alliances that go beyond institutional borders.

We plan to use research to draw productive parallels to work at other institutions. For instance, we are in the process of replicating George Mason University's multimethod study of doctoral students and advisors (see Rogers, Zawacki, and Baker 2016). We are already seeing valuable patterns across our two institutions that demonstrate the ongoing need to support advanced graduate writers in the areas we have already described above as well as a need to develop support and training for dissertation advisors (for one model of such support and training, see Perdue, this volume). We also hope to contribute to the growing coalition of support for graduate student writing by presenting and publishing our work so that we all continue to learn from each other's experiences.

We are excited, for instance, by the efforts of the Consortium on Graduate Communication (co-founded by Nigel Caplan, University of Delaware, and Michelle Cox, Cornell University) and by the scholarly work collected and edited by Steve Simpson et al. (2016) in *Supporting Graduate Student Writers: Research, Curriculum, and Program Design*. We have already cited Rogers, Zawacki, and Baker's study of doctoral students and advisors as well Sundstrom's cautionary tale (both in this collection). We simply do not have the space to pursue the implications of other compelling studies in the collection that look at the inner struggles of dissertation writers (Casanave 2016), the challenges of international students (Fairbanks and Dias 2016; Mallett, Haan, and Habib 2016), and issues of program and curriculum design through a series of program profiles such as those at Ohio Univeristy or the University of Toronto (Phillips 2016; Freeman 2016). We are also grateful for special issues of *Across the Disciplines* (2015) and *WLN: A Journal of Writing Center Scholarship* (2016) that have focused on support for graduate writers. Sustained support for graduate student writing ultimately relies on the collective and collaborative actions of small groups of faculty and students working not only across campus but also across institutions.

APPENDIX
Reading List for Graduate Consultants
Graduate Writing Consultancy—Selected Readings
- Megan Kittle Autry and Michael Carter. "Unblocking Occluded Genres in Graduate Writing." *Composition Forum* 31 (Spring 2015). http://compositionforum.com/issue/31/north-carolina-state.php
- Michelle Cox, "WAC: Closing Doors or Opening Doors for Second Language Writers?" *Across the Disciplines*, vol. 8, issue 4, 2011. http://wac.colostate.edu/atd/ell/cox.cfm
- Sue Dinitz and Susanmarie Harrington, "The Role of Disciplinary Expertise in Shaping Writing Tutorials." *The Writing Center Journal*, vol. 33, issue 2, Fall/Winter 2014, pp. 73–98. Stable URL: http://www.jstor.org/stable/43443372

- Anthony Paré, Doreen Starke-Meyerring, and Lynn McAlpine. "The Dissertation as Multigenre: Many Readers, Many Readings." *Genre in a Changing World*, edited by Charles Bazerman, Adair Bonini, and Débora Figueiredo. Perspectives on Writing Series, The WAC Clearinghouse and Parlor Press, 2009, pp. 179–93. http://wac.colostate.edu/books/genre/chapter9.pdf
- Heather M. Robinson and Jonathan Hall. "Connecting WID and the Writing Center: Tools for Collaboration." *The WAC Journal* 24 (2013): 29–47. http://wac.colostate.edu/journal/vol24/robinson.pdf
- Steve Simpson, "Introduction." *Supporting Graduate Student Writers: Research, Curriculum, and Program Design*, edited by Steve Simpson, Nigel A. Caplan, Michelle Cox, and Talinn Phillips, U of Michigan P, 2016, pp. 1–20. https://www.press.umich.edu/pdf/9780472036684-intro.pdf

Writing across the Curriculum: A Critical Sourcebook
- Michael Carter, "Ways of Knowing, Doing, and Writing in the Disciplines," pp. 212–38.
- Michael Pemberton, "*Rethinking* the *WAC*/Writing Center Connection," 366–79.
- Christopher Thaiss, "Theory in WAC: Where Have We Been, Where Are We Going?" pp. 85–101.

St. Martin's Sourcebook for Writing Tutors
- Part I. Tutoring Process: Exploring Paradigms and Practices, pp. 1–32
- Steven North, "The Idea of a Writing Center," pp. 44–57
- Jeff Brooks, "Minimalist Tutoring: Making the Student Do All the Work," pp. 128–32
- Linda Shamoon and Deborah Burns, "A Critique of Pure Tutoring," pp. 133–47
- Terese Thonus, "Tutoring and Students Assessments of Academic Writing Tutorials: What is 'Success'?", pp. 175–99
- Julie Neff, "Learning Disabilities and the Writing Center," pp. 249–62
- Sharon Myers, "Reassessing the 'Proof Reading Trap': ESL Tutoring and Writing Instruction," pp. 284–301
- Nancy Barron and Nancy Grimm, "Addressing Racial Diversity in a Writing Center: Stories and Lessons from Two Beginners," pp. 302–25
- David Sheridan, "Words, Images, Sounds: Writing Centers as Multiliteracy Centers," pp. 334–43

ESL Writers: A Guide for Writing Center Tutors
- Nancy Hayward, "Insights into Cultural Divides," pp. 1–15
- Paul Kei Matsuda and Michelle Cox, "Reading an ESL Writer's Text," pp. 39–47
- Carol Severino. "Avoiding Appropriation," pp. 48–59
- Jennifer Staben and Kathryn Dempsey Nordhaus. "Looking at the Whole Text," pp. 71–83
- Cynthia Linville, "Editing Line By Line," pp. 84–93
- Kurt Bouman, "Raising Questions about Plagiarism," pp. 105–16

Online Resources
- Brooks-Gillies, Marilee, Garcia, Elena G., Kim, Soo Hyon, Manthey, Katie, and Smith, Trixie. (2015, August 25). Graduate Writing across the Disciplines, Introduction [Special issue on graduate writing across the disciplines]. *Across the Disciplines, 12*(3). Retrieved December 3, 2015, from http://wac.colostate.edu/atd/graduate_wac/intro.cfm
- Consortium on Graduate Communication
- "Dissertations" handout from the UNC Writing Center: http://writingcenter.unc.edu/handouts/dissertations/
- SpeakWrite Studio pages—especially https://speakwrite.wvu.edu/writing-studio/writing-handouts
- The WAC Clearinghouse: https://wac.colostate.edu/
- *The WAC Journal*: https://wac.colostate.edu/journal/

REFERENCES

Aitchison, Claire, and Anthony Paré. 2012. "Writing as Craft and Practice in Doctoral Education." In *Reshaping Doctoral Education: International Approaches and Pedagogies*, ed. Alison Lee and Susan Danby, 12–25. London: Routledge.

Boquet, Elizabeth. 1999. "'Our Little Secret': A History of Writing Centers, Pre- to Post-Open Admissions." *College Composition and Communication* 50 (3): 463–82. https://doi.org/10.2307/358861.

Brady, Laura. 2006. "A Greenhouse for Writing Program Change." *WPA. Writing Program Administration* 29 (3): 27–43.

Brady, Laura. 2013. "Evolutionary Metaphors for Understanding WAC/WID." *WAC Journal* 24:7–27.

Brady, Laura, and Nathalie Singh-Corcoran. 2016. "A Space for Change: Writing Center Partnerships to Support Graduate Writing." *WLN: A Journal of Writing Center Scholarship* 40 (5–6): 2–9.

The Carnegie Classification of Institutions of Higher Education. 2015. "About Carnegie Classification." http://carnegieclassifications.iu.edu/.

Carter, Michael. 2007. "Ways of Knowing, Doing, and Writing in the Disciplines." *College Composition and Communication* 58 (3): 385–418.

Casanave, Christine Pearson. 2014. *Before the Dissertation: A Textual Mentor for Doctoral Students at Early Stages of a Research Project*. Ann Arbor: University of Michigan Press. https://doi.org/10.3998/mpub.7111486.

Casanave, Christine Pearson. 2016. "What Advisors Need to Know about the Invisible 'Real-Life' Struggles of Doctoral Dissertation Writers." In *Supporting Graduate Student Writers: Research, Curriculum, and Program Design*, ed. Steve Simpson, Nigel A. Caplan, Michelle Cox, and Talinn Phillips, 97–116. Ann Arbor: University of Michigan Press.

Casanave, Christine Pearson, and Xiaoming Li, eds. 2008. *Learning the Literacy Practices of Graduate School: Insiders' Reflections on Academic Enculturation*. Ann Arbor: University of Michigan Press. https://doi.org/10.3998/mpub.231189.

Curry, Mary Jane, and Theresa Lillis. 2013. *A Scholar's Guide to Publishing Journal Articles in English: Critical Choices, Practical Strategies*. Clevedon, UK: Multilingual Matters. https://doi.org/10.21832/9781783090617.

Dinitz, Sue, and Susanmarie Harrington. 2014. "The Role of Disciplinary Expertise in Shaping Writing Tutorials." *Writing Center Journal* 33 (2): 73–98.

Downs, Douglas, and Elizabeth Wardle. 2007. "Teaching about Writing, Righting Misconceptions: (Re)Envisioning 'First-Year Composition' as 'Introduction to Writing Studies.'." *College Composition and Communication* 58 (4): 552–84.

Fairbanks, Katya, and Shamini Dias. 2016. "Going Beyond L2 Graduate Writing: Redesigning an ESL Program to Meet the Needs of Both L2 and L1 Graduate Students." In *Supporting Graduate Student Writers: Research, Curriculum, and Program Design*, ed. Steve Simpson, Nigel A. Caplan, Michelle Cox, and Talinn Phillips, 139–58. Ann Arbor: University of Michigan Press.

Freeman, Jane. 2016. "Designing and Building a Graduate Communication Program at the University of Toronto." In *Supporting Graduate Student Writers: Research, Curriculum, and Program Design*, ed. Steve Simpson, Nigel A. Caplan, Michelle Cox, and Talinn Phillips, 222–38. Ann Arbor: University of Michigan Press.

Kamler, Barbara, and Pat Thomson. 2008. "The Failure of Dissertation Advice Books: Toward Alternative Pedagogies for Doctoral Writing." *Educational Researcher* 37 (8): 507–14.

Kamler, Barbara, and Pat Thomson. 2014. *Helping Doctoral Students Write: Pedagogies for Supervision*, 2nd ed. New York: Routledge.

Lee, Sohui, and Chris Golde. 2013. "Completing the Dissertation and Beyond: Writing Centers and Dissertation Boot Camps." *Writing Lab Newsletter* 37 (7–8): 1–6.

Mallett, Karyn E., Jennifer Haan, and Anna Sophia Habib. 2016. "Graduate Pathway Programs as Sites for Strategic, Language-Supported Internationalization: Four Pedagogical Innovations." In *Supporting Graduate Student Writers: Research, Curriculum, and Program Design*, ed. Steve Simpson, Nigel A. Caplan, Michelle Cox, and Talinn Phillips, 118–38. Ann Arbor: University of Michigan Press.

Melzer, Dan. 2013. "Using Systems Thinking to Transform Writing Programs." *WPA: Writing Program Administration* 36 (2): 75–94.

Paltridge, Brian, and Sue Starfield. 2007. *Thesis and Dissertation Writing in a Second Language: A Handbook for Supervisors*. New York: Routledge.

Paré, Anthony. 2011. "Speaking of Writing: Supervisory Feedback and the Dissertation." In *Doctoral Education: Research-Based Strategies for Doctoral, Supervisors, and Administrators*, ed. Lynn McAlpine and Cheryl Amundsen, 59–74. New York: Springer. https://doi.org/10.1007/978-94-007-0507-4_4.

Paré, Anthony, Doreen Starke-Meyerring, and Lynn McAlpine. 2011. "Knowledge and Identity Work in the Supervision of Doctoral Student Writing: Shaping Rhetorical Subjects." In *Writing in Knowledge Societies*, ed. Doreen Starke-Meyerring, Anthony Paré, Natasha Artemeva, Miriam Horne, and Larissa Yousoubova, 215–36. Anderson, SC: Parlor Press.

Phillips, Talinn. 2016. "Writing Center Support for Graduate Students: An Integrated Model." In *Supporting Graduate Student Writers: Research, Curriculum, and Program Design*, ed. Steve Simpson, Nigel A. Caplan, Michelle Cox, and Talinn Phillips, 159–70. Ann Arbor: University of Michigan Press.

Reid, E. Shelley. 2003. "A Changing for the Better: Curriculum Revision as Reflective Practice in Teaching and Administration." *WPA. Writing Program Administration* 26:10–27.

Robinson, Heather M., and Jonathan Hall. 2013. "Connecting WID and the Writing Center: Tools for Collaboration." *WAC Journal* 24:29–47. http://wac.colostate.edu/journal/vol24/robinson.pdf.

Rogers, Paul, Terry Myers Zawacki, and Sarah E. Baker. 2016. "Uncovering Challenges and Pedagogical Complications in Dissertation Writing and Supervisory Practices: A Multimethod Study of Doctoral Students and Advisors." In *Supporting Graduate Student Writers: Research, Curriculum, and Program Design*, ed. Steve Simpson, Nigel A. Caplan, Michelle Cox, and Talinn Phillips, 52–77. Ann Arbor: University of Michigan Press.

Shook, John. 2010. "How to Change a Culture: Lessons from NUMMI." *Sloan Management Review* (Winter). https://sloanreview.mit.edu/article/how-to-change-a-culture-lessons-from-nummi/.

Simpson, Steve. 2012. "The Problem of Graduate-Level Writing Support: Building a Cross-Campus Graduate Writing Initiative." *WPA. Writing Program Administration* 36 (1): 95–118.

Simpson, Steve, Nigel A. Caplan, Michelle Cox, and Talinn Phillips, eds. 2016. *Supporting Graduate Student Writers: Research, Curriculum, and Program Design*. Ann Arbor: University of Michigan Press. https://doi.org/10.3998/mpub.8772400.

SpeakWrite. 2015. *Eberly College of Arts and Sciences*. West Virginia University. https://speakwrite.wvu.edu.

Sundstrom, Christine Jensen. 2014. "The Graduate Writing Program at the University of Kansas: An Inter-Disciplinary, Rhetorical Genre-Based Approach to Developing Professional Identities." *Composition Forum* 29. http://compositionforum.com/issue/29/.

Sundstrom, Christine Jensen. 2016. "Graduate Writing Instruction: A Cautionary Tale." In *Supporting Graduate Student Writers: Research, Curriculum, and Program Design*, ed. Steve Simpson, Nigel A. Caplan, Michelle Cox, and Talinn Phillips, 192–205. Ann Arbor: University of Michigan Press.

Vaught-Alexander, Karen. 1999. "Situating Writing Centers and Writing across the Curriculum Programs in the Academy: Creating Partnerships for Change with Organizational Development Theory." In *Writing Centers and Writing across the Curriculum Programs: Building Interdisciplinary Partnerships*, ed. Robert W. Barnett and Jacob S. Blumner, 119–40. Westport, CT: Greenwood Press.

Weiner, Bryan. 2009. "A Theory of Organizational Readiness for Change." *Implementation Science; IS* 4 (1): 67. https://doi.org/10.1186/1748-5908-4-67; http://implementationscience.biomedcentral.com/articles/10.1186/1748-5908-4-67.

10
"FIND SOMETHING YOU KNOW YOU CAN BELIEVE IN"
The Effect of Dissertation Retreats on Graduate Students' Identities as Writers

Ashly Bender Smith, Tika Lamsal, Adam Robinson, and Bronwyn T. Williams

Graduate students are often told by well-meaning mentors that they should envision their writing as joining a conversation among a "community of scholars." They are not writing simply to display information, as often happens as undergraduates, but instead taking their part in an ongoing scholarly conversation. Yet the use of this common metaphor does not always include detailed guidance as to how, in fact, a person engages this conversation through writing. For many faculty, the strategies they used in learning to write as a scholar rather than a student are hazy memories at best. Even remembering the strategies, however, may not address questions of confidence and agency that can be troubling to graduate students, often hindering their ability to write effectively at the graduate level. Such anxieties and uncertainties about writing can become particularly vivid, and potentially debilitating, when students are writing their doctoral dissertations. Negotiating the writing demanded by a dissertation is a challenge on a number of levels, including dealing with concerns of genre, authorial position, and style. Also important, but not necessarily as explicitly addressed, is how graduate students perceive themselves as writers and how their attitudes toward writing facilitate or obstruct their abilities to finish their projects. Negotiating the demands of these new writing contexts can be particularly frustrating for graduate students who, after having achieved significant success in their academic lives, are faced with challenges to their confidence as they embark on what is often the highest stakes writing project they have yet to encounter.

To help graduate students negotiate these challenges, the University Writing Center at the University of Louisville has held a series of Dissertation Writing Retreats for doctoral students each May, beginning in 2011. The purpose of the Dissertation Writing Retreat, like many others across the country, is to provide doctoral students the opportunity to focus on their writing, offer feedback on their writing, and help them establish effective writing habits. As we conducted the retreats, however, we also noticed that, in addition to helping students with individual writing concerns, the events influenced how the students thought about themselves as writers, their attitudes toward writing, and their positions as part of a community of writers. In an attempt to assess the efficacy of the retreats, we interviewed a number of participants before one of the retreats and then again six months later. The interviews covered topics such as the students' writing processes, their concerns about completing their dissertations, and their perceptions of themselves as writers. The interview responses illustrated the important role writing centers can play in explicitly engaging graduate students' perceptions of their literate identities. While the message of some dissertation writing retreats is that success should be measured in the number of pages produced by the writers during the retreat, our research offers support for an approach that puts an equal emphasis on less immediately tangible goals such as a more nuanced understanding of writing processes and an enhanced sense of agency as scholarly writers. Writing centers have long noted that writers who attend consultations seem to feel empowered and more confident when they leave. We argue that addressing perceptions of agency by making issues of literate identities part of an ongoing conversation can be a more explicit goal of writing center work with graduate students. For doctoral students in particular, we believe that explicitly engaging conceptions of their emerging scholarly identities, as we do in events such as our dissertation writing retreats, is an important part of our writing center's graduate student mission.

In this chapter we draw on the pre- and post-retreat interviews to discuss the doctoral student participants' perceptions of how the retreat influenced their sense of confidence about their identities as writers and allowed them to be more reflective on and conscious about their writing processes. We maintain that the opportunity provided to the retreat participants to discuss and reflect on their writing processes during workshops, individual sessions with Writing Center consultants, and conversations with fellow retreat participants from across disciplines helped them to continue to develop their identities as emerging scholars. In particular, the participants noted in their post-retreat interviews that the combination of ongoing conversations about writing processes with both peers and writing center consultants, as well as the effects of a shared, social setting for writing, helped them understand more about how they worked most effectively as writers and how they imagined themselves as scholars. The confidence the students expressed can be understood as a crucial element in perceptions of authorial agency that, we believe, can be one of the long-term benefits of a retreat.

We begin the chapter with a brief review of how we situate our approach to retreats in the context of recent discussions of graduate student writing. Then we turn to the reasons the participants expressed in their pre-retreat interviews for wanting to attend the retreat and how those reasons reflected their expectations but also many of their anxieties as writers. While participants noted in their post-retreat interviews a range of experiences from the retreat that they found productive, we focus on two of the experiences that came up frequently as having a positive effect on how they discussed their sense of scholarly writing identity. The first experience was the opportunity to develop and reflect on new writing processes and habits while the second was writing in a common space with a community of fellow writers. Both experiences helped the participants not only to develop a sense of their individual identities as writers and scholars but also to gain a sense of agency in their writing, which, in turn, helped them to perceive themselves as members of their larger scholarly communities. We conclude with implications of our findings for writing centers holding similar retreats as well as for our ongoing writing center work with graduate students.

DISSERTATION WRITING RETREATS—PROCESS AND COMMUNITY

Many dissertation writing retreats—sometimes referred to as camps or boot camps[1]—follow one of two models, according to Sohui Lee and Chris Golde (2013). Retreats are designed with a "Just Write" model that emphasizes producing words or a "Writing Process" model that emphasizes conversations about writing processes and contexts, as well as developing habits for writing productivity. While "Just Write" models are alluring for administrators, advisors, and participants, these models often focus on short-term goals as opposed to preparing participants for longer-term writing success. Our retreat works on the "Writing Process" model as a means toward assisting participants in becoming more effective members of their scholarly community. Our approach is consistent with Lee and Golde's (2013) recommendations that retreats should emphasize the collaborative process of writing through one-hour consultations with Writing Center consultants as well as interactive workshops. Scholarship on doctoral students' writing groups finds that such conversations are influential in helping participants better understand their writing processes and their projects, as well as helping them to provide more effective feedback to other writers (Maher et al. 2008; Aitchison 2009). Although writing groups typically meet over longer periods than retreats, the focus of such groups is similar to that in the consultations and workshops provided in many retreats. Writing consultations in our retreat were often marked by critical, reflective conversations about the structure and conventions of the reviewed text, for example how different sections within a chapter could be organized to more effectively reveal an argument. In addition, one of the interactive workshops covered the function of literature reviews and their forms in different disciplines. Consultations and workshops can help prepare students by engaging them in the kind of informative "talk" about their writing that Kevin Leander and Paul Prior find is influential in improving writing (Leander and Prior 2004).

Even when participants aren't discussing writing conventions and process or reflecting on their own writing, retreats encourage a sense of community through shared space and time, as well as the shared objective of dissertation completion. Damien Maher et al. (2008) found that in writing groups of doctoral students the shared dissertation-completion goal fostered a sense of community because the participants developed an emotional connection with each other that stemmed from the belief that fellow members understood the difficulties of the process and were providing support throughout the process (273). The bond between retreat and writing group members also encourages a sense of accountability among members. In her review of the Dissercamp at Florida State University, Elizabeth Powers (2014) explains that participants "tuned into this ambiance of productivity" marked by a sense of both support and friendly competition (15). Uta Papen and Virginie Theriault found that participants in their writing retreats reported being similarly motivated by the presence of others in the room, such that they would keep writing even when they might otherwise have stopped for the day (Papen and Theriault 2016). Writing group members in another study explained that the community they developed provided an important source of support for their written products as well as their developing academic identities (Badenhorst et al. 2013). These findings emphasize that the protected time and space provided by a dissertation writing retreat is afforded by the physical context, which also allows for a sense of community to develop.

Overall, much of the scholarship on dissertation writing retreats and groups finds that those that are designed with a Writing Process focus are effective in helping participants develop effective writing habits and perspectives about productive writing. Moreover, the Writing Process focus helps academic writers learn from and support one another. This scholarship certainly reveals many of the benefits of Writing Process–focused retreats and groups, particularly with attention to providing focused time and space and emotional support for dissertation completion. An under-considered advantage is the ability for Writing Process–focused retreats to support participants' developing sense of agency as academic writers and members of scholarly communities of practice.

Before moving on to a description of our retreats, it is important to offer a brief definition for how we are employing the concept of "agency" in this chapter. We see agency as reflecting writers' perceptions of their positions in given contexts, as well as their practices. Agency involves not only the skills necessary to undertake a task, but also the perception that one is able—or permitted—to undertake the task at hand. We conceive of agency as a space in which the individual builds upon previous experiences and decisions in order to act, make decisions, and make meaning, in specific social and historical context (Williams 2018). People can have the skills to complete a writing project, but feel their agency is obstructed in some way, such as having to write in a new genre or dealing with discouraging memories of criticism. Many students, including the participants in our study, do not specifically use the term "agency" when they talk about their literacy practices. Even so, when students talk about issues such as having a sense of confidence, putting skills into action, or being able to overcome obstacles in their writing, they are talking about perceptions of agency. We believe that perceptions of agency can be facilitated through mentoring, response, and other forms of support such as the social act of writing together.

BACKGROUND OF OUR RETREAT AND STUDY

The University Writing Center at the University of Louisville held its first dissertation writing retreat in May 2011 and has held one every year since, along with occasional retreats in the summer and online. The May dissertation writing retreats usually comprise twelve to fourteen doctoral students from disciplines and colleges across the university, and six or seven consultants, each of whom works with two writers during the week (the consultants are doctoral students enrolled in the Rhetoric and Composition program; most have writing center experience and are in the dissertation stage themselves). Retreat applicants submit a cover letter explaining their goals in applying for the retreat, a letter of support from their advisor, and their dissertation prospectus or sample chapters. Before the retreat, writers are asked to reflect on their projects and their writing concerns and set goals for the retreat week. In the weeks leading up to the retreat, the writing consultants contact their assigned writers to begin building a relationship that will be key to the success of the retreat.

The retreat runs daily from 8:00 AM to 4:00 PM. The participants write for three hours in the morning, engage in a writing workshop and discussion about a relevant writing issue before lunch, write for a few more hours after lunch, and finish the day with an hour-long consultation. The interactive writing workshops cover a range of topics that doctoral students deal with while writing their dissertations: structuring large writing projects, setting appropriate goals and time management, writing the literature review, responding to committee feedback, and building on effective writing processes learned during the retreat. The retreat takes place at the University Writing Center, where, from the first day, writers establish their personal writing space equipped with the books, data, computers, and other relevant materials they may need. Working in the same space, as well as chatting during lunch and workshops, also builds community, establishes accountability, and emphasizes the social nature of writing.

The research for this chapter resulted from our interest in gauging the effectiveness of the retreats. We decided to do a series of pre- and post-retreat interviews to examine what the participants said about a broad range of questions about their writing. We were interested in any effects the students reported to us. The data for this chapter were gathered before and after the 2014 dissertation writing retreat.[2] Students registered for the retreat were invited to participate in a pre-retreat interview with Bronwyn, the writing center director, to talk about their attitudes toward writing, their conceptions of themselves as writers, their experiences of writing as graduate students, their writing processes, and their goals for the retreat. The interviews took place at the University Writing Center and lasted about an hour. Seven of the fourteen participants took part in all the interviews.[3] Follow-up interviews took place six months after the retreat. In the follow-up interviews, participants were asked to talk again about the points covered in the pre-retreat interviews, as well as their thoughts about how the retreat had or had not been helpful for their writing and their sense of their scholarly identities. Participants were offered the chance to use pseudonyms for publication, but all chose to use their real names.

FINDINGS FROM PRE- AND POST-RETREAT INTERVIEWS
Expectations of the Retreat

The pre-conference interviews revealed several common writing concerns by the participants, including issues around space and community, writing processes, and the nature of their identities as scholars.

In the pre-retreat interviews one theme that emerged from the participants was their lack of focus and time management as key hurdles to writing the dissertation. George, a doctoral student in physics, said that he felt that one of the obstacles he had in writing the dissertation came from trying to focus on writing in the setting of his home department. "That's one reason that I want the retreat because I've got a desk and stuff and workspace, but there are other students in there and one of them, whom I love, is just so hyper doing other things and he's really bright, but there's a lot of distraction there. I need the discipline of coming to another place." Several participants expressed the hope that the retreat would provide a quiet space where they could focus on writing. They spoke about the struggle they often felt from the underlying tensions of balancing their academic work and their daily lives, tensions which included finding time and space for writing. At the same time, the idea of having a space to write did not necessarily mean they wanted to write in isolation. Several participants specifically mentioned that they were looking forward to the idea of being with other people who were working on their dissertations.

The participants' expectations of what they would experience at the retreat were varied. Not all of the writers were sure what to expect at the retreat, and some participants were initially hoping for the "Just Write" retreat model, with no time being spent on consultations and workshops. Other participants were excited to be exposed to different perspectives about their writing and their writing processes from the workshops and consultations. Katie, a doctoral student in comparative humanities, specifically pointed out that she hoped the retreat would give her the opportunity to "talk about ways to actually be writing this next year." She said one of her goals would to "create a writing approach that will maximize my efforts . . . but also . . . be transferred to my future lengthier writing and research projects that I will be completing the rest of my academic career." Katie also said she thought the retreat, with its diversity of disciplines, could provide her with new strategies and perspectives that might be helpful to her own process.

In the pre-retreat interviews, the students expressed concerns about whether their writing habits were as productive as they might be. Though they often did not use the term "writing process," they did talk about their writing practices and wondered if they were taking the most effective approach to dissertation writing, even though most of them also felt that, in general, they were already good writers. Carol, a student in comparative humanities, said that, during her studies, "A couple of my professors had reinforced the fact that I was actually a very good writer. That I was apparently much better at it than many of my colleagues." Yet she said those previous experiences had not necessarily left her feeling prepared for writing her dissertation. She said she felt confident in her knowledge of the scholarship, but not as confident in how to progress through the writing of her dissertation. "That's something I feel like I've struggled with, while getting the PhD, that I still am missing some fundamental bare bones of how to build things."

Along with concerns about process, participants such as Carol also talked about their concerns about writing in isolation and establishing and communicating an appropriate scholarly identity. Carol noted that, after she had finished her doctoral exams, she was not sure what to do next toward working on her dissertation and did not get much guidance from her director, a pattern that had continued. "There was a period of time after I finished my comps where there was just kind of silence from all around me, and I thought, 'Oh, oh I see, I'm just supposed to go and do stuff, and then come back with a thing.' That's kind of how our relationship works." In addition to concerns such as Carol's, many graduate students feel, at some point, the uncertainty of the liminal space between student and scholar. Given this uncertainty, it's not surprising that many graduate students experience some level of impostor syndrome, the belief that they haven't earned their place in their program or field (Parkman 2016). Katie said, for example, that a lack of confidence in her writing made her reluctant to think of herself as a scholar in her academic setting because she "felt like a counterfeit." Unfortunately, as Cecile Badenhorst et al. (2015) explain in their review of graduate writing pedagogies, many practices within graduate programs reinforce the belief that scholars are independent agents, and in this model unproductive students or students who produce unsatisfactory work are often treated as having deficit writing skills (3–4). Graduate students who succeed will, at some point, shift toward feeling that they are more scholar than student, with more in common with their faculty mentors than with fellow students.

While the pre-retreat interviews revealed, not surprisingly, that the participants recognized that they were in a transition period, having moved from being graduate students completing coursework for their professors to scholars who would be expected to produce work that offered something new and meaningful to their field, the "how" and the "what" attached to this expectation were less clear to these writers. George, for example, expressed frustration about not being sure about the audience for which he was writing. He pointed to his uncertainty about how to move from literature review to his own argument as a problem rooted in his position as a graduate student. "I'm having to write chunks of stuff where all I'm doing is summarizing what's known in the field and it's just a chore. It's not necessarily that I'm learning anymore. It's that I'm elaborating this whole (research) process." He said that he felt the content summaries requested by his director were more like background knowledge a student would have to display and were not typical in the published research George read. George's experience was not only shared by other retreat participants, but also reflects attitudes described in other research on dissertation writing (Rogers, Zawacki, and Baker 2016).

In addition to concerns around expectations that the dissertation will add something new to the field, students in pre-retreat interviews also talked about how their positions as graduate students presented challenges to how they approached their writing." Meg, a doctoral student in Psychology, had returned to graduate school after a number of years doing professional writing in the business world. In her pre-retreat interview she talked about her frustrations with trying to write the dissertation in the academic discourse required by her faculty committee members. "I'm trying to find that voice, but also meet the requirements of the people I'm writing for here," she said. "I'm hoping that I can write my dissertation in a way that's very clear, that flows well, that doesn't have too much extraneous information. It's one of the things that is, I think, a struggle with the people I write for." Meg said that she felt that the language of some scholars in her discipline "obfuscates the point in favor of sounding very academic." Instead, she preferred to emulate other scholars in her field who have a "style that's very, very clear . . . that seems to be more genuine . . . and straightforward." Yet she remained unsure if the style of these other scholars would satisfy her committee members. Meg's comment illustrates how the emerging scholarly identity of a graduate student is often bound up in issues of the relationships writers are trying to negotiate, both with their professors and with their larger disciplinary field. They understand that they need to be establishing a position as a scholar in their field, but that they also still needed to be responsive to the demands, and idiosyncrasies, of their advisor and committee members. The pre-retreat interview participants' comments indicate an uncertainty about whether they were adopting the appropriate tone and professional identity in their dissertations. Research on authorship and agency (Haswell and Haswell 2010; Walker 2015) supports the conclusion that such uncertainties about authorial position in regard to potential audiences can construct obstacles to perceptions of agency.

Conversations about Process

In planning for the retreat, we wanted to include in our workshops and consultations explicit conversations about participants' writing processes. Even when the students did not use the term, "writing process," their concerns about productivity and progress were often connected to concerns about process. Our conceptions of writing processes are not limited to rigid definitions of composing and revising. Instead, like Donald Murray (1982), we regard writing habits and dispositions about writing that individuals develop to be crucial aspects of their writing processes. One of our central goals of our dissertation writing retreats is to help the writers, through conversations and reflections, to develop productive writing habits for a large-scale project. For example, writing center consultants begin their first appointments with their writers with a discussion about the writers' processes. Those conversations lay the foundation for ongoing discussion and reflection throughout the week about how the participants are writing, what changes they are making in their processes, and how they might build on those changes in the future. We know that during a one-week retreat even the most prolific writers will only produce a fraction of the words needed complete their dissertations. And certainly an attention to process is not a radical approach to teaching writing. Yet the post-retreat interviews revealed that the practices of writing during the retreat, and the vital role of reflecting on, and perhaps modifying, individual writing processes was one of the more important experiences for participants. Recent research in psychology demonstrates that a change in practice, combined with effective reflection on such practice, can have a marked effect on confidence and perceptions of agency (Wilson 2011). In post-retreat interviews, the 2014 participants talked about how they had developed more productive writing processes, and also how those practices and the discussions about writing helped increase their sense of confidence and agency.

The retreat heightened awareness among the participants that being a productive scholar requires habits and approaches that are sustainable and generative. Katie praised the retreat, stating that it "helped me find my rhythm and develop better writing habits, as a life-time writer of both scholarly and creative work." Tiffany, in comparative humanities, explained that she was relying on some strategies she developed in meetings with her consultant and also that she was trading strategies with her brother, who was also working on his dissertation. Carol also said she used the structure of the retreat "to figure out kind of my own rhythms, what kind of writing works best at different times of day, and how can I adapt that structure to something that's really useful to me in the long run." Talking about her writing habits and progress with another dissertation writer was so helpful to Katie that she subsequently established weekly progress report discussions with a specific group of other dissertation writers. These participants' responses show that dissertation writing retreats can motivate participants to establish and continue some of the writing habits that scholars maintain can be effective for graduate students, such as creating writing groups that focus on flexible accountability, dedicated time, supportive feedback, and goal-setting (Aitchison 2009; Murray and Newton 2009; Badenhorst et al. 2013).

In addition to discussions about developing productive writing habits, the individual consultations and ongoing conversations with peers about their writing helped some of the participants gain more confidence in their abilities as dissertation writers. In her post-retreat interview, Meg indicated that she felt more confident about her ability to write the dissertation. "I have learned to trust the process, specifically, the part of the process where I back away from the writing and let my brain work on a problem in the background," she said. "When I reach an impasse with my writing, I give myself permission to back away from it for a bit in the knowledge that some part of my intellect will continue looking for a solution. It's like waiting for toast to pop up." The enhanced sense of agency in working through difficult or frustrating writing situations is essential to the ability to sustain a career as a scholarly writer. The retreat demonstrated to the writers that they could be productive scholarly writers and also helped them reflect on how they'd accomplished what they did during the week. The confidence that participants describe in their reflections on changes in their writing process are consistent with what is described in research on motivation, where experiences that offer a sense of mastery and accomplishment not only make a project seem less intimidating, but also regulate feelings of anxiety (Pajares and Miller 1994; Bandura 1997). In addition, such experiences of accomplishment can become self-perpetuating as people usually want to engage in activities in which they can foresee a possibility of success. The more confidence people feel in a given activity, the more willing they will be to expend effort on it and the more persistence and resilience they will show in the face of potential obstacles (Pajares and Schunk 2001). Tiffany said that the retreat helped her gain a better sense of what was possible when she found the best writing process for her. She described the confidence that she gained by committing to the daily work that the retreat asked of her: "Once you find something you know you can believe in, it starts working triple, quadruple well . . . it's amazing what confidence . . . can do with your writing, but it's really hard to get to that point."

What's more, some of the participants said the attention to process helped them lessen their sense of feeling the "impostor syndrome," so often described by graduate students. Katie said, for example,

> The retreat helped me realize that these feelings are, to a degree, another form of imposter syndrome. . . . Yet, the retreat reminded me that part of my writing habit needs to be giving precedence to my writing. I don't need to necessarily keep the same hours every day, but I do need to schedule and keep my writing times. And, as the afterglow of the retreat reinforced, I'm much happier when I follow these practices. I'm a writer. And the retreat helped me remember that writing completes a part of myself in a way nothing else can.

The comments from participants in the post-retreat interviews indicate the value in attending to writing processes as more than simply sets of composing skills. In addition, such conversations illustrate how they can contribute to an evolution in identity that can change how people will approach subsequent writing projects.

Experiences Sharing a Writing Space and Community

Another element of the dissertation writing retreat that participants mentioned in the post-retreat interviews as having a positive effect both on their practice and their emerging scholarly identities was writing in a shared space among a community of peers. Almost all of the participants mentioned that hearing the perspectives of other dissertation writers—both the retreat participants and the consultants who were all also working on their dissertations—was ultimately helpful for their own progress. Several mentioned that this was a somewhat surprising outcome.

Understandably, the physical space of the writing center itself, which is quiet with natural lighting, was appreciated by some of the writers. Katie explicitly addressed this in describing the space as "tranquil, full of ambient light, and sort of a magical place," an "atmosphere" that she attempted to emulate at home. More than just a physical space, the retreat offered a social space that provided emotional support and an important change from feeling they were writing in isolation, according to many of the participants. Participants indicated that they developed this sense of community through shared writing time, during which they worked independently and sometimes bounced ideas off one another, and also through interactive workshops and during lunch when a variety of strategies were offered for dissertation completion as well as successful academic life. As Powers (2014) noted about Florida State's dissertation camp, the week of intensive time working together with the same people fosters quick familiarity. When asked if the retreat helped her make progress on her dissertation, the first reason that Katie offered for why it was "absolutely" helpful was that "I was there with people in the same boat—fellow dissertators struggling to complete—and this increased my level of comfort, which in turn helped me to loosen up enough to put pen to paper." For Katie, it was helpful to be with "other people in the deep end that also feel like they can't swim." For doctoral students, this kind of community can be especially important because graduate students, as we noted earlier, are often concerned about the significance and scholarly contribution of their work when, as in academia, "texts and their authors are inseparable" (Kamler and Thomson 2008, 508). Scholarship on both writing retreats and writing groups shows that, when academics consistently work around others with a common purpose, they create bonds beyond sharing physical and temporal space (Maher et al. 2008; Badenhorst et al. 2013; Maher, Fallucca, and Halasz 2013; Powers 2014).

For some participants, the perceived value of writing in a common space was based on the sense of accountability they expected during the retreat. When signing up, applicants to the retreat knew that the expectation was that they would attend for the full time each day of the week. This provided some accountability for the week of the retreat, but participants who engaged with their fellow dissertation writers also felt accountable to each other. For example, Brandon, from comparative humanities, mentioned that working in the same space as other writers often makes the work easier because the situation can "keep you in your seat if other people are still in theirs," and he did not want his fellow writers to "see me wandering away for too long." The accountability that is fostered in this community of dissertation writers is more about mutual accountability and encouraging each other to stay productive, rather than about a person being reprimanded.

Participants also noted that the disciplinary diversity within the community of dissertation writers helped them understand and articulate a variety of writing approaches that they found valuable. Much of this talk focused on comparing the similarities and differences between disciplinary writing conventions. Participants in retreats are sometimes at the beginning of the dissertation writing process. Discussing the components of a dissertation during workshops, consultations, and informal conversations helped participants to conceptualize the broad scope of their dissertation's structure and also to see how the parts of the dissertation worked together. In addition, explaining the complex ideas within their dissertations to consultants and participants who were not in the same discipline helped the dissertators to clarify their ideas in their writing. Thus, in addition to helping participants develop empowering strategies and improve their sense of belonging to their scholarly community, the disciplinary diversity was also beneficial in helping them establish a community connected by the similar short-term goal of completing the dissertation.

Each of the participants interviewed either maintained or re-created the community developed during the retreat in part because the shared purpose offered emotional support. Participants continued to seek out this community not just because, as Tiffany claimed, "Misery loves company." Many participants agreed after the retreat that their community hopes were fulfilled during the retreat, and that this element, among others, helped them to develop agentive skills and perspectives that helped them sustain their writing momentum.

A final benefit of the social writing space was the opportunity it provided the writers to talk with others in the group about how they were dealing with other challenges in their lives, from family illness to financial worries that were affecting their ability to focus on writing their dissertations. Such conversations are an important reminder that we should address such tensions that underlie the writerly lives of the dissertators beyond the formal boundaries of scholarly writing so that we can offer better support to empower their writing process (see Gray's argument, this volume). This kind of social and cultural context of writing becomes meaningful, especially for dissertators at a retreat, when they are encouraged to write as community of writers facing similar challenges, which do not only arise out of academic performance, but also out of social, cultural, and even behavioral practices.

Effects on Emergent Scholarly Identities and Agency

Although many dissertation writing retreats—as well as other writing center activities—have at least an implicit goal of empowering writers, the interviews with our participants illustrated that it may be helpful to think about changes in their perspectives of themselves as writers as an enhanced perception of agency. Each year, the retreat targets these concerns by helping participants gain a better understanding of what it means to join a community of scholars while also helping them discover work habits and writing processes that they can hone in order to be a productive member of their fields. Comments from post-retreat interviews illustrate how the retreat instilled in the participants a belief that they were capable writers and that they could accomplish their goals if they found a writing environment in the company of fellow writers who were undergoing similar experiences.

As one example of this shift in identity it is useful to focus on one of the participants, Brandon, whose reflections are particularly illustrative of how the emphasis on process, as well as the shared space and community, helped facilitate a shift in agency and professional identity that carried on well after the event itself. In the pre-retreat interviews, he discussed his uncertainties and anxieties about the prospect of joining the scholarly community of his field. As one might expect, much of his anxiety centered on the feeling that he was being asked to produce work that was of a higher quality and level of sophistication than his previous work. He described how his dissertation differed from his BA and MA theses because the work that would emerge from his dissertation would need to "go out into the world and be something meaningful to more than just me and my committee who has to read my work." While Brandon felt that his professors had evaluated his previous work based on how well he had demonstrated his learning, with his dissertation, he now understood that he must construct and support a point of view that could stand up to the scrutiny of knowledgeable scholars in his field.

In the post-retreat interview, Brandon said that the experiences during the retreat, including the discussions of process and the community of writers, had changed his conception of himself as a scholar by offering support and by taking him to the dissertation phase "where I feel like the veil was lifted, and I'm 'okay. I've to say something, without knowing everything I have to say something of value, but I have to be reasonable with myself,' so that was helpful." Brandon complimented the retreat's overall efforts and specifically its workshops by stating, "One thing . . . the retreat did is that we don't really get taught how to shift from being a graduate student to a scholar. We've been writing research papers . . . but that was something that the workshops did together over lunch . . . This is a large project, and the way I approach it has to be different. I'm no longer a student. I'm a scholar." Like Brandon, many of the participants highlighted in their post-retreat interviews some of the ways that the retreat had helped them more effectively grapple with the demands that come with navigating the continuing transition of moving from being graduate student to emerging scholar.

IMPLICATIONS

Dissertation writing retreats often advertise themselves to graduate students as events that facilitate writing progress and provide thoughtful feedback on their drafts. We agree on the importance of these more conventional aspects of writing retreats. Yet our research demonstrates that the participants' development of stronger perceptions of agency and more confident literate identities are equally important, if less explicitly addressed, benefits of writing retreats. It is important not to overlook the seemingly simple, yet important role that the combination of writing with others, as well as material and structural support, has on feelings of agency and confidence. While a typical day in the writing center is more focused on individual consultations, the retreat provides the social, supportive environment of a community of writers at work. Simply the opportunity to collaborate, to feel connected to, or appreciated by the people around them was a powerful, productive experience for participants during the retreat. There is an ineffable quality to having a group of people writing together that makes the writing contagious. What's more, the material support of the writing center, from the dedicated space to the conversations about time management also creates an atmosphere where the focus can be on writing, away from the distractions of other places in which graduate students may write. Maintaining such a focus after the retreat can be more difficult, though every year some of the participants from our retreats continue to return to the writing center as a space for writing, as well as consultations. In an attempt to support this kind of writing community we have also begun to facilitate ongoing graduate student writing groups during the academic year where time is available for writers to gather, write together, and talk with each other about their writing concerns.

The results of this research have also reinforced our commitment to talk with writers—at all levels—about their sense of identity and agency in the course of consultations. We teach consultants to help students who visit the center to think about their identities as writers and often to help them re-frame these identities toward a greater sense of agency in the future. For us, the conversation we have with a writer is a moment on a continuum that stretches both to the past and the future. We hope to help writers plan for ways to revise their drafts in the future, but also to revise their perceptions of themselves as writers, which are often more negative than is evidenced by their writing.

Research on motivation often emphasizes the importance of relationships, along with a sense of control and meaning, in developing strong internal motivations and the accompanying resilience to see a project through (Sheldon and Schuler 2011). The communities created and nurtured by dissertation writing retreats clearly establish important senses of community for the graduate students who participate. The writers at the retreat responded to the sense of shared purpose and activity they developed with their fellow graduate students as well as with the consultants with whom they worked. In addition, the responses the writers received from their consultants helped them gain confidence in their work, which in turn helped them feel more like the "writers" and "scholars" they hoped to become through their doctoral work. The shifts in identity that the participants described in post-retreat interviews also indicated a difference in how they conceived of their future as writers and readers. Having what psychologists call an "authentic mastery experience" (Pajares and Schunk 2001) not only provided them with a greater sense of confidence about their writing, but also resulted in shifts in identity that appeared to last well after the event itself. It can be too easy for faculty to overlook, or misunderstand, the uncertainty many graduate students feel, particularly as they begin their dissertations. Discussions of "imposter syndrome" often do not address the seemingly crucial role of writing in such graduate student anxieties. While the dissertation writing retreat is not panacea for such anxieties, the evidence of our research indicates that it may provide a useful and timely intervention that helps participants move toward thinking of themselves as more scholar and writer than student, both in conversations with others, and more crucially in their internal narratives.

NOTES

1. We specifically chose to call our event a "retreat" rather than a "boot camp." The former word has connotations of relaxation, reflection, and refuge while the latter we felt was associated with stress, conformity, and abuse.
2. During the 2014 retreat, Bronwyn was director of the University Writing Center, Adam was associate director, and Ashly and Tika were assistant directors and doctoral students in rhetoric and composition. Ashly and Tika also served as consultants during the retreat.
3. Of the fourteen participants in the 2014 retreat, five were from Comparative Humanities, two from Education, and one each from Biology, Engineering, Fine Art, Nursing, Physics, Psychology, and Public Health.

REFERENCES

Aitchison, Claire. 2009. "Writing Groups for Doctoral Education." *Studies in Higher Education* 34 (8): 905–16. https://doi.org/10.1080/03075070902785580.

Badenhorst, Cecile, Sharon Penney, Sarah Pickett, Rhonda Joy, Jacqueline Hesson, Gabrielle Young, Heather McLeod, Dorothy Vaandering, and Xuemei Li. 2013. "Writing Relationships: Collaboration in a Faculty Writing Group." *AISHE-J* 5 (1): 1001–26.

Badenhorst, Cecile, Cecilia Moloney, Janna Rosales, Jennifer Dyer, and Lina Ru. 2015. "Beyond Deficit: Graduate Student Research-Writing Pedagogies." *Teaching in Higher Education* 20 (1): 1–11. https://doi.org/10.1080/13562517.2014.945160.

Bandura, Albert. 1997. *Self-Efficacy: The Exercise of Control.* New York: Freeman.

Haswell, Janis, and Richard Haswell. 2010. *Authoring: An Essay for the English Profession on Potentiality and Singularity.* Logan: Utah State University Press. https://doi.org/10.2307/j.ctt4cgq15.

Kamler, Barbara, and Pat Thomson. 2008. "The Failure of Dissertation Advice Books: Toward Alternative Pedagogies for Doctoral Writing." *Educational Researcher* 37 (8): 507–14. https://doi.org/10.3102/0013189X08327390.

Leander, Kevin, and Paul Prior. 2004. "Speaking and Writing: How Talk and Text Interact in Situated Practices." In *What Writing Does and How It Does It: An Introduction to Analyzing Texts and Textual Practices,* ed. Charles Bazerman and Paul Prior, 201–37. Mahwah, NJ: Lawrence Erlbaum Associates.

Lee, Sohui, and Chris Golde. 2013. "Completing the Dissertation and Beyond: Writing Centers and Dissertation Boot Camps." *Writing Lab Newsletter* 37 (7–8): 1–5.

Maher, Damian, Leonie Seaton, Cathi McMullen, Terry Fitzgerald, Emi Otsuji, and Alison Lee. 2008. "'Becoming and Being Writers': The Experiences of Doctoral Students in Writing Groups." *Studies in Continuing Education* 30 (3): 263–75. https://doi.org/10.1080/01580370802439870.

Maher, Michelle, Amber Fallucca, and Helen Mulhern Halasz. 2013. "Write on! Through to the PhD: Using Writing Groups to Facilitate Doctoral Degree Progress." *Studies in Continuing Education* 35 (2): 193–208. https://doi.org/10.1080/0158037X.2012.736381.

Murray, Donald. 1982. *Learning by Teaching: Selected Articles on Writing and Teaching.* Portsmouth, NH: Boynton/Cook Heinemann Press.

Murray, Rowena, and Mary Newton. 2009. "Writing Retreat as Structured Intervention: Margin or Mainstream?" *Higher Education Research & Development* 28 (5): 541–53. https://doi.org/10.1080/07294360903154126.

Pajares, Frank, and M. David Miller. 1994. "The Role of Self-Efficacy and Self-Concept Beliefs in Mathematical Problem-Solving: A Path Analysis." *Journal of Educational Psychology* 86 (2): 193–203. https://doi.org/10.1037/0022-0663.86.2.193.

Pajares, Frank, and Dale H. Schunk. 2001. "Self-Beliefs and School Success: Self-Efficacy, Self-Concept, and School Achievement." In *Perception,* ed. R. Riding and S. Rayner, 239–66. London: Ablex.

Papen, Uta, and Virginie Theriault. 2016. "'It Helped Me Feel Like a Legitimate Academic Writer': Writing Retreats as a Milestone in the Development of Ph.D. Students' Sense of Self as Researchers." Language, Literacy and Identity Conference, University of Sheffield, United Kingdom.

Parkman, Anna. 2016. "The Impostor Phenomenon in Higher Education: Incidence and Impact." *Journal of Higher Education Theory and Practice* 16 (1): 51–60.

Powers, Elizabeth. 2014. "Dissercamp: Dissertation Boot Camp 'Lite'." *Writing Lab Newsletter* 38 (5–60): 14–15.

Rogers, Paul M., Terry Myers Zawacki, and Sarah E. Baker. 2016. "Uncovering Challenges and Pedagogical Complications in Dissertation Writing and Supervisory Practices: A Multimethod Study of Doctoral Students and Advisors." In *Supporting Graduate Writers: Research, Curriculum, and Program Design,* ed. Steve Simpson, Nigel A. Caplan, Michelle Cox, and Talinn Phillips, 52–77. Ann Arbor: University of Michigan Press.

Sheldon, Kennon M., and Julia Schuler. 2011. "Wanting, Having, and Needing: Integrating Motive Disposition Theory and Self-Determination Theory." *Journal of Personality and Social Psychology* 101 (5): 1106–23. https://doi.org/10.1037/a0024952.

Walker, Clay. 2015. "Composing Agency: Theorizing the Readiness Potentials of Literacy Practices." *Literacy in Composition Studies* 3 (2): 1–21. https://doi.org/10.21623/1.3.2.2.

Williams, Bronwyn T. 2018. *Literacy Practices and Perceptions of Agency: Composing Identities*. London: Routledge.

Wilson, Timothy. 2011. *Redirect: Changing the Stories We Live By*. London: Penguin.

11
MORE THAN DISSERTATION SUPPORT
Aligning Our Programs with Doctoral Students' Well-Being and Professional Development Needs

Marilyn Gray

Like all writing centers, the University of California at Los Angeles (UCLA) Graduate Writing Center (GWC) is shaped by the particulars of our local context and resource base. The UCLA GWC began as a graduate student initiative: the UCLA Graduate Students Association developed a proposal for the GWC in consultation with Student Affairs and passed a special fee through a referendum vote to fund the center. The referendum set up an oversight committee so that the GWC always has graduate student input from across the disciplines. As the GWC director, I collaborate with the oversight committee to determine program direction and allocate resources. Ongoing assessment of programs and graduate student needs informs program development as well. The student-initiated inception, the ongoing student oversight, the collaborative nature of program development, and the institutional location in Student Affairs have resulted in a GWC that is very responsive to graduate student needs and input. The GWC in turn has experienced considerable growth. Between the academic years 2007–2008 and 2015–2016, the number of annual writing appointment registrations increased 160 percent.[1] The student staff has also approximately doubled. Even though the GWC fee has been raised by a second referendum vote, demand for programs and services outpaces available resources.

As a consequence of the demand, and at the request of the oversight committee members, we have started to explore how our services and programs might qualify for additional support from other funding sources. Many of the programs within Student Affairs receive funding from student service fees, which may fund only those non-academic services that are ineligible for state funding. According to University of California policy, student service fees may support "services related to the physical and psychological health and well-being of students;

DOI: 10.7330/9781607327516.c011

social, recreational, and cultural activities and programs; services related to campus life and campus community; technology expenses directly related to the services; and career support" (Regents Policy 3101: The University of California Student Tuition and Fee Policy n.d.). If our programs go beyond writing support and contribute to academic progress, well-being, and professional development, then our office meets graduate student needs in a much broader sense, an impact that this chapter will discuss primarily in connection with programs that support dissertation writers—boot camps, retreats, workshops, and writing groups. This broader impact potentially qualifies our office for an expanded resources base, such as the aforementioned student service fee funding.

If we think about it, most writing support at the graduate level, particularly at the doctoral level, relates to academic progress and professional development. It is worth considering, then, to what extent those of us directing GWCs actually organize and articulate our program outcomes in light of this relationship. Now that professional development and writing support for doctoral students have become more widely acknowledged needs, at least separately,[2] it is important that we conceptualize the relationship between the two carefully to inform graduate writing program design, especially support for dissertation writers. Further, if we do not present writing support more explicitly in terms of well-being and professional development, then I believe we are doing our stakeholders and doctoral students a disservice.

At UCLA, presenting our work in these terms has enabled our GWC to receive some additional student service fee funding. To argue for that funding, we track the writing genres that students bring to appointments, and that information helps us document our support for academic writing, which we classify as fulfilling formal academic requirements (e.g., course papers, theses, dissertation proposals, and dissertations) and support for professionally oriented writing (e.g., fellowship essays, conference proposals and presentations, personal statements, and articles for publication). Our appointment data for the last four years show that about 35–50 percent of our appointments are devoted to professional genres, depending on how you classify different genres,[3] which clearly demonstrates our contribution to career support. Although our taxonomy classifies the dissertation as an academic genre rather than a professional genre, I would make the case that dissertation writers should be supported through programs that emphasize professional development, given that the students are developing writing and rhetorical knowledge and project management strategies that will enable them to have successful careers, whether inside or outside academia.

In addition to professional development, however, programs that support dissertation writing can address an even wider range of doctoral student needs, as we can see very readily from our institutional location within Student Affairs. Whether one looks at academic progress issues or issues around social support, mental health, and wellness (often bound up with academic progress), it's clear that dissertation writing support programs (and graduate writing centers in general) are well positioned to have a positive impact. One particularly important area is student well-being, given the challenges, stressors, and isolation frequently experienced during the dissertation process; the combination of dissertation writing and job applications can be particularly stressful for late-stage doctoral students, especially those in fields with challenging job markets.

Our experience at UCLA suggests that writing center directors (WCDs) who would like to provide more writing support to doctoral students should explore data on doctoral student needs at their own institutions or comparable institutions if their home campuses do not have available data. If doctoral education stakeholders see an alignment of writing support with other areas of demonstrated need—not just academic progress, but professional development and well-being issues as well—then WCDs have the potential to establish a broader base of support and related resources. In addition, engaging with other stakeholders around areas of doctoral student need brings WCDs into important conversations happening at their institution and institutions across the country about how to improve doctoral education in the context of current economic and job market realities. Given these potential benefits, I argue in this chapter that professional development and well-being outcomes should become intentional elements in our design of dissertation support programs rather than merely welcome byproducts. Further, I argue that designing support programs with a meta-disciplinary focus (humanities, social sciences, and STEM), such as the workshops and dissertation boot camps/retreats we developed at UCLA, can help us meet these outcomes more effectively than programs targeted to more general dissertation support needs. To that end, I describe doctoral students' well-being needs, deeply connected to academic progress, and their professional goals related to writing. I then describe the focused meta-disciplinary dissertation boot camps/retreats and workshops our GWC has designed to meet these needs and goals and finally what participants tell us about the effectiveness of our efforts.

ACADEMIC PROGRESS, WELL-BEING, AND WRITING THE DISSERTATION

Concerns about academic progress—retention, low PhD completion rates, and lengthy time-to-degree—are clear and sufficient reasons to advocate for graduate writing support (Council of Graduate Schools 2010, 57–60). Low PhD completion rates and lengthy time-to-degree patterns are well-documented problems, with data from the Council of Graduate Schools PhD Completion Project showing that only 56.6 percent of the PhD students in their sample had completed their PhD by the tenth year (Council of Graduate Schools 2008, 15).[4] UCLA has reasonably good completion numbers compared to the national average, and yet some 30 percent of our doctoral students are still not finishing programs within ten years, especially in humanities and social sciences (UCLA Graduate Division n.d., A-41–A-43). With so many PhD students not completing the degree, any program that can help doctoral students not just finish, but finish in a timely way, would be very beneficial. Dissertation writing support in particular has the obvious potential to improve completion rates and time-to-degree.

Academic progress is not just a concern of administrators, however; graduate students themselves acutely feel the academic and time pressures associated with graduate school. The UCLA Student Affairs Graduate and Professional Student Survey conducted in 2014[5] asks students about their perceptions and concerns related to academic progress. The data from this survey show that 36.3 percent of doctoral student respondents felt "slightly behind schedule" and 11.7 percent felt "significantly behind schedule" concerning their academic progress (N = 1,462). A somewhat higher percentage of respondents expressed concerns about their academic progress overall, with 47.7 percent being "concerned" and 18 percent being "very concerned" about their academic progress (N = 1,441). About 42 percent of doctoral student respondents agreed or strongly agreed that they "have seriously considered leaving my graduate/professional program before completing the degree" (N = 1,440). Furthermore, when asked about mental health and academic progress, 40.5 percent of respondents said that "feeling depressed, stressed, or upset" had "somewhat slowed" their academic progress, and 15.3 percent said that these feelings had "significantly slowed" their academic progress (N = 1,454). These numbers indicate that many doctoral students worry about academic progress and that wellness issues could impede that progress.

Graduate students' mental health and well-being are critical for their academic performance and timely progress. In 2006, a University of California-wide committee on student mental health issues found that graduate students were at a higher risk for mental health issues because of high academic demands, financial pressures, and family responsibilities, as well as greater potential for isolation (University of California, Office of the President 2006).[6] The UC-wide mental health report included findings from a 2004 Berkeley Graduate Student Survey Mental Health Report. The Berkeley report found that "In the last twelve months, 45.3 percent of respondents had experienced an emotional or stress-related problem that *significantly* affected their well-being and/or academic performance."[7] The executive summary of the Berkeley report closes with this statement recommending that the university attend to graduate student mental health:

> It is anticipated that this survey will provide relevant information to the campus; we hope that it additionally motivates action. Graduate students contribute significantly to the academic mission of UC Berkeley, by performing cutting-edge research, teaching undergraduate students, and publishing in scholarly journals. Maintenance of strong academic performance within the university requires social support and emotional well-being; therefore it is in the university's best interests to prioritize graduate student mental health. (4)

The UC report concurred with the Berkeley report's recommendations, which led to UC-wide mandates and additional funding for mental health support for UC students. The mental health support recommended by the UC report was conceptualized in three tiers. While the first tier recommendations focused on improving mental health services for students and the second tier on support and interventions that target at-risk populations, the third tier emphasized support for healthy learning communities in general, specifically mentioning "academic support and learning support" for writing among other subjects.[8] Although the UC report is over ten years old, it illustrates values and mandates that are still in effect at UC campuses, even if additional resources are not available to allocate under this particular mandate. As I have learned, dissertation writing support programs, such as the boot camps/retreats we sponsor at the UCLA GWC, can be shown to meet second or third tier objectives from this report, or to support healthy learning communities as the local UCLA criteria for student service fee funding specifies.

These are the kinds of institutional contexts that, I would argue, are worth researching carefully when seeking funding for programs. Since mental health and well-being are categories often supported by student service fees, it is useful to provide evidence of the close relationship between academic progress, well-being, and writing (e.g., see Smith et al., this volume) and to explain how our dissertation support program objectives are intentionally designed with that relationship in mind. Dissertation writing support programs, like boot camps/retreats and writing groups can, for example, reduce isolation and provide social support during graduate school in general and the dissertation process in particular (Council of Graduate Schools 2010, 59).[9]

CAREER GOALS, PROFESSIONAL DEVELOPMENT, AND DISSERTATION WRITING SUPPORT

In a 2014 study of graduate student well-being, UC Berkeley researchers demonstrated a striking correlation between graduate student well-being and their perspectives on career prospects. The researchers defined two major indicators of well-being—a positive one, "satisfaction with life," and a negative one, "depression" (The Graduate Assembly 2014). They then analyzed the top predictors for graduate student well-being and found that the number one predictor of well-being related directly to graduate students' perception of career prospects: "Graduate students' beliefs about their career prospects are overall the top predictor of their well-being, strongly predicting their satisfaction with life and depression. Students who feel upbeat about their career prospects are significantly happier and less depressed than students who do not feel the same optimism. Concern with career prospects was a major theme of students' written comments" (The Graduate Assembly 2014, 2). Not surprisingly, feelings about career prospects play a critical role in graduate students' sense of well-being. We believe that emphasizing professional skill development in our support programs, particularly writing for the purposes of this chapter, can help to improve doctoral students' confidence in their career prospects.

Doctoral students often need support for developing their writing and rhetorical skills beyond the resources their departments currently offer. When given a self-assessment of skills, UCLA doctoral students rated themselves lower on a number of writing-related skills than on other types of skills. The self-rating questions used the following five-point scale: lowest 10 percent, below average, average, above average, highest 10 percent. For writing a dissertation, 22.9 percent of doctoral student respondents ranked themselves in the lower two ratings, and 50.7 percent ranked themselves as average (N = 1,430). For writing a journal article, 25.8 percent of doctoral respondents ranked themselves in the lower two ratings, and 44.6 percent ranked themselves as average

(N = 1,433). For writing grants, 35.2 percent ranked themselves in the lower two categories, and 40.1 percent ranked themselves as average (n = 1,422).[10] While only one question on the survey asked about dissertations directly, journal articles and grant writing are relevant for dissertation writing. Those who write article-compilation dissertations need support for journal articles. Those who are not confident about grant writing and/or dissertation writing likely will need support for writing dissertation proposals. Since many doctoral programs do not provide much formal writing support, the GWC can play a critical support role by offering programs, such as boot camps, retreats, workshops, and writing groups, that target disciplinary genres, including the subgenres comprising a dissertation, and that focus on professional development related to writing and career goals.

To target career support needs for graduate and professional students more effectively, some universities have started to define professional skills and competencies for their graduate students.[11] During the 2014–2015 academic year, for example, a UCLA faculty committee was convened by the vice provost of Graduate Studies and the vice chancellor of Student Affairs to develop a set of core competencies for graduate education professional development. That committee has established the following core competencies for UCLA graduate students: career path preparation; communication skills; self-assessment and development; project management, leadership, and collaboration; teaching and mentorship; and scholarly expertise and integrity. Another important and related trend in formulating professional competencies for graduate education is the increasing use of Independent Development Programs (IDPs), tools that help graduate students monitor their own development of skills within the core competencies. Members of the Graduate Careers Consortium developed an IDP for STEM graduate students and postdocs, a resource that is hosted by the American Association for the Advancement of Science (AAAS) and available for anyone to use.[12] At the time of this writing, an IDP for social sciences and humanities is under development by a subcommittee of the Graduate Career Consortium.[13] As professional development competencies, which always include communication skills, become more common at universities, it will become increasingly important for GWCs to articulate their dissertation writing support objectives with these competencies in mind and to align their programs with other graduate support programs. And because communication and writing skills are often defined very generally in competency rubrics, GWCs may even have opportunities to shape the specific dimensions of these competencies, as well as to demonstrate that GWC programs develop competencies beyond just writing and communication, like project management, for example.

DISCIPLINE-FOCUSED "COURSE MODEL" BOOT CAMPS/RETREATS

While dissertation writing support programs—boot camps, retreats, workshops, and writing groups—contribute most obviously to writing development, they can additionally support well-being and professional development around writing, as I have argued. In the remainder of this chapter, I focus on the discipline-focused GWC boot camps and retreats we designed to develop core academic and professional communication competencies as well as to provide personal and professional development opportunities.

Some background: when I began my oversight of the GWC dissertation writing support programs in summer 2008, I was aware of the University of Pennsylvania boot camp structure with its two weeks of mandatory half days of writing, individual appointments, and supplemental workshops. Instead of using this shorter, writing intensive structure, however, we decided to develop what Anita Mastroieni and Deanna Cheung refer to as a "course model" boot camp with one session per week for five or six weeks (Mastroieni and Cheung 2011).[14] We chose this structure because we thought that a program spanning a longer period of time would give participants more ongoing social support and accountability and more time to develop effective writing habits and project management strategies.

We also chose the "course model" structure because of the pedagogical implication of the intensive "boot camp" structure itself, which seemed to promote what Robert Boice (1990, 2000) calls the "binge" approach to writing. We were also influenced by Boice's findings on faculty writing productivity, which showed that faculty who wrote regularly (preferably daily, in moderation) had more insights, wrote more, published more, and had higher rates of tenure than those who wrote in binges. We still adopted the name "dissertation boot camp," however, to communicate the bottom-line learning outcome—that we want to help participants get their dissertation writing into shape and ramp up their productivity. At the first session, we explain boot camp goals and promise that it will not involve pushups and jumping jacks.

While we want participants in our boot camps to push themselves to write a lot, more importantly we want them to develop writing habits that will sustain a writing routine throughout the dissertation and into their professional lives. We think of productivity as both a goal and a learning outcome, since cultivating writing productivity requires other skills like good project management, resource management, and drafting techniques, in addition to good time management and goal setting, all of which we address in our boot camp. We are both a "writing process" boot camp in the sense that Sohui Lee and Chris Golde use the term, and, at the same time, we aspire to be a "professional development" boot camp, a program goal that we continue to try to strengthen (Lee and Golde 2013).

Dissertation writing support programs, more generally, are especially well poised to enhance professional development if they have sufficient disciplinary and generic focus such that program content can be tailored to the participants' research contexts, methods, and genre conventions. Others have also acknowledged the appropriateness of genre pedagogy in graduate writing support (e.g., see Sundstrom 2014; Autry and Carter 2015; Vorhies 2015). We believe that, while cross-disciplinary programs—whether workshops, writing groups, or boot camps/retreats—are valuable for bringing dissertators together to address writing strategies and provide emotional and social support, programs designed for participants from closely related disciplines, or meta-disciplines, and focused on field-specific methods, genres, and conventions may be able to provide more effective professional development opportunities around writing.

In our GWC, we divide our boot camp/retreat support programs by meta-disciplines and by proposal and dissertation stages. For the dissertation proposal stage, we have separate boot camp programs for humanities and social sciences, and we offer different support options for STEM. We used to run all three proposal programs as multi-session boot camps, but we found that the STEM PhDs were writing much shorter proposal documents, often in a grant format, so we now offer single-session workshops on the STEM dissertation proposal, as well as individual workshops on specific fellowships like the NIH National Research Service Awards throughout the year. STEM dissertation proposal writers may also participate in STEM writing retreats, which are described in more detail below. Moreover, separate proposal-stage boot camps for humanities and social sciences allow us to address the features of their proposals more specifically. Social science proposals are much more likely to have research questions, problem statements, methods, and preliminary results sections. Humanities proposals tend to be less structured, to address methods and theory differently than in social sciences (or possibly not at all), and to require projected chapter breakdowns and summaries. In addition, dividing programs by disciplinary areas allows presentations and discussions that are targeted to actual research and writing practices, thus contributing to professional development in a more contextualized way.

Our dissertation-stage boot camps were originally also divided into two meta-disciplinary groups based on a generic difference—one camp was for the results chapter within an IMRaD-structured (introduction, methods, results, and discussion) dissertation, either the whole dissertation or each article chapter, and the other was for an analytical chapter in a humanities or arts dissertation. As could be predicted, however, the results-chapter camp, which ranged from hard sciences to purely qualitative dissertations, ended up being too broad for any disciplinary cohesion. We now divide dissertation-stage programs into three sections—quantitative (STEM and social sciences), qualitative (and sometimes mixed methods), and humanities/arts. The three-way division provides the most cohesive groups that we can currently support, and the relative similarities of genre, process, disciplinary area, and epistemology (broadly speaking) contribute to more focused, substantive discussions among participants about their research projects and writing process.[15] For example, although writing in the humanities has some similarities to writing in the qualitative social sciences, keeping the two in separate programs gives the qualitative researchers space to discuss specific qualitative research and writing issues such as human subjects research, software tools for qualitative research, coding, grounded theory, positionality, and the transition from data analysis to writing in qualitative research contexts.

The dissertation boot camps for humanities and qualitative social sciences also help participants conceptualize the project management side of dissertation writing and learn better organizational skills for managing long writing projects. I would also argue that project management and drafting strategies as procedural knowledge are among the genre's most occluded aspects. We frame the humanities and qualitative boot camps as focusing on how to write an analytical dissertation chapter, which we treat as a sub-genre of the dissertation. We believe that if you can write a dissertation chapter, you can write a dissertation. We also prioritize reviewing the drafting process in depth because, although participants may know about drafting in theory, in practice they may find it difficult to apply this knowledge to long texts that need extensive revision and often undergo major changes in ideas, structure, and argument.

The quantitative social sciences and STEM grouping still spans a broad disciplinary range, but the participants usually share experimental, hypothesis-driven research methods, and their dissertations are more similar from the standpoint of genre. Besides the IMRaD structure, STEM dissertations are almost exclusively compilations of research article manuscripts (generally each article is a chapter), and we have found that social science fields (particularly for studies using predominantly quantitative methods) have adopted article-compilation dissertations more frequently as well. Expectations for dissertation introductions in this social science/STEM grouping vary widely, however, ranging from no introduction at all to fairly lengthy introductions with comprehensive literature reviews. Doctoral students in STEM fields usually invest more time in writing publishable articles, so the period when they actually put the dissertation together often occurs at the very end of their time in the degree program. If they have published a few papers during graduate school, the dissertation stage mainly involves writing a global introduction and possibly a conclusion. If they are behind in their writing, then they may also need to draft several papers in a very compressed timeframe. These issues of genre and timing are important considerations in program design for these students' professions.

Because the writing needs and habits of STEM students are different from students in other fields, our support model for this group, as I noted above, has actually evolved away from the course-model boot camp and into writing retreats, workshops, and writing groups facilitated by graduate writing consultants from these fields.[16] STEM students usually work in laboratory settings, so what they often need in order to make progress on writing is more isolation rather than less—a break in their routine and an opportunity to regroup. The retreat format gives STEM graduate students a valid reason to leave their labs for a few days and refocus on their writing. While this change in program structure relates more to facilitating academic progress than to professional development per se, we retain professional development components from the boot camp as much as possible. Required morning sessions, for example, address goal-setting, time management, and project management, as well as provide an opportunity for participants to interact with peers. Optional but well-attended writing workshops offered during the retreat cover scientific writing, writing process strategies, dissertation structure, and dissertation introductions and conclusions. Because all of the writing workshops in the STEM retreat are designed for these students, we use appropriate examples from scientific articles and dissertations to illustrate best practices for the genre and professional communication more generally.

SOME PROMISING FEEDBACK ON DISSERTATION BOOT CAMPS/RETREATS

To understand the impact of our dissertation boot camps (DBCs) and retreats on students' professional development, as well as on their academic progress, productivity, and well-being, we asked scaled and open-ended questions in a post-program evaluation of our 2015 humanities and qualitative DBCs[17] and the 2015 and 2016 STEM retreats.[18] The evaluation survey responses show that participants perceived some gains in all of these areas.

We assessed participants' perceptions of the impact of the boot camps/retreats on their productivity through open-ended and scaled questions. In a scaled question, 79 percent of participants in the humanities and qualitative DBCs agreed or strongly agreed that participation in the DBC increased their writing productivity. In open-ended questions, we asked them how many pages they wrote during the camp, and whether they thought they had written more pages than they would have if they had not participated in the camp. In their written responses, we received some straightforward quantitative answers on the number of pages attributed to program participation. The majority credited the DBC with allowing them to produce more pages than they would have otherwise produced if they had not participated in the camp, and their answers were typically in the five-to-twenty-page range. Other responses included a few participants who did not write, a few who did not feel their output was affected by the program, and a few who felt the program improved quality rather than quantity. For the STEM retreat participants, rather than just asking the number of pages written, we asked how much writing or other work they were able to accomplish. Those who responded to this question indicated progress on writing, analysis, organizational, and/or planning tasks.

We also asked humanities and qualitative participants scaled questions on their perception of the program's impact on their writing habits. Ninety-three percent agreed or strongly agreed that the program helped them improve their habits as a writer. Participants also agreed or strongly agreed that the DBC had given them effective strategies to write an individual dissertation chapter (93%), and a dissertation overall (90%). While good writing habits take time and effort to develop, let alone sustain, we hope that the self-assessment, discussions about writing processes, genres, and conventions, and strategies shared by both facilitators and participants will help participants make continued growth in these areas. While we do not currently assess the impact of our boot camps and retreats on time-to-degree and completion directly, we believe that the writing knowledge and strategies these programs provide can ultimately improve these academic progress outcomes.[19]

Project management, time management, organizational strategies, and drafting strategies are important professional development learning outcomes of these boot camp/retreat programs as well. All humanities and qualitative participants who responded (N = 28) agreed or strongly agreed that the DBC helped them develop project management and organization strategies for complex writing projects. Eighty-six percent indicated that the DBC helped them develop effective strategies for planning work and setting realistic writing goals, skills transferrable to other forms of work. Ninety percent of the boot camp participants agreed or strongly agreed that the program gave them effective strategies to use at different stages of the drafting process. A deeper understanding of their writing processes can put doctoral students in a better position to mentor others around writing, as several participants noted on the program evaluation.[20] One student wrote of having "acquired a lot of conceptual tools to increase . . . my progress as a writer. I feel that now I can help other students in the same position that I am." Interestingly, when we asked directly whether the boot camp had helped participants' professional development, 72 percent agreed or strongly agreed—a lower percentage than other questions, which may indicate that some participants are not connecting the learning outcomes noted here to their professional development. A few evaluation comments indicate as well that there was likely some variation in how the term "professional development" was interpreted.

Our evaluative feedback from humanities and qualitative social sciences participants indicates that DBCs can also contribute to participants' well-being through increased confidence and motivation. Ninety percent of participants agreed or strongly agreed that participating in the boot camp increased their confidence to manage their dissertation projects with one participant commenting that the program "reinforced general life skills of balance and goal setting."[21] Eighty-six percent reported increased motivation to write, which we attribute to the boot camps demystifying the writing process, and, by doing so, helping to alleviate imposter thinking when dissertators see that their challenges are not unique. As one participant said in an evaluation comment, the program provided "an opportunity to see the common struggles and concerns." (See Smith et al., this volume on imposter syndrome, literate identities, and the effects of retreats on motivation and confidence.) As I noted earlier, these are findings that are closely connected to UCLA's core competencies related to wellness, life balance, and healthy work habits, and so conceptualizing our efforts as well-being and professional development outcomes has been an effective way to align our programs with broader university goals for graduate education.

Writing centers have a real opportunity to contribute to doctoral education by providing carefully and strategically designed programs to support dissertation writers and prepare them for their careers, whether inside or outside of academia. To that end, our UCLA GWC dissertation programs are designed to address multiple professional development and well-being outcomes, not just the expected skills more narrowly related to written communication. Whatever doctoral students' career goals may be, all of these learning outcomes are critical for their future success, and so, as I have argued, they should shape not only the design of our dissertation support programs but also graduate writing support more generally. Besides facilitating the well-being and professional development of graduate students, our GWC programs can be part of the cultural shift at universities to support all PhD pathways in a more inclusive manner (See Council of Graduate Schools and Educational Testing Service 2012). Further, when we articulate and document the range of outcomes our Graduate Writing Centers writing support programs achieve, the more likelihood there is that we will be able to persuade university stakeholders to provide us with more resources to provide the kinds of targeted and comprehensive dissertation writing support I've described. But it is the doctoral students who stand to benefit the most when our programmatic support addresses their needs and experiences in a more integrated manner. In the end, framing our work as contributing to graduate students' broader career and well-being goals will resonate well with them, with administrators, and with graduate faculty who understand the current challenges of doctoral education.

NOTES

1. From 1,055 to 2,747 appointment registrations.
2. For example, the Council of Graduate Schools (2010) treats them separately. Their recommendations include writing support, dissertation support, and professional development, but professional development comes across as everything other than writing. A "writing clinic" on writing a journal article manuscript is suggested under the category of "writing assistance" instead of professional development (57–60).
3. The percentage was 35.2 when including fellowships, personal statements, CVs/resumes, and all job application documents. It rose to 49.1 percent when including abstracts, journal articles, and conference presentations as well.
4. The completion rate by the end of the seventh year is only 45.5 percent.
5. Data summarizing responses from all UCLA graduate and professional school survey respondents are available online (https://www.sairo.ucla.edu/By-Survey/GRAD

More than Dissertation Support 237

-Survey). The Student Affairs Institutional Research Office provided the data in this chapter for just doctoral student respondents (degrees included PhD, DrPH, EdD, DMA, DEnv).

6. In addition to graduate students, the other "high risk student populations" identified by the report were international students, LGBT students, and students from underrepresented racial and ethnic groups.
7. The Berkeley report is Appendix E of the University of California, Office of the President (2006) report.
8. Tier 3 recommendations include: "Expand key academic support and learning services (e.g., in math, science, foreign language, writing clinics, course-specific tutoring, staffed study groups, and assistance in courses known to be difficult) to enhance students' ability to manage academically related stress." Unfortunately, Tier 3 recommendations were never funded due to the economic recession of the late 2000's.
9. See Wolfsberger (2014) for a doctoral writing group that particularly emphasized social support.
10. The data here also come from the doctoral student respondents of the 2014 UCLA Student Affairs Graduate and Professional Student Survey.
11. Some competency rubrics are for graduate students overall, and some are specifically for doctoral students. Two models for reference are Stanford University's Graduate Professional Development Framework (https://vpge.stanford.edu/professional-development/framework) and UC Davis's GradPathways with eight competency areas (https://gradstudies.ucdavis.edu/professional-development/gradpathways).
12. https://myidp.sciencecareers.org/ A major impetus for developing an IDP for STEM postdocs and graduate students was to help principal investigators and trainees meet NIH grant training and mentoring requirements.
13. The tool under development is called ImaginePhD. For more information see https://www.gradcareerconsortium.org/imaginephd.php.
14. Technically, there had been "course model" dissertation programs at UCLA in summers 2006 in 2007. These were four-week programs called "dissertation institutes" and were not facilitated by the writing center. In 2008, in consultation with colleagues and graduate student staff, I extended the programs to six weeks and changed the name to "boot camp," taking the name from the "just write" camps at University of Pennsylvania even though we didn't follow their intensive format.
15. Wendy Bastalich (2011) also argues for grouping students in fields with broadly similar methods when designing doctoral writing support; their program feedback became more favorable after STEM disciplines were divided from humanities and social sciences. I suggest slightly narrower divisions, but the overall reasoning for the disciplinary divisions is similar.
16. Writing group participants bring three-to-five pages of new writing to each session, and the facilitator and two or three peers review the drafts and then give feedback. The writing group format works well for students motivated to produce writing regularly and receive feedback, such as those who are near the end of their programs. The writing groups demonstrate how to give and receive constructive writing feedback and develop participants' professional skills and scholarly identities. In our experience, putting similar fields in writing groups works better for the reasons of cohesion mentioned earlier. We also try to introduce best practices for writing groups at the end of our retreats and boot camps, and we sometimes help organize writing groups that will run independently as follow-up peer support for the dissertation boot camps and retreats. (See Phillips [2012], Guerin et al. [2013], and Aitchison and Guerin's [2014] edited volume for diverse writing group models and their role in doctoral education.)

17. These numbers reflect an aggregate (N=29 unless otherwise noted) from the two programs (Humanities DBC—eighteen respondents, Qualitative DBC—eleven respondents). Most evaluations were anonymous paper surveys completed at the end of the last session, but a few were done through an equivalent Google form. All respondents attended at least three of six sessions.
18. We have fifteen paper evaluations from the 2015 and 2016 STEM dissertation/thesis retreats.
19. Lee and Golde (2013) asked boot camp participants in a follow-up survey whether the program had improved their time-to-degree, and about one third felt that they had reduced time-to-degree by one or more quarters.
20. See also Autry and Carter (2015) on the potential benefit of dissertation support programs for cultivating future faculty mentors.
21. Busl, Donnelly, and Capdevielle (2015) also reported gains in confidence and reductions in anxiety for participants in intensive boot camps with writing process components.

REFERENCES

Aitchison, Claire, and Cally Guerin. 2014. *Writing Groups for Doctoral Education and Beyond: Innovations in Practice and Theory.* New York: Routledge.

Autry, Meagan Kittle, and Michael Carter. 2015. "Unblocking Occluded Genres in Graduate Writing: Thesis and Dissertation Support Services at North Carolina State University." *Composition Forum* 31. http://compositionforum.com/issue/31/.

Bastalich, Wendy. 2011. "Beyond the Local/General Divide: English for Academic Purposes and Process Approaches to Cross Disciplinary, Doctoral Writing Support." *Higher Education Research & Development* 30 (4): 449–62. https://doi.org/10.1080/07294360.2010.518954.

Boice, Robert. 1990. *Professors as Writers: A Self-Help Guide to Productive Writing.* Stillwater, OK: New Forums Press.

Boice, Robert. 2000. *Advice for New Faculty Members: Nihil Nimus.* Boston: Allyn and Bacon.

Busl, Gretchen, Kara Lee Donnelly, and Matthew Capdevielle. 2015. "Camping in the Disciplines: Assessing the Effect of Writing Camps on Graduate Student Writers." Special Issue, *Across the Disciplines* 12 (3). http://wac.colostate.edu/atd/graduate_wac/busletal2015.cfm.

Council of Graduate Schools. 2008. *Ph.D. Completion and Attrition: Analysis of Baseline Data from the Ph.D. Completion Project.* Washington, DC: Council of Graduate Schools.

Council of Graduate Schools. 2010. *Ph.D. Completion and Attrition: Policies and Practices to Promote Student Success.* Washington, DC: Council of Graduate Schools.

Council of Graduate Schools and Educational Testing Service. 2012. *Pathways Through Graduate School and Into Careers. Report from the Commission on Pathways Through Graduate School and Into Careers.* Princeton, NJ: Educational Testing Service.

The Graduate Assembly. 2014. *The Graduate Student Happiness and Well Being Report.* Berkeley: University of California. http://ga.berkeley.edu/wellbeingreport/.

Guerin, Cally, Vicki Xafis, Diana V. Doda, Marianne H. Gillam, Allison J. Larg, Helene Luckner, Nasreen Jahan, Aris Widayati, and Chuangzhou Xu. 2013. "Diversity in Collaborative Research Communities: A Multicultural, Multidisciplinary Thesis Writing Group in Public Health." *Studies in Continuing Education* 35 (1): 65–81. https://doi.org/10.1080/0158037X.2012.684375.

Lee, Sohui, and Chris Golde. 2013. "Completing the Dissertation and Beyond: Writing Centers and Dissertation Boot Camps." *The Writing Lab Newsletter* 37 (8): 1–5.

Mastroieni, Anita, and Deanna Cheung. 2011. "The Few, the Proud, the Finished: Dissertation Boot Camp as a Model for Doctoral Student Support." *NASPA: Excellence in Practice*, 4–6. http://www.academia.edu/2116848/Excellence_in_Practice-A_Knowledge_Community_Publication.

Phillips, Talinn. 2012. "Graduate Writing Groups: Shaping Writing and Writers from Student to Scholar." *Praxis: A Writing Center Journal* 10 (1): 45–51. http://www.praxisuwc.com/phillips-101.

Regents Policy 3101: The University of California Student Tuition and Fee Policy. n.d. http://regents.universityofcalifornia.edu/governance/policies/3101.html.

Sundstrom, Christine Jensen. 2014. "The Graduate Writing Program at the University of Kansas: An Inter-Disciplinary, Rhetorical Genre-Based Approach to Developing Professional Identities." *Composition Forum* 29. http://compositionforum.com/issue/29/.

University of California, Office of the President. 2006. *Final Report of Student Mental Health Committee*. http://regents.universityofcalifornia.edu/regmeet/sept06/303attach.pdf.

UCLA Graduate Division. n.d. *UCLA Graduate Programs Annual Report, 2010–2011*. https://grad.ucla.edu/asis/report/arentire.pdf.

Vorhies, Heather Blain. 2015. "Building Professional Scholars: The Writing Center at the Graduate Level." *Writing Lab Newsletter* 39 (5–6): 6–9.

Wolfsberger, Judith. 2014. "A Weekly Dose of Applause!" In *Writing Groups for Doctoral Education and Beyond: Innovations in Practice and Theory*, ed. Claire Aitchison and Cally Guerin, 177–89. New York: Routledge.

12
REVISITING THE REMEDIAL FRAMEWORK
How Writing Centers Can Better Serve Graduate Students and Themselves

Elizabeth Lenaghan

Writing is essential to graduate education, especially at the doctoral level. As emergent specialists, doctoral students write to communicate novel ideas and research. And in an increasingly competitive academic job market, they must excel by writing competitive grant applications, presenting at specialized conferences, and publishing in top-tier journals (Kamler 2008; Brooks-Gillies et al. 2015). Likewise, those doctoral students who have no intention of pursuing an academic career must know how to write effectively to succeed as professionals in our increasingly globalized and interdisciplinary world (Lee and Aitchison 2009). To fully realize such writing accomplishments, doctoral students need to do far more than simply complete the writing associated with degree requirements. They need to develop sophisticated understandings of how writing operates in and outside of academia.

More than a product or a fixed set of skills, academic writing is an iterative process through which knowledge is made and identities are formed (Kamler and Thomson 2006; Paré 2007). To encourage students to appreciate these rich dimensions of writing, Anthony Paré (2007) explains, "We need to create invitations or opportunities that exploit the heuristic power of writing—not just writing to *display* knowledge, but writing to explore, to problem-solve, to take chances, to *make* knowledge. And we need to help students develop their writing, over time, as expert writers do, with moments of planning, organizing, drafting, and revising" ("Conclusion"). Crucially, graduate students who are provided such opportunities are less likely to believe writing is "ancillary or marginal to the real work of research," as Barbara Kamler and Pat Thomson point out (Kamler and Thomson 2006, 3). On the contrary, they will embrace writing as a "situated social *practice*" (4) and

DOI: 10.7330/9781607327516.c012

"a vital part of the research process" (3). Beyond being more accurate, such understandings of writing are essential for developing disciplinary expertise and fundamental to cultivating an identity as a writer that accommodates the emotional, physical, and aesthetic labor associated with the writing process (Kamler and Thomson 2006; Lee and Danby 2011; Rose and McClafferty 2001).

Given both the importance of and complexities surrounding writing at the graduate-level, I have been surprised by the exigence that much recent literature on graduate writing services provides for creating such services: the need to decrease attrition rates and time-to-degree among graduate students. For instance, several recent publications describing both graduate schools' and departmental efforts to assist graduate student writers frame the development of writing groups (Maher, Fallucca, and Mulhern Halasz 2013), courses (Sundstrom 2014), mentorship programs (Holley and Caldwell 2012), and thesis and dissertation support services programs (Autry and Carter 2015) as attempts to address challenges associated with student retention and/or timely degree completion. Writing centers, too, evoke these challenges as an impetus for serving graduate students. The call for proposals for a 2016 *WLN* special issue on graduate support (by the co-editors of this collection), for example, cited "vigorous campus conversations focused on improving graduate completion rates and time to degree" as justification for its focus ("WLN: Special Issue Call" 2014). Likewise, an even more recent article in *Praxis: A Writing Center Journal* explicitly locates writing centers as "well positioned" to address the Council on Graduate Education's 2014 recommendation to provide writing support as a means of improving retention and shortening degree completion (Mannon 2016, 59).

On the one hand, the prevalence of such citations reflects the challenges that characterize graduate education today—challenges to which writing centers, alongside other university departments and programs, can and should respond. On the other hand, I fear that the impulse to equate the need for graduate writing services with the desire to decrease attrition and time-to-degree suggests that writing centers prioritize conversations about written products over conversations about the processes of production. Such a priority seems to minimize the important role that writing centers play in providing low-stakes opportunities for students to evoke, rehearse, and refine their disciplinary knowledge and to shape and reshape appropriate scholarly identities. In addition to providing graduate students with opportunities to shape their scholarly identities through performances of disciplinary expertise, such conversations can also prompt students to see how the rhetorical, disciplinary, and genre-based features of writing combine to communicate meaning (see Reineke et al., this volume, for examples of the latter).

A second problem with seeming to emphasize product-oriented outcomes is that doing so has the potential to confirm what Steve Simpson (2013) identifies as a "perennial issue in writing center work": the idea of "the writing center as the 'fix-it' or 'triage' center" (1). As Simpson notes, this idea not only reproduces false notions of the writing center's services as being solely remedial; it is also likely to create inaccurate expectations of what writing centers can or should achieve. More fundamentally, the notion of writing center as a "triage" or remedial space is likely to alienate potential users who may not be struggling with their writing but would nonetheless benefit from the holistic feedback and collaborative conversation they could find in writing centers.

Alongside the negative impacts that positioning writing centers as product-oriented or remedial might have for graduate students, such positioning can also damage writing centers' reputations at the institutional level by marginalizing and compartmentalizing the role that writing center services can play in graduate student education. In her recent analysis of how almost four hundred writing centers from a wide range of colleges and universities across the country publically brand themselves, Lori Salem (2014) reveals a connection between how writing centers brand themselves and the ideas about literacy that colleges and universities aim to cultivate. She explains, "Writing centers allow universities to signal the kind of literacy they sponsor, and they give universities a concrete venue for operationalizing institutional goals and agendas" (37). At best, then, a graduate writing center that brands itself as sponsoring only (or even mostly) the kind of "fix-it" literacies associated with degree completion may actually be doing so at the expense of the more commonly espoused goals of graduate education that foreground the development of researchers over research (Park 2007).

With a more holistic aim for graduate study as a frame, this chapter suggests how writing centers might better position themselves as participants in doctoral education by drawing on my own experiences as the creator and director of the graduate writing center at Northwestern University. Funded by The Graduate School and the Weinberg College of Arts and Sciences, The Graduate Writing Place (GWP) was established in the fall of 2010 to supplement our extant Writing Place, which is staffed by advanced undergraduates. The GWP, whose origins, design, and day-to-day operations I explain in greater detail below, is currently housed in a different location and staffed by me and a group of ten Graduate Writing Fellows, advanced PhD candidates from across the university; together, the fellows and I design and carry out the services of the GWP. Annually, these typically include over 1,000 hours of one-to-one writing consultations, thirty discipline-specific and cross-disciplinary workshops, fifteen interdisciplinary writing groups, and three dissertation writing retreats.

In what follows, I describe how aspects of the design, execution, and marketing of these services aim to counter product-oriented or remedial narratives that associate participation in graduate writing center services primarily with decreases in time-to-degree or attrition. In particular, I focus on the relationship of all of our services to the one that, while the core of all writing center practice, is also most likely to be perceived as remedial: the one-to-one consultation. Through designing, conducting, and promoting writing consultations in ways that cultivate students' development as writers and scholars, I argue, writing centers can rise above, if not fully eclipse, their remedial reputations. Indeed, in striving to establish their relevance to all types of students, writing centers can also showcase their relevance to their institutions and to the professional and scholarly aims of doctoral education.

CREATING THE GRADUATE WRITING PLACE (GWP)

The decision to found the GWP was made by Northwestern's Writing Place director and graduate school administrators. Their impetus was twofold: to decrease graduate student use of the extant Writing Place, making more consultations available to undergraduate students, and to provide graduate students with a peer interlocutor who had experience with many of the genres associated with graduate-level writing. With these goals in mind, The Graduate School provided funding to hire a graduate assistant to help develop writing services for graduate students while being mentored and trained by the Writing Place director. Then a PhD candidate in the School of Communication (and now the director of the GWP), I was selected for this assistantship in August 2010.

The first year of my assistantship was focused on providing one-to-one writing consultations for graduate students. Suspecting that graduate students would appreciate the privacy afforded by a more intimate location than the extant Writing Place provided, as well as the exclusivity afforded by a differentiated schedule and name, the Writing Place director and I converted an unused program office into a room where consultations could be conducted, and we set up a separate schedule on the Writing Place's online scheduling system. Recognizing that the complexity and length of much graduate student writing warrants increased attention and time, we increased the duration of GWP consultations. Unlike the thirty-minute consultations available in the Writing Place, GWP clients must book *at least* an hour-long consultation and are also invited to book two-hour consultations. Moreover, during two-hour consultations, writers may choose to work synchronously for the full two hours or elect to email their writing to be read during the first hour and then come in during the second hour for discussion (see Kallestinova's findings, this volume, on effectiveness of hybrid read-ahead sessions). We also allow students to schedule four hours of consultations a month in an effort to foster the writers' ongoing development through sustained support and regular feedback, an important provision for doctoral students (Starke-Meyerring 2011).

My growing awareness of the importance of providing this kind of flexible assistance was, in part, informed by my experience entering an interdisciplinary PhD program with prior degrees in English literature and seeing that different disciplines had different communicative expectations and that writing—genres, conventions, language—needed to align with those expectations. In GWP consultations with my then graduate student peers, I drew on my newly gained understandings of the ways that the rhetorical, disciplinary, and genre-based features of writing communicate and create knowledge, asking my peers questions about the genres and conventions in their disciplines, thereby creating opportunities for them to articulate their own understandings. Similar to Michael Carter's (2007) aims for training faculty to cultivate "greater awareness" of how "the process of doing and writing research" coalesce to "shape disciplinary ways of knowing" (407), I hoped these conversations would help writers see the deep connection between writing, knowledge making, and disciplinary expertise and also to see how meaning can be shaped and refined through the types of collaborative conversations that characterize GWP consultations.

After a year of GWP consultations, there were limited but positive indications that GWP clients were developing this kind of meta-orientation toward writing and their writing processes. Of the fifty-four graduate students and postdoctoral writers who had consultations during the 2010–2011 academic year, thirty-six (67 percent) booked more than one consultation, suggesting an understanding that the GWP isn't a source of "quick fixes," but a venue where writers can expect to engage in ongoing conversations about writing as a practice through which disciplinary knowledge is formed and disciplinary identities are performed. That many writers engaged in consultations in such a way is further suggested by how many of them chose to focus on higher-order topics during their consultations: 70 percent discussed the clarity of their argument/contribution; 65 percent discussed organization (often, though not exclusively, related to genre conventions); 56 percent discussed providing requisite and/or convincing evidence/analysis/synthesis; and 52 percent discussed framing their work to suit a particular audience. In addition, of the twenty-one graduate students who completed an anonymous evaluation survey circulated in March 2011, sixteen strongly agreed that "using the Graduate Writing Place has transformed my understanding of writing and the writing process in a way that will have a lasting impact." In written responses to open-ended questions, students expressed appreciation for the dialogic quality of the consultations, identifying "exchanging ideas," "addressing [substantive] issues," "improving . . . my ability to communicate ideas to a broad audience" and, indeed, "dialogue" as elements of sessions they valued.[1]

EXPANDING THE GWP

The number of repeat consultations and the positive evaluations also pointed to opportunities for expanding the GWP to serve graduate students in other ways while also still showcasing the appeal and potential of consultations. To assess the specific types of writing support students were aware of, used, and/or desired, I surveyed students across the graduate school.[2] I also met with twenty-seven directors of graduate programs and other university administrators across the university to advertise and explain the mission of the GWP and to hear from them what types of writing requirements and resources existed in their departments and programs, as well as what services they thought the GWP might offer to meet student needs.

Results of the survey and findings from meetings with faculty and administrators indicated that the GWP could expand to provide more focused support for dissertation writers. In designing and facilitating a two-week dissertation writing retreat as well as three cross-disciplinary writing workshops, I aimed to mitigate students' reported lack of preparedness to write their dissertations in comparison with other writing required for their degrees (78 percent of surveyed PhD students reported feeling prepared to complete writing required for coursework and candidacy, whereas only 59 percent of respondents who had achieved candidacy felt prepared to write their dissertations). To better prepare doctoral students for writing their dissertations, both the writing retreats and the workshops aim to provide them with generalizable insights into key components of dissertation writing (e.g., how to synthesize research into a literature review).

The retreats and workshops also aimed to mimic GWP consultations by providing forums where cross-disciplinary conversations could enable participants to rehearse their disciplinary and genre knowledge in a low-stakes atmosphere (Cuthbert, Spark, and Burke 2009), and, in turn, they also showcased GWP expertise in particular topics and genres, assuring participants that they could get valuable feedback on those same topics in an individual consultation. Finally, in relocating the services of the GWP outside of the physical locale where individual consultations take place, writing retreats and workshops helped make visible much of the "invisible work" that happens in writing centers (Jackson and Grutsch McKinney 2011). Most obviously, they did so by introducing the GWP to students who may not otherwise have seen themselves as beneficiaries of writing center consultations.

Nonetheless, these expanded services could not reproduce a key feature of GWP consultations: their capacity to offer sustained, individualized support. Therefore, highlighting the potential utility of GWP consultations to retreat and workshop participants was—and continues to be—crucial to reinforcing the idea that the development of a disciplinary writing identity is an ongoing process that requires continuous practice and support from multiple parties (Paré 2007). Specifically, consultations provide the opportunity for students to explore and explain their disciplinary writing knowledge—moves and conventions—*before* this knowledge becomes tacit (Lovitts 2007). These explanations not only help them to become more reflective about their own writing processes and identities as writers, but also increase the likelihood that they will go on to become successful mentors of their own students, should they remain in academia, rather than fall into the shockingly high proportion of dissertation supervisors who have been identified as unprepared to teach students to write in their disciplines (Starke-Meyerring 2011). For those who do not remain in academia, the consultations, along with retreats and workshops, offer students the opportunity to communicate across disciplinary lines, an essential skill in the "alt-ac" careers many will be pursuing.

The extent to which writing retreats and workshops have succeeded in increasing students' awareness of the non-remedial, process-oriented nature of writing center consultations is suggested by the higher percentage of retreat and cross-disciplinary workshop participants who have attended writing consultations in subsequent years. As of summer 2016, 59 percent of the 355 students who participated in one of the 16 dissertation retreats have subsequently elected to attend GWP consultations. Similarly, of the 603 students who attended cross-disciplinary workshops between September 2011 and July 2016, 45 percent have also subsequently attended GWP consultations.

STAFFING THE GWP

One substantial contributor to students electing to use GWP consultations in process-oriented and non-remedial ways has been the addition of graduate writing fellows who serve as tutors. The Graduate Writing Fellows Program was implemented in 2012 to augment existing GWP services, that is, the number of writing consultations available and number of cross-disciplinary workshops held, and to provide graduate student writers with more discipline-specific entry points into the process-oriented work of GWP consultations. The advanced PhD candidates who are selected as fellows are awarded an annual honorarium of $3,000, an amount that is over and above whatever they may already earn through assistantships or other fellowships; in return, they tutor and help with the continued development and operations of graduate writing services. Specifically, fellows perform three triangulated roles: First, they hold 120 hours of GWP consultations over the course of the academic year. Second, they co-design, develop, and facilitate two sessions of a cross-disciplinary writing workshop on a topic of their choosing. And third, they work with relevant faculty and students in their own departments to create discipline-specific writing workshops and resources.

The fellows are selected following a competitive application process that includes a personal statement about their desire to serve as a fellow, a scholarly writing sample, consultation with their advisors, and an interview. Fellows must have demonstrated success at writing in their fields based on having presented at competitive conferences, winning a significant grant, and/or publishing in peer-reviewed outlets. The most competitive fellows not only have expertise with the genres and methods appropriate to their disciplinary work, they also have familiarity with the conventions of other disciplines, typically achieved through prior degrees and work experience and/or previous writing center and editorial work, as well as by conducting interdisciplinary research. Thus, while the current and former fellows represent an impressive twenty of the university's fifty-eight PhD granting departments and programs, even this number may not do justice to any one fellow's disciplinary breadth.

To ensure such quality and breadth among applicants, we showcase the Fellows Program to prospective applicants as an exceptional professional development opportunity. Recruitment materials draw attention to the unique potential of the fellowship to help graduate students develop as teachers and mentors, particularly of their fellow graduate students. Our materials explain how the program stands out to potential employers, particularly universities that may ask fellows to immediately begin teaching and mentoring graduate students. Based on these recruitment tactics, we have, over the last five years, received at least three times as many qualified applicants as positions available, a wealth of talent that has enabled a particularly discerning selection process. Selection criteria include the candidate's attitude toward writing, experience writing in a wide variety of genres and/or for different audiences, prior experiences with writing centers generally and with GWP services specifically. Particularly for candidates who have not participated in GWP consultations, I try to invoke the atmosphere of our consultations in my interview with the goal of gauging candidates' empathy for the struggles and difficulties that can animate graduate-level writing and, equally important, evaluate candidates' willingness and ability to think about their own writing processes at a meta-level.

Fellows' initial and ongoing training provides them with more opportunities for cultivating an understanding of the writing process as both a knowledge- and identity-making activity, emphasizing how they can both use and impart this understanding in their individual consultations with writers. Prior to the beginning of fall quarter, new fellows participate in a two-day orientation and read materials that provide them with background into the history of writing centers and graduate writing instruction, as well as common practices and characteristics of writing consultations. Fellows read, for example, Anne Beaufort's (2007) explanation of disciplinary expertise as made up of five domains of knowledge: discourse community, writing process, rhetorical, genre, and subject matter. Building on Catherine Savani's (2011) suggestion that asking questions in line with these domains might help bridge disciplinary divides in the writing center, we use the questions she developed for each domain as a starting point for thinking about what other questions might be pertinent at a graduate level. Beyond thinking about how and when writing might operate differently in graduate contexts, this exercise also helps fellows to think about the utility that answering such questions (and thinking about expertise in such a way) might have for a graduate writer.

To put these ideas into immediate use, the fellows engage in practice consultations with each other and several returning or former fellows. We reflect on these practice consultations in the context of the disciplinary backgrounds and genres that graduate student writers bring to GWP consultations. Rather than aiming to develop fellows' familiarity with areas outside their current disciplinary and genre knowledge, we talk about how they can use their extant expertise to help writers articulate and uncover their own understandings of the rhetorical, disciplinary, and genre features germane to the writing at hand (see Reineke et al., this volume, for a "moves" approach to uncovering such features). As Rebecca Nowacek and Brad Hughes explain in their discussion of the generalist consultants who work in undergraduate-focused writing centers, such an "expert outsider" stance enables writing consultants to draw on their understanding of the rhetorical and disciplinary purposes that writing serves while also ceding field and subject matter expertise to the writer. When used effectively, this expert-outsider positioning "can help writers better engage the social and rhetorical dimensions of their writing" (Nowacek and Hughes 2015, 151). In other words, it's not just what fellows know about writing in a particular genre or discipline that can make a consultation relevant for a writer; it's what fellows know about how writing shapes disciplinary knowledge and is, at the same time, shaped by that knowledge. Through this collaborative, dialogic process, then, GWP consultations reinforce the idea that writing is an iterative and social process that is informed by and responsive to its readers, in this case fellows acting as interlocutors.

To evaluate the extent to which GWP clients achieve and are satisfied with such process-based aims, we rely on a combination of anonymous client surveys and the reports that fellows write about each consultation. Following every consultation in the GWP, writers are sent a brief automated survey asking them to evaluate and comment on their experience. Between fall 2012, when the Graduate Writing Fellows Program was established, and August 2016, 1,124 survey evaluations were completed, representing 32 percent of the 3,529 consultations held during the same time period. The survey results provide overwhelmingly positive indications of graduate writers' satisfaction with their experiences in writing consultations. In response to the first survey question "How would you rate your writing consultation?" 84 percent answered "Excellent." The other two questions—"Will you return to the Graduate Writing Place?" and "Will you recommend the Graduate Writing Place?"—garnered even more positive responses, with over 97 percent of students answering yes to both.

The survey respondents supplemented these positive responses with optional qualitative feedback, helping to illuminate why they evaluate sessions so positively. For example, one comment that captures themes frequently invoked by writers who receive both reader- and genre-oriented feedback during their consultations, explained: "I'd reached an impasse in my proposal and didn't know how to diagnose the problem or proceed. But Seth had lots of probing questions to offer that were helpful in clarifying my argument. His suggestions for how to approach structuring the proposal document were also spot-on."

Fellows' own follow-up reports, which are also sent to the writers with whom they consulted after each session, help corroborate how fellows attempt to combine instruction with questioning to scaffold writers' development, particularly in ways that facilitate writers' meta-understandings of the rhetorical, disciplinary, or genre features underlying writing. The primary intent of these reports is to summarize key aspects of a consultation that a writer might use in the future, such as methods for reverse outlining or providing functional definitions of complex terms. In addition to re-articulating whatever feedback they provided during the session, then, fellows often supplement their feedback (and thus corroborate their expertise) with links to advice about or models of specific genres and conventions. In addition, fellows often explicitly call writers' attention to moments of confusion or misunderstanding that occurred during the consultation. Fellows remind writers that these moments are spots when they might consider what inspired that confusion (e.g., uncertain use of disciplinary conventions/jargon; lack of clarity about rhetorical aims, purposes, and audiences; insufficient content knowledge). Fellows' reports therefore aim to compel writers into considering these kinds of issues as they revise and compose in the future.

Over the course of their fellowships, fellows continue to hone their own meta-understandings of how writing works within and across disciplines through the work they do to fulfill the other requirements of the Graduate Writing Fellows Program: the planning and facilitating of cross-disciplinary and discipline-specific workshops. The topics, content, format, and activities for these workshops are developed collectively. Fellows work with me, with each other, and with stakeholders and peers in their home departments to identify the best way to present materials. By discussing and collaborating on these workshop materials, fellows learn from each other's knowledge of certain discipline- and genre-specific writing conventions, augmenting what Sarah Summers (2016) labels the "expertise-based tools" that can be used during GWP consultations to help writers cultivate meta-understandings of how genre and discipline-specific moves and conventions operate in their fields.

In addition, fellows are encouraged to design cross-disciplinary and discipline-specific workshops that model the kinds of dialogue and interaction that take place in GWP consultations. Often, they also assemble panels of speakers from their programs or departments (or even outside of the university). Whether leading the workshop solely or as part of a panel, fellows use a dialogic format to engage their peers in conversations about the nature of writing and research in their programs and in broader meta-disciplines.

PROMOTING THE GWP AS MENTOR AND PARTNER

To correct remedial impressions of the GWP at the student, program and institutional level, we have been fortunate enough to have funding that allows us to staff the center exclusively with advanced PhD candidates, thus also correcting the common misperception that writing center work is most appropriate for providing novice graduate students with training in working with writers before they begin the "real" work of teaching their own classes (Nicolas 2005). Likewise, selecting fellows from a variety of disciplines rectifies the common practice of staffing writing centers with graduate students from English or rhetoric programs, which can suggest that writing and the ability to teach it fall within the purview of those disciplines only.

But wider institutional visibility is also important. For example, I attend resource fairs and graduate student orientations, sit on panels related to graduate writing, and facilitate workshops about dissertation writing for department-based, graduate student-led professional development groups who may have been charged with coordinating professional development colloquia for their doctoral programs. Less frequently, departmental administrators or faculty will see advertisements for cross-disciplinary workshops and contact me about modifying presentations for a particular department or program. Similar to the ways in which the fellows' discipline-specific programming aims to provide departmental entry points to GWP services, I hope that my presence in such varied venues cultivates an image of the writing center that emphasizes outreach, mentoring, and support for all advanced graduate writers.

These pedagogical opportunities also allow me to perform the task that Emily Issacs and Melinda Knight identify as crucial to maintaining the institutional position and longevity of a writing center: telling the story of what GWPs have achieved and what they aspire to achieve to as many stakeholders as will grant me access (Issacs and Knight 2014). Such narratives emphasize the importance of support from and partnerships with graduate faculty, advisors, graduate programs, departments, and graduate schools, along with other campus-wide graduate support offices (e.g., see Gray, this volume), and those responsible for allocating funding. Positioning our services as important supplements to existing mentorship and other graduate programming demonstrates the central role writing support can and should play in graduate education given its fundamental importance to the making of both scholars and scholarship (Aitchison and Paré 2012).

While the GWP, like nearly all graduate writing centers, is still in its early stages, I see evidence that its relevance and importance is beginning to resonate for more than just graduate writers. In addition to the growing numbers of PhD candidates we've been serving over the last six years, we are also seeing postdoctoral students and faculty schedule one-to-one consultations; taken together, these clients, in fact, comprised 48 percent of our overall clientele in the 2015–2016 academic year vs. 30 percent in the 2010–2011 academic year. Further, among our growing population are a substantial percentage of the high achieving fellows themselves. As of August 2016, twenty of the thirty-one current and former Graduate Writing Fellows have booked one-to-one writing consultations with each other.

Such evidence suggests the importance of communicating a persistent and consistent message about writing as a dynamic, ongoing developmental and educational process. Alongside providing appropriate and appropriately trained graduate consultants, emphasizing this process can demonstrate the relevance of writing centers to writers of all levels. In turn, writing centers can transcend their remedial reputations and reaffirm the key role that writing and our services play in graduate education as a whole.

NOTES

1. These topics stem from my coding of the follow-up reports written after each consultation. Since consultations rarely focused on a single aspect of writing, and writers often elected to focus on different elements of their writing during different consultations, the total number of students focusing on all writing topics exceeds the number of students who held consultations. Other coded topics (and corresponding numbers of students) for 2010–2011 are grammar and syntax (56% of writers) and citation conventions/concerns (15% of writers).
2. Though there was only a 10 percent response rate (n=351 of the 3,621 graduate students invited to take the survey), the students who did respond represented all eight of Northwestern's graduate degree granting schools and fifty-one of its eighty degree-granting departments and programs. Moreover, 84 percent of the respondents described themselves as "fluent" in English. Finally, the vast majority of respondents (87%) was enrolled in PhD granting programs, and 64 percent of these students were writing their dissertation proposals and/or had already achieved candidacy. Together, these statistics suggest the survey results should provide a fairly representative slice of Northwestern's graduate students.

REFERENCES

Aitchison, Claire, and Anthony Paré. 2012. "Writing as Craft and Practice in the Doctoral Curriculum." In *Reshaping Doctoral Education*, ed. Alison Lee and Susan Danby, 12–25. London: Routledge.

Autry, Megan Kittle, and Michael Carter. 2015. "Unblocking Occluded Genres in Graduate Writing: Thesis and Dissertation Support Services at North Carolina State University." *Composition Forum* 31. http://compositionforum.com/issue/31/north-carolina-state.php.

Beaufort, Anne. 2007. *College Writing and Beyond: A New Framework for University Writing Instruction*. Logan: Utah State University Press.

Brooks-Gillies, Marilee, Elena G. Garcia, Soo Hyon Kim, Katie Manthey, and Trixie Smith. 2015. "Graduate Writing Across the Disciplines, Introduction." *Across the Disciplines* 12 (3). http://wac.colostate.edu/atd/graduate_wac/intro.cfm.

Carter, Michael. 2007. "Ways of Knowing, Doing, and Writing in the Disciplines." *College Composition and Communication* 58 (3): 385–407.

Cuthbert, Denise, Ceridwen Spark, and Eliza Burke. 2009. "Disciplining Writing: The Case for Multi-Disciplinary Writing Groups to Support Writing for Publication by Higher Degree Research Candidates in the Humanities, Arts and Social Sciences." *Higher Education Research & Development* 28 (2): 137–49. https://doi.org/10.1080/07294360902725025.

Holley, Karri A., and Mary Lee Caldwell. 2012. "The Challenges of Designing and Implementing a Doctoral Student Mentoring Program." *Innovative Higher Education* 37 (3): 243–53. https://doi.org/10.1007/s10755-011-9203-y.

Issacs, Emily, and Melinda Knight. 2014. "A Bird's Eye View of Writing Centers." *WPA: Writing Program Administration* 37 (2): 36–67.

Jackson, Rebecca, and Jackie Grutsch McKinney. 2011. "Beyond Tutoring: Mapping the Invisible Landscape of Writing Center Work." *Praxis: A Writing Center Journal* 9 (1): 1–11. http://www.praxisuwc.com/jackson-mckinney-91.

Kamler, Barbara, and Pat Thomson. 2006. *Helping Doctoral Students Write: Pedagogies for Supervision*. London: Routledge.

Kamler, Barbara. 2008. "Rethinking Doctoral Publication Practices: Writing From and Beyond the Thesis." *Studies in Higher Education* 33 (3): 283–94. https://doi.org/10.1080/03075070802049236.

Lee, Alison, and Claire Aitchison. 2009. "Writing for the Doctorate and Beyond." In *Changing Practices of Doctoral Education*, ed. David Boud and Alison Lee, 87–99. London: Routledge.

Lee, Alison, and Susan Danby. 2011. *Reshaping Doctoral Education: International Approaches and Pedagogies*. London: Routledge.

Lovitts, Barbara E. 2007. *Making the Implicit Explicit: Creating Performance Expectations for the Dissertation*. Sterling, VA: Stylus Publishing.

Maher, Michelle, Amber Fallucca, and Helen Mulhern Halasz. 2013. "Write On! Through to the Ph.D.: Using Writing Groups to Facilitate Doctoral Degree Progress." *Studies in Continuing Education* 35 (2): 193–208. https://doi.org/10.1080/0158037X.2012.736381.

Mannon, Bethany Ober. 2016. "What Do Graduate Students Want from the Writing Center?." *Praxis: A Writing Center Journal* 13 (2): 59–64. http://www.praxisuwc.com/new-page-29-1.Ait.

Nicolas, Melissa. 2005. "Writing Centers as Training Wheels." *Praxis: A Writing Center Journal* 3 (1). http://www.praxisuwc.com/nicolas-3-1.

Nowacek, Rebecca, and Brad Hughes. 2015. "Threshold Concepts in the Writing Center." In *Naming What We Know: Threshold Concepts of Writing Studies*, ed. Linda Adler-Kassner and Elizabeth Wardle, 171–85. Logan: Utah State University Press.

Paré, Anthony. 2007. "What We Know about Writing, and Why it Matters." Keynote presented at the Annual Dalhousie Conference on University Teaching and Learning, Halifax, Nova Scotia, May 2. http://citeseerx.ist.psu.edu/viewdoc/download?doi=10.1.1.574.4120&rep=rep1&type=pdf.

Park, Chris. 2007. *Redefining the Doctorate: A Discussion Paper.* York: Higher Education Academy.

Rose, Mike, and Karen A. McClafferty. 2001. "A Call for the Teaching of Writing in Graduate Education." *Educational Researcher* 30 (2): 27–33. https://doi.org/10.3102/0013189X030002027.

Salem, Lori. 2014. "Opportunity and Transformation: How Writing Centers are Positioned in the Political Landscape of Higher Education in the United States." *Writing Center Journal* 34 (1): 15–43.

Savani, Catherine. 2011. "An Alternative Approach to Bridging Disciplinary Divides." *Writing Lab Newsletter* 35 (7/8): 1–5.

Simpson, Steve. 2013. "Building for Sustainability: Dissertation Boot Camp as Nexus of Graduate Writing Support." *Praxis: A Writing Center Journal* 10 (2): 1–8. http://www.praxisuwc.com/simpson-102.

Starke-Meyerring, Doreen. 2011. "The Paradox of Writing in Doctoral Education." In *Doctoral Education: Research-Based Strategies for Doctoral Students, Supervisors, and Administrators*, ed. Lynn McAlpine and Cheryl Amundsen, 75–95. Houten: Springer Netherlands. https://doi.org/10.1007/978-94-007-0507-4_5.

Summers, Sarah. 2016. "Building Expertise: The Toolkit in UCLA's Graduate Writing Center." *Writing Center Journal* 35 (2): 117–46.

Sundstrom, Christine Jensen. 2014. "The Graduate Writing Program at the University of Kansas: An Inter-Disciplinary, Rhetorical Genre-Based Approach to Developing Professional Identities." *Composition Forum* 29. http://compositionforum.com/issue/29/kansas.php.

"WLN: Special Issue Call—Graduate Student Support." 2014. *The WLN Blog*, October 20, 2014. https://www.wlnjournal.org/blog/2014/10/wln-special-issue-call-graduate-student-support/.

Epilogue

CENTER-ING DISSERTATION SUPERVISION
What Was, What Is, and What Can Be

Sherry Wynn Perdue

Nearly a decade ago, when I commenced my own query into the support needs of graduate writers and the role that writing centers might play in meeting them, I located few voices from within the field to guide my search. Of those, most authors lamented the writing center's inability to effectively guide the disciplinary specialist, limited their interventions to ESL writers, or addressed graduate writers only to the extent that they were employed within the writing center. Equally discouraging, none of the articles and book chapters I located was grounded in empirical research. This book, the 2016 special issue of *WLN: A Journal of Writing Center Scholarship* that preceded it, and a 2016 special issue of *Praxis* signal an important change in our relationship to graduate writers, moving from institutional neglect toward *center*-ed support.

In this epilogue, I examine ways to extend the work we are already doing to support individual graduate writers within the center by building collaborations with and providing professional learning opportunities for graduate supervisors. Although such collaborations were not the focus of the chapters that comprise this book, its contributors affirm the need to enlarge the center of our work. Joan Turner, for example, acknowledges the perception gap that plagues our consulting on behalf of graduate writers. Many faculty supervisors' conception of graduate writing and the role of a writing consultation within it is akin to the graduate student simply "writing up" the research (Kamler and Thomson 2014) and the writing consultant intervening to help the individual "fix up" the mechanics that the writer failed to learn. Such a scheme fails to comprehend the complex act of the graduate student writing him- or herself into the discipline, an understanding that eludes most graduate supervisors but that compositionists and writing center practitioners have gained from recent scholarship in rhetorical genre studies by the

DOI: 10.7330/9781607327516.c013

likes of Anis Bawarshi and Mary Jo Reiff (Bawarshi and Reiff 2010), Charles Bazerman (2009), and Anthony Paré (2011, 2014).

In response to gaps and misconceptions about graduate writers themselves and to the writing center's role in addressing their needs, Steve Simpson (this volume) asks writing centers to "position [ourselves] as resources for advisors and graduate faculty" thereby enhancing their understanding of writing and its necessary relationship to disciplinary mentorship as well as acknowledging the importance of scaffolded graduate support. Although Simpson would concede that the needs of graduate writers are inadequately addressed at the departmental level, he clearly indicates that the writing challenges confronting graduate students cannot be mediated solely by academic support units like the writing center. Decontextualized stand-alone services reinforce a prominent belief that "the graduate writing problem" is synonymous with an individual writer who enters graduate school with a skills deficit (Goodchild, Green, Katz, and Kluever 1997; Gardner 2008; Kamler and Thomson 2014). In actuality, the graduate writing problem is less about individual writers' skill deficits than about task novelty, cognitive overload, information (il)literacy, authority, and supervision training gaps (Peelo 2011; Aitchison and Guerin 2014; Kamler and Thomson 2014;).

If we are to reconceive the writing center's role and to act as change agents in support of graduate writers, then I advise writing centers to embrace Michael Pemberton's recommendation to become "'co-sponsors' of graduate students' disciplinary enculturation through the medium of writing." In the next few pages, I briefly share one model for this co-sponsorship, a dissertation supervision fellowship program I designed and piloted at my own institution in 2016.

CENTER-SUPPORTED SUPERVISION

Before introducing the model, I must acknowledge the role that one early essay, Judith Powers's "Assisting the Graduate Thesis Writer through Faculty and Writing Center Collaboration," played in its development. In Powers's (1995) call for a collaborative conferencing method, I found a germ of an idea that grew from "trialogue," her team's effort to triangulate the writing consultation among the graduate writer, the consultant, and the supervisor to facilitate better understanding of the writing task within all parties (15). Over time and with the input of many others, it yielded the sponsored dissertation supervision model I implemented within the Rosen Supervision Fellows Program described below. Although Powers was perhaps too quick to dismiss the writing consultant's ability to address advanced disciplinary content and technical matters, the trialogue was an early effort to better facilitate genre awareness across all parties and it fueled my determination to do the same. But the more I consulted one-on-one with graduate writers, particularly dissertators, the gap between what was expected from them and their supervisors' ability to model or convey those expectations (even when I consulted with individual supervisors throughout the process) gnawed at my consciousness. Graduate writers deserved better from me, from their supervisors, from their graduate schools, and from their institutions.

Anecdotal evidence from my own sessions suggested that if graduate students were to become better prepared to compose complex, disciplinary-situated high stakes texts like the dissertation—if they were going to conceive of themselves as knowledge makers—their supervisors needed more explicit preparation for and knowledge of the writing process than their own experience as supervisees had provided. And while I was not finding what I needed in writing center studies or in US discussions of graduate writing when I began this quest on behalf of graduate writers, I was fortunate to discover a body of scholarship devoted to doctoral supervision in Canada, the United Kingdom, Australia, and New Zealand that encouraged me to place the supervisor rather than the graduate writer at the center of my efforts.

Within this international scholarship, I found a theoretical framework and empirical evidence for my growing belief that the doctoral supervisor was the most important resource in the graduate writer's journey to internalize her or his discipline's "norms and values" (Lee 2008; Bitchener, Basturkmen, and East 2010). I also found support for one important caveat that would justify my role as what my domestic writing center colleagues call an "expert outsider" (Nowacek and Hughes 2015). Although supervisors generally possess the genre-specific writing ability that novices like their supervisees lack, they often struggle "to articulate their knowledge of disciplinary discourse," a form of implicit knowledge (Paré 2011, 60–62). When supervisors lack explicit awareness of the rhetorical moves writers need to make within a discipline-specific genre for a department-specific audience, the resulting feedback is akin to "fuzzy bits of advice" (Paré 2011, 60–62), which may frustrate rather than clarify the dissertator's task.

The sponsored dissertation supervision program described herein is more explicit than the writing center intervention detailed by Powers. It leverages the writing center scholar's role as an expert outsider (Nowacek and Hughes 2015) who holds explicit knowledge of writing that she can share by sponsoring doctoral supervisors, the genre natives who hold implicit knowledge of writing in the field. It is my belief—and one I hope you might come to share—that writing center scholars can effect greater change for more dissertators when they mentor graduate supervisors.

ROSEN DISSERTATION SUPERVISION FELLOWSHIP PROGRAM

As my appreciation grew for the role that writing centers might play in helping graduate writers by supporting graduate faculty, particularly by providing "workshops to support supervisors in identifying and diagnosing problems in student writing" (Bitchener et al. 2011, 5), the dean of the College of Arts and Sciences asked me to create a writing center program that would honor the College of Arts and Science's (CAS) 2016 annual theme, which emphasized twenty-first century literacies. The Oakland University Writing Center, which reports to Academic Affairs, was once overseen by the CAS dean and the writing center's modest endowment, a generous gift of Joan and Robert Rosen, continues to be administered by the college's development staff. Although I knew the dean was asking for an endowment-worthy program to support undergraduate writers, I countered with a two-pronged proposal that included support for graduate writers. The writing center would sponsor eight faculty-undergraduate research teams to engage in disciplinary-specific research with the benefit of a $1,000 stipend for each faculty member and an additional $1,000 for research and travel funds for each undergraduate if I could concurrently fund a fellowship experience for faculty members who supervise doctoral dissertations. Because the dean understands the distinct literacies represented within the disciplines and across the undergraduate and graduate programs he oversees, he endorsed the plan and approved the allocation without concessions. Talk about kairos!

In October 2015, I recruited faculty members who both teach graduate courses and supervise dissertations. Ten applicants were accepted into the program: seven associate professors and three assistant professors, each tenure-line or tenured, from psychology (5), educational leadership (2), early childhood education (2), and counseling (1). Although I sought participants from each of the three schools/colleges that award doctoral degrees, only the College of Arts and Sciences and School of Education and Human Sciences are represented in the cohort. All fellows were awarded a $1,000 stipend to join the pilot supervision program advertised as an opportunity to investigate their supervision beliefs, knowledge, and practices, particularly their delivery of feedback, in the context of best practices as identified within the literature and as informed by Rhetorical Genre Theory.

Throughout 2016, the cohort met once a month for an hour and half in a seminar format to consume scholarship and food (an important incentive that the program provides). We discussed assigned resources; explored fellows' supervision challenges; practiced revision-focused feedback to de-identified dissertation excerpts; mapped out supervisor-supervisee contractual language; and prioritized program goals for future supervision cohorts. To guide our early work, I compiled a syllabus-of-sorts, with potential talking points for each session and with practitioner and research resources to inform our exploration. Fellows commenced study of their roles as mentors and evaluators via such topics as graduate student identity and effective feedback practices by reading Barbara Kamler and Patricia Thomson's (2014) *Helping Doctoral Students Write: Pedagogies for Supervision*, which I purchased for each participant (Kamler and Thomson 2014). As a natural outgrowth of the book discussion, I asked fellows to identify salient supervision challenges. These fellows, like the supervisors described in the extant literature we would later consult, articulated their own struggles to meet the needs of multiple supervisees—each with different personalities, expectations, writing styles, and paces (Eley and Jennings 2005; Lange and Baillie 2008)—and to balance their own work/writing preferences with those of their supervisees (Pyhältö, Vekkaila, and Keskinen 2012). Rather than sticking to the "syllabus script" after the first two sessions, I allowed the participants' questions and goals to determine what we would address in each subsequent meeting. And, to parrot Dr. Seuss, *Oh, the places we [went]* because I prioritized flexibility as a cornerstone of our time together. I would encourage anyone exploring a similar program to do the same.

EXPLORING "WHAT CAN BE"

With the first iteration of the Rosen Dissertation Supervision Fellowship complete, I look forward to empirically investigating the degree to which interventions like mine might build upon and extend the work described within this book. To that end and because dissertation supervision is less robustly supported and studied within the United States, I will represent the program within a case study (Stake 1995, 2003; Baxter and Jack 2008; Creswell 2012; Yin 2013) that explores participants' supervision experiences, beliefs, genre knowledge, and feedback practices as well as their perceptions about this writing center program's potential to enhance their ability to guide dissertators' transition from students to disciplinary colleagues. Conceived in this way, my focus will be local and the degree to which I may extrapolate my findings is more circumscribed: to represent what exists at my institution, to examine how these faculty members experience their supervision, to learn what they know and believe, to discern what they expect from their students and themselves, and to better understand the role that the writing center might play in facilitating their growth.

While I have yet to complete the data collection and analysis of the in-depth interviews, observation notes, feedback practice excerpts, and program evaluations that will inform this case, I can affirm that the existing literature helped me to anticipate supervisory challenges such as participants' tendency to privilege later order concerns too early in the feedback process (Rogers, Zawacki, and Baker 2016) and the belief that their dissertators' writing problems reflected individual deficits or laziness more than the complexity of the dissertation challenge (Goodchild, Green, Katz, and Kluever 1997; Gardner 2008; Kamler and Thomson 2014). And while I currently cannot cite findings to support a claim that the center is well positioned to sponsor dissertation supervision, I can report that the faculty fellows have overwhelmingly welcomed this opportunity to hone revision-focused feedback in a knowledge-rich and supportive environment. Perhaps more important to my purpose here, these faculty supervisors claim to better appreciate both the challenges graduate writers face and the role that the writing center can play in their own development as supervisors, particularly their growing awareness of their role in honing dissertators' genre knowledge.

As a testament to the program and their self-efficacy as supervisors, the participants have agreed to help me refine the fellows program for the next generation of fellows, to serve as liaisons to departmental and college/school colleagues, and to collaborate on a proposal for the graduate school to build more sustainable support for supervisors and graduate writers. And, none of these commitments are accompanied by a stipend or a course release.

Before I conclude, I must concede that some conditions of this program might be difficult for others to replicate. In most writing centers, stipends and food are luxuries, and many graduate faculty members are not eager to embrace another undervalued responsibility. With that said, my goal in sharing this program is to encourage others not only to envision what we can do under a traditional model of writing center support but also to follow Michael Pemberton's (this volume) and Ben

Rafoth's (2015) suggestions that we rhetorically reimagine writing center roles beyond "what has been" and "what is" to "what can be."

REFERENCES

Aitchison, Claire, and Cally Guerin, eds. 2014. *Writing Groups for Doctoral Education and Beyond: Innovations in Practice and Theory*. London: Routledge.

Bawarshi, Anis S., and Mary Jo Reiff. 2010. *Genres: An Introduction to History, Theory, Research, and Pedagogy*. West Lafayette, IN: Parlor Press and The WAC Clearinghouse.

Baxter, Pamela, and Susan Jack. 2008. "Qualitative Case Study Methodology: Study Design and Implementation for Novice Researchers." *Qualitative Report* 13 (4): 544–59. https://nsuworks.nova.edu/tqr/vol13/iss4/2.

Bazerman, Charles. 2009. "Genre and Cognitive Development: Beyond Writing to Learn." In *Genre in a Changing World*, ed. Charles Bazerman, Adair Bonini, and Dbora Figueiredo, 279–94. Fort Collins, CO: The WAC Clearinghouse. https://doi.org/10.4000/pratiques.1419.

Bitchener, John, Helen Basturkmen, and Martin East. 2010. "The Focus of Supervisor Written Feedback to Thesis/Dissertation Students." *International Journal of English Studies* 10 (2): 79–97. https://doi.org/10.6018/ijes/2010/2/119201.

Bitchener, John, Helen Basturkmen, Martin East, and Heather Meyer. 2011. *Best Practice in Supervisor Feedback to Thesis Students*. [Research report sponsored by the National Project Fund]. https://akoaotearoa.ac.nz/best-practice-supervisor-feedback.

Creswell, John W. 2012. *Qualitative Inquiry and Research Design: Choosing among Five Approaches*. 3rd ed. Thousand Oaks, CA: SAGE Publications.

Eley, Adrain R., and Roy Jennings. 2005. *Effective Postgraduate Supervision: Improving the Student/Supervisor Relationship*. Maidenhead, UK: Open University Press.

Gardner, Susan K. 2008. "Student and Faculty Attributions of Attrition in High and Low-Completing Doctoral Programs in the United States." *Higher Education* 58 (1): 97–112. https://doi.org/10.1007/s10734-008-9184-7.

Goodchild, Lester F., Kathy E. Green, Elinor L. Katz, and Raymond C. Kluever, eds. 1997. *Rethinking the Dissertation Process: Tackling Personal and Institutional Obstacles*. New Directions for Higher Education Series No. 99 (Fall 1997). San Francisco, CA: Jossey-Bass Publishers.

Kamler, Barbara, and Patricia Thomson. 2014. *Helping Doctoral Students Write: Pedagogies for Supervision*. London: Routledge.

Lange, Karina, and Caroline Baillie. 2008. "Exploring Graduate Student Learning in Applied Science and Student-Supervisor Relationships: Views of Supervisors and Their Students." *Engineering Education* 3 (1): 30–43. https://doi.org/10.11120/ened.2008.03010030.

Lee, Anne. 2008. "How Are Doctoral Students Supervised? Concepts of Doctoral Research Supervision." *Studies in Higher Education* 33 (3): 267–81. https://doi.org/10.1080/03075070802049202.

Nowacek, Roberta, and Brad Hughes. 2015. "Threshold Concepts in the Writing Center: Scaffolding the Development of Tutor Expertise." In *Naming What We Know: Threshold Concepts of Writing Studies*, ed. Linda Adler Kassner and Elizabeth Wardle, 171–85. Logan: Utah State University Press. https://doi.org/10.7330/9780874219906.c011.

Paré, Anthony. 2014. "Rhetorical Genre Theory and Academic Literacy." *Journal of Academic Language and Learning* 8 (1): A83–A94.

Paré, Anthony. 2011. "Speaking of Writing: Supervisory Feedback and the Dissertation." In *Doctoral Education: Research-Based Strategies for Doctoral Students, Supervisors and Admin-*

istrators, ed. Lynn McAlpine and Cheryl Amundsen, 59–74. London: Springer. doi: 10.1007/978-94-007-0507-4_4.

Peelo, Moira. 2011. *Understanding Supervision and the PhD*. London: Continuum.

Powers, Judith K. 1995. "Assisting the Graduate Thesis Writer through Faculty and Writing Center Collaboration." *The Writing Lab Newsletter* 20 (2): 13–16.

Pyhältö, Kirsi, Jenna Vekkaila, and Jenni Keskinen. 2012. "Exploring the Fit between Doctoral Students' and Supervisors' Perceptions of Resources and Challenges vis-à-vis the Doctoral Journey." *International Journal of Doctoral Studies* 7:395–414. https://doi.org/10.28945/1745.

Rafoth, Ben. 2015. "Face, Factories, and Warhols: A r(Evolutionary) Future for Writing Centers." Keynote Address presented to the International Writing Centers Association Conference, Pittsburgh, Pennsylvania, 2015.

Rogers, Paul, Terry Myers Zawacki, and Sarah E. Baker. 2016. "Uncovering Challenges and Pedagogical Complications in Dissertation Writing and Supervisory Practices: A Multimethod Study of Doctoral Students and Advisors." In *Supporting Graduate Writers: Research, Curriculum, & Program Design*, ed. Steve Simpson, Nigel A. Caplan, Michelle Cox, and Talinn Phillips, 52–77. Ann Arbor: University of Michigan Press.

Stake, Robert E. 1995. *The Art of Case Study Research*. London: Sage Publications.

Stake, Robert E. 2003. "Case Studies." In *Strategies of Qualitative Inquiry*, 2nd ed., ed. Norman K. Denzin. and Yvonna S. Lincoln, 134–64. London: Sage Publications.

Yin, Robert K. 2013. *Case Study Research: Design and Methods*. 5th ed. Thousand Oaks, CA: SAGE Publications.

ABOUT THE CONTRIBUTORS

SUSAN LAWRENCE is term associate professor of English and director of the George Mason University Writing Center, which supports graduate students though individual consultations, workshops, and writing groups. She teaches graduate courses in research methods and writing center theory and has published on writing in the disciplines and tutoring online. She coedited, with Terry Myers Zawacki, a special issue of *Writing Lab Newsletter* focused on writing center support for graduate student writers.

TERRY MYERS ZAWACKI is emerita director of Writing Across the Curriculum and the writing center at George Mason University where she was recognized for significant long-term contributions to the overall excellence of the university. Her publications include *Engaged Writers and Dynamic Disciplines* and coedited collections *WAC and Second Language Writers* and *Writing Across the Curriculum: A Critical Sourcebook*, as well as articles on WAC, writing centers, assessment, WAC and L2 writers, and challenges around dissertation writing. She is lead editor of the book series *International Exchanges on the Study of Writing*.

LAURA BRADY is Eberly Professor of Outstanding Teaching within the English Department at West Virginia University. She currently codirects a communication-across-curriculum program that includes support for graduate student writing. Her research (often collaborative) focuses on writing pedagogy and WAC/WID with articles in journals such as *College English, Composition Forum, The WAC Journal, WLN: A Journal of Writing Center Scholarship,* and *WPA: Writing Program Administration* as well as several edited collections.

MICHELLE COX is the founding director of Cornell University's English Language Support Office, which provides writing and speaking support to international multilingual graduate students. She is the inaugural chair of the CCCC WAC Standing Group and founding co-chair of the Consortium on Graduate Communication. Her publications include coedited collections, chapters, and articles on second language writing, WAC and L2 writing, WAC program administration, and graduate communication support.

THOMAS DEANS is professor of English and director of the Writing Center at the University of Connecticut. He serves as series coeditor for the *Oxford Brief Guides to Writing in the Disciplines* and has ongoing interests in university-community partnerships, writing centers, writing assessment, and representations of writers in literary and sacred texts.

PAULA GILLESPIE directed the Center for Excellence in Writing at Florida International University until retiring in 2017. A past president of the International Writing Center Association (IWCA), she received the Ron Maxwell award for her work with peer tutors and the Muriel Harris award for service. Her publications include the coauthored *Longman Guide to Peer Tutoring* and coedited *Writing Center Research: Extending the Conversation*, as well as the Peer Tutor Alumni Research Project, for which she and coauthors received an IWCA outstanding article award.

ABOUT THE CONTRIBUTORS

MARY GLAVAN, formerly an assistant to the director at Carnegie Mellon University's Global Communication Center, is a lecturer in the writing program at the University of Southern California. Her work explores the intersections of writing studies, disability rhetoric, and community advocacy.

MARILYN GRAY is the founding director of the Graduate Writing Center at the University of California, Los Angeles. In this role she has led writing workshops and dissertation support programs for UCLA graduate students from a wide range of disciplines. She particularly enjoys working with doctoral students when they are developing their research proposals. Her research interests range widely from Slavic literature to doctoral education reform.

JAMES HOLSINGER is Director of Learning Assistance at Elon University. He previously served as Writing Center Director at Longwood University. His work focuses on the intersections of learning centers and retention among at-risk populations.

ELENA KALLESTINOVA is the founding director of the Graduate Writing Laboratory at Yale University. She designs and implements writing and communication programs for graduate and professional school students through workshops, writing groups, dissertation writing retreats, and individual consultations. She is passionate about graduate communication, second language writing, language acquisition, and mentoring graduate student writers. Her publications include articles on topics in linguistics, scientific writing, graduate student writing needs, and writing center studies.

TIKA LAMSAL is assistant professor in the Department of Rhetoric and Language at the University of San Francisco. He teaches undergraduate and graduate courses on multilingual and multimodal writing and professional communication across languages and cultures. His research focuses on multilingual and multimodal literacies, non-Western rhetorics, refugee literacies, cross-cultural and cross language composition, and has appeared in *JAC: Journal of Advanced Composition* and *Journal of Global Literacies, Technologies, and Emerging Pedagogies*.

PATRICK S. LAWRENCE is assistant professor of English at the University of South Carolina, Lancaster. He is a past Coordinator for Graduate Writing Support at the University of Connecticut, and he also researches intersecting issues of race, ethnicity, gender, and sexuality in late twentieth-century American literature and culture. His work has been published in *Mosaic*, *Asian American Literature: Discourses and Pedagogies*, and *Intertexts*.

ELIZABETH LENAGHAN is assistant professor of instruction in the Cook Family Writing Program at Northwestern University and the founding director of Northwestern's Graduate Writing Place. Her research and teaching focus on the impact new media have on the reception, consumption, and production of traditional cultural objects and modes of expression, and her work on graduate writing centers has been published in *Academic Exchange Quarterly*.

MICHAEL A. PEMBERTON is professor of Writing and Linguistics at Georgia Southern University and director of the University Writing Center. A past president of the International Writing Centers Association, he has published six books, including *Labored: The State(ment) and Future of Work in Composition*, *The Center Will Hold*, and *The Ethics of Writing Instruction*, as well as articles and book chapters on writing center theory, tutoring ethics, and writing technologies. He is editor of the journal *Across the Disciplines* and the *Across the Disciplines Books* series.

SHERRY WYNN PERDUE is writing center director at Oakland University. Her work has appeared in *Writing Center Journal*, *Education Libraries*, *Writing Lab Newsletter*, and *Perspectives in Undergraduate Research and Mentoring*. In 2012, she and Dana Lynn Driscoll earned IWCA's Outstanding Article Award for "Theory, Lore, and More: An Analysis of RAD

Research in *The Writing Center Journal*, 1980–2009." She is a founding coeditor of *The Peer Review* and a past president of the East Central Writing Center Association.

DOUG PHILLIPS is teaching assistant professor and academic advisor in the Department of English at West Virginia University. He teaches courses in technical writing and business writing. At Carnegie Mellon University, where he earned his PhD, he served as assistant to the director at the Global Communication Center.

JULIANN REINEKE is associate director of Carnegie Mellon's Global Communication Center, where she develops workshops for the campus-wide community and trains undergraduate and graduate tutors. Her research focuses on scientific poster design and methods for teaching the English article system.

ADAM ROBINSON is the Learning Center coordinator at Penn State New Kensington where he oversees the campus' tutoring and disability services. He previously served as associate director in the Writing Center at the University of Louisville, where he earned an MA in English.

STEVE SIMPSON, formerly the Writing and Oral Presentation Center director, is chair of the Department of Communication, Liberal Arts, and Social Sciences at New Mexico Institute of Mining and Technology (New Mexico Tech), where he develops writing programs for graduate students in STEM disciplines. Simpson is coeditor of *Supporting Graduate Student Writers* (Michigan) and has published numerous articles on graduate student support program development. He is also a founding board member and current co-chair of the Consortium on Graduate Communication.

NATHALIE SINGH-CORCORAN is clinical associate professor of English at West Virginia University where she directs the Eberly Writing Studio. She is a former president of the International Writing Centers Association. Her collaborative scholarship has appeared in the *ADE Bulletin, College English, Composition Forum, Kairos,* and *WLN: A Journal of Writing Center Scholarship.*

ASHLY BENDER SMITH is assistant professor of Business Communication at Sam Houston State University. In addition to writing centers, her research focuses on business communication pedagogy, veteran studies, and course-based opportunities for civic engagement.

SARAH SUMMERS is assistant professor of English at Rose-Hulman Institute of Technology. Her scholarly work focuses on graduate writing centers and using design thinking to teach writing and includes articles in *Writing Center Journal, Writing Lab Newsletter,* and *Computers and Composition.* She teaches advanced writing courses in grant writing and digital writing as well as courses in disability studies and visual rhetoric.

MOLLY TETREAULT is director of the Connors Writing Center at the University of New Hampshire. She also teaches first-year writing and writing center theory and practice. Her research interests include writing centers, first-year writing, the transition from high school to college, and writing across the curriculum.

JOAN TURNER is emeritus professor in the department of English and Comparative Literature, and former director of the Centre for English Language and Academic Writing, at Goldsmiths, University of London. She has published widely in writing research, English for Academic Purposes, and intercultural communication. Her latest book is *On Writtenness: The Cultural Politics of Academic Writing,* published by Bloomsbury. She is also the author of *Language in the Academy: Cultural Reflexivity and Intercultural Dynamics,* and coeditor of *Students Writing in the University: Cultural and Epistemological Issues.*

BRONWYN T. WILLIAMS is professor of English and director of the University Writing Center at the University of Louisville. He writes and teaches on issues of literacy, identity, digital media, and popular culture. His most recent book is *Literacy Practices and Perceptions of Agency: Composing Identities*. Previous books include *New Media Literacies and Participatory Popular Culture Across Borders*; *Shimmering Literacies: Popular Culture and Reading and Writing Online*; and *Identity Papers: Literacy and Power in Higher Education*.

JOANNA WOLFE is director of the Global Communications Center and teaching professor in the Department of English at Carnegie Mellon University. She is author of the textbooks *Team Writing* and *Digging into Literature: Strategies for Reading and Writing Literary Analyses*, both published by Bedford St. Martins, and has written multiple award-winning articles in technical communication and writing studies.

INDEX

Academic Writing for Graduate Students, 153, 154
Across the Disciplines, special issue on "Graduate Reading and Writing across the Curriculum," 199, 201
administration. *See* location: within the institution; staffing: directors
advisors/advising, 35–36, 185, 189–90, 246, 257
    advisor training, 22, 199, 258–261
    cultural barriers to working with, 73–74
    expectations for graduate writers/writing, 75, 96–97, 98, 189
    directive feedback from, 13
    perceptions of graduate writing, 6, 10, 22, 255
    perceptions of the writing center, 78, 80, 88, 92
    writing center collaborations with. *See* collaborations: with graduate faculty and advisors
affective dimensions/concerns, 9, 36, 95, 116–17, 140–41, 207, 217, 231, 241
    confidence: tutors', 126, 170, 172; writers', 10, 34, 72, 95, 126, 189, 204, 205–6, 208, 213, 214–15, 219–20, 235
    health, 21, 224, 225, 226–27, 228, 236
    sense of agency, 21, 205–6, 208, 214, 217–19
    sense of isolation, 39, 110, 117, 121, 211, 216, 225, 227, 228, 233
Aitchison, Claire, 88, 194
Anson, Chris, 60
attrition and completion, 8, 18, 49, 51–52, 54, 77, 91, 226, 234, 238, 241, 243
Austin, Liz, 96
Autry, Megan, 12, 199

Badenhorst, Cecile, 211
Baker, Sarah, 189, 199
BALEAP (The British Association of Lecturers in English for Academic Purposes), 90, 92
Barnett, Bruce, 34, 141
Barron, Nancy, 200
Bastalich, Wendy, 238
Bawarshi, Anis, 256
Bazerman, Charles, 256
Bean, John, 97
Beaufort, Anne, 112, 248
Bennet, John Godolphin, 148
Boice, Robert, 230
boot camps. *See* retreats
Bouman, Kurt, 201
Bouquet, Elizabeth, 53, 191
Bourdieu, Pierre, 87
Brooks, Jeff, 200
budget. *See* funding sources
Burns, Deborah, 8, 12, 200

Caffarella, Rosemary, 34, 141
Caplan, Nigel, 157, 199
Canagarajah, Suresh, 70, 76
Carr, Allison, 57
CARS (Creating a Research Space, Swales Model), 20, 165, 166
Carter, Michael, 12, 168, 174, 199, 244
Cheung, Deanna, 28, 230
collaboration with other units, 6, 17, 20, 41, 43–44, 77, 79, 88, 196–198, 251
    with college of arts & sciences, 256
    with graduate faculty and advisors, 79, 189, 193, 256–61
    with graduate student organizations, 223
    with WAC/WID, 21, 37, 43, 185–99
communities of practice, 10, 37, 208. *See also* discourse communities
concept map, 196
Consortium on Graduate Communication (CGC), 62–63, 77, 124, 199
Council of Graduate Schools, 4, 23, 49, 50, 51, 68, 226
courses, graduate writing, 35, 37, 70, 87–88, 150, 151, 194, 241
Cox, Michelle, 199, 201
Critical Systems Thinking, 196
Cumming, Alister, 14
Curry, Mary Jane, 66, 82

Deans, Tom, 16
Devet, Bonnie, 32, 164, 17
Dinitz, Sue, 32, 192, 193, 199
director. *See* staffing
disciplinary enculturation, 11, 15, 29–30, 33, 35–37, 40, 43, 256
discourse communities, 33, 34, 36–37, 173
Donahue, Christiane, 94
Downs, Doug, 191

EATAW (European Association of Teachers of Academic Writing), 4, 90
emotional dimensions. *See* affective dimensions/concerns
English language centers, 86–87
English L2 writers, 10, 14, 18, 20, 62, 67–69, 86, 87, 93, 95, 98–100, 151, 152, 155
    distinctive needs of, 67, 69–76, 78
    programmatic approaches for, 78–79, 81, 149–50
    tutoring approaches for, 80–81, 100, 146–161
ESL writers. *See* English L2 writers
ESL Writers: A Guide for Writing Center Tutors, 201
evaluation, of services, 19–20, 127, 128–140, 205, 209–219, 234–35, 245, 249–50, 260

Fallucca, Amber, 39
Farrell, John Thomas, 7, 50
Feak, Christine, 88, 153, 155
fellows programs, 22, 30, 41, 81, 242, 247–48, 251
Ferris, Dana, 52
Fitzgerald, Lauren, 45
Freeman, Traci, 50, 55, 61
Frota, Sylvia, 146, 147
funding sources for graduate writing support, 16, 20, 21, 41–42, 60–62, 186, 195, 203, 227, 243
    grants, 60–61
    student fees, 61, 223–24

Gillespie, Paula, 41, 45, 52
generalist/specialist debates, 8, 11–12, 18, 29–37, 192–93, 249
Golde, Chris, 38, 206, 231
Graduate writing center. *See* location
Grammar Choices for Graduate and Professional Writers, 157
Grimm, Nancy, 200
Guerin, Cally, p. 237

Halasz, Helen Mulhern, 30
Hall, Jonathan, 193, 200
Harrington, Susanmarie, 192, 193, 199
Harris, Muriel, 9
Harwood, Nigel, 92
Haviland, Carol, 94
Hayward, Nancy, 201
Helping Doctoral Students Write: Pedagogies for Supervision, 259
Hemmeter, Tom, 57
Holmes, Betty, 141, 144
Horner, Bruce, 93, 94
Howard, Rebecca, 75
Hubbuch, Susan, 32, 163
Hughes, Brad, 249

Ianetta, Melissa, 44
imposter syndrome, 220, 235
intellectual property, 75
internationalization, 67–68, 88, 102
    as driver of grad writing support, 18, 50, 53
Issacs, Emily, 251
iThenticate, 74, 75

Jolly, Peggy, 61

Kamler, Barbara, 88, 110, 189, 240, 259
Kiedaisch, Jean, 32
Knight, Melinda, 251

Lancaster, Zak, 155
Larsen-Freeman, Diane, 93
Latino/a students, 66, 68, 71–72, 73, 80
Leander, Kevin, 207
Lee, Alison, 88
Lee, Sohui, 38, 206, 231
Leki, Ilona, 14
Lerner, Neal, 7, 45
Linville, Cynthia, 201
literature review, 34, 132, 188, 193, 212
location
    of graduate writing center, 36, 55
    housed with undergraduate, 57–58
    stand-alone, 40, 242, 243
    within the institution, 22, 57–58, 196–7, 225, 258
Longman Guide to Peer Tutoring, The, 45
Lunsford, Andrea, 174–176

Macaulay, Rosemary, 92
Mackiewicz, Jo, 164
Maher, Damian, 39
Maher, Michelle, 39
Manchón, Rosa, 147
Mastroieni, Anita, 230

Matsuda, Paul Kei, 201
Maykel, Cheryl, 16
McAlpine, Lynne, 189, 200
McKinney, Jackie Grutsch, 15, 16, 39
Mee, Carolyn, 57
Melzer, Dan, 196, 198
Micciche, Laura, 57
Mullen, Joan, 94
multilingual grad writers. *See* English L2 writers
Murray, Donald, 213
Murray, Rowena, 90
Myers, Sharon, 200

National Center for Education Statistics, 68
Necamp, Samantha, 94
needs analysis, 77–78
Neff, Julie, 200
network of support, writing center as, 16–17, 42–44
North, Stephen, 43, 200
"novelty moves," 165–166
Noticing Hypothesis, 147
Nowacek, Rebecca, 249

occluded genres, 10, 232
Olson, Barrie, 165
Olson, Gary, 59
online tutoring, 56, 124, 125
Organizational Development Theory, 186, 198
"'Our Little Secret': A History of Writing Centers, Pre- to Post-Open Admissions," 53
Output Hypothesis, 147
Oxford Guide for Writing Tutors, The, 45

Paltridge, Brian, 88
Papen, Uta, 207
Pare, Anthony, 194, 241, 256
partnerships. *See* collaboration with other units
Passeron, Jean-Claude, 87
patchwriting, 76
pedagogy. *See* tutoring approaches
Pemberton, Michael, 200
perceptions of graduate writing centers and support, 22, 57, 58, 88–89, 113, 118–121, 251, 255–56
Phillips, Talinn, 14, 31, 39, 62, 76, 79, 108, 237
plagiarism, 74–76, 153. *See also* iThenticate; patchwriting; intellectual property
Powers, Elizabeth, 207

Powers, Judith, 7, 50, 125, 164, 256
Praxis, special issue on "Access and Equity in Graduate Writing Support," 16, 49, 62, 241, 255
Prentice, Cheryl, 50, 55, 61
Prior, Paul, 207

Rafoth, Ben, 261
Reardon, Kristina, 16, 109
reading in/for tutorial sessions, 12, 19–20, 124–145
Reiff, Mary Jo, 256
research skills, support for, 79
resources for graduate writers
    online, 37–38, 56, 154, 155, 156, 168
    print, 56
"Rethinking the WAC/Writing Center Connection," 18, 29, 200
retreats, 5–6, 15, 21–22, 38, 49, 61, 204–20, 225, 228, 230–35, 237, 238, 245–47
Roam, Dan ("The Back of a Napkin"), 81
Robinson, Heather, 193, 200
Rogers, Paul, 89, 189, 199
Rubdy, Rani, 94

Salem, Lori, 242
Schmidt, Richard W., 146, 147
Seidlhofer, Barbara, 93
Severino, Carol, 201
Shamoon, Linda, 8, 12, 200
Sheridan, David, 200
Simpson, Steve, 199, 200, 242, 256
Snively, Helen, 35, 40, 49, 51, 55, 61
St. Martin's Sourcebook for Writing Tutors, 201
staffing, 3–4, 34, 40–42, 51, 242
    directors, 3, 43, 59–60, 62, 195
    graduate tutors, 40–41, 58–59, 79, 111, 149, 195, 247–48, 251
    undergraduate tutors, 29–30, 37, 167
Starfield, Sue, 88
Starke-Meyerring, Doreen, 15, 188, 200
STEM, 18, 41, 67–76, 79–82, 163, 168, 192, 225, 229, 231–34
Sundstrom, Christine Jensen, 195, 199
supervisors/supervising. *See* advisors/advising
Supporting Graduate Student Writers: Research, Curriculum, and Program Design, 62, 199, 200
Sutherland-Smith, Wendy, 75
sustaining graduate writing support, 20–21, 62–63, 187, 196, 198, 260
Swain, Merrill, 147
Swales, John, 20, 88, 153, 155, 165, 166

Tardy, Chris, 13
Thaiss, Chris, 45, 52, 93, 200
Theriault, Virginia, 207
Thomson, Pat, 88, 110, 189, 240, 259
Thonus, Terese, 200
translingual approach, 93–94
tutor training, 13, 58–59, 248–49
    to work across the disciplines, 192–93, 199–201
    to work with English L2 writers, 20, 146, 151–161
    to work with technical content, 41, 164–179
tutoring approaches, 8, 12
    corpora, 151, 154, 156–157
    directive/non–directive, 12–13, 100, 176
    generalist/specialist, 29–32, 164, 192–93, 249
    genre based, 20, 164–179, 244
    HOC/LOC, 13, 126, 128, 136–37, 143
    noticing, 147–49, 151–57, 161
    sentence level, 14, 20, 76, 148, 149, 150, 156–57, 160
    visualization exercises, 81
tutorial formats, 14–15
    asynchronous online, 124–25
    group/distributed, 80–81
    hybrid/read-ahead, 19–20, 124–145, 244
    individual, 11, 55–56, 107
    synchronous online, 56
Tutor's Guide: Helping Writers One to One, A, 45

Vaught–Alexander, Karen, 187
Vorhies, Heather Blain, 121

WAC for the New Millennium, 31
Wardle, Elizabeth, 45, 192
WCOnline, 114, 126–127, 129, 138, 144
well-being. *See* affective concerns/dimensions: health
Wilder, Laura, 165
WLN: A Journal of Writing Center Scholarship, special issue Support for Graduate Writers, 7, 49, 199, 241, 255
Wolfe, Joanna, 165, 176
workshops, 15, 56, 79, 245–47
    developed by graduate tutors, 194, 247, 249–51
    fees for, 61
    in writing retreats, 207, 209, 218, 225, 231, 233
Writing across the Curriculum: A Critical Sourcebook, 200
Writing Center Resource Guide, 31
Writing Centers and Writing Across the Curriculum Programs, 186
writing groups, 15, 39–40, 56, 80–81, 206–7, 233, 237n16
Writing Across the Curriculum. *See* collaboration with other units
Writing in the Disciplines. *See* collaboration with other units
Writing Lab Newsletter, 7, 50
Writing Science: How to Write Papers that Get Cited and Proposals that Get Funded, 154

Zawacki, Terry Myers, 45, 93, 189, 199
Zenger, Amy, 94

www.ingramcontent.com/pod-product-compliance
Lightning Source LLC
Chambersburg PA
CBHW060516080526
44586CB00012B/508